# ON ELIOT

# NCQ TITLES

Though each can be read independently,
these NCQ publications, taken together,
comprise a single hyper-text collection.

# ON ELIOT

## these fragments

Bernard Sharratt

New Crisis Quarterly
2015

NEW CRISIS QUARTERLY

ncq@newcrisisquarterly.myzen.co.uk

First published 2015

For
Gabriel Josipovici
& Tamar Wang

*… without whom…*

# CONTENTS

# FOREWORD

This book traces, in a somewhat idiosyncratic manner, my intermittent responses to T. S. Eliot over the past fifty years or so, as a reader who has remained frustratingly puzzled by Eliot's poems.

In particular, it includes two accounts of *The Waste Land* which differ considerably from each other and which may well be regarded as incompatible. I leave it to my reader to decide. Since an engagement with any writer, and especially with such a paradigmatic yet problematic figure as Eliot, may go through several changes over a lifetime, I see no need to regard any particular critical argument as definitive. The book is more concerned with reflecting such changes of response than with making a contribution to the academic industry around Eliot.

That industry is formidable. Thankfully, I ceased being a professional literary critic long ago, and I have no intention of trawling through the sea of scholarship to see if my own arguments and suggestions have been either anticipated or already refuted by previous commentators. Though my concern is partly with how the practices of literary criticism have been affected by, among other factors, transformations in the very apparatuses of scholarship and of publication, and particularly the implications of current developments in the digital domain.

Moreover, this is not the book on T. S. Eliot that I set out to write a few months ago. The original notion was simply to put together two short essays, already published, with some substantial unpublished material on Eliot and the Moot Group. I still regard Eliot's involvement with that self-declared 'Christian conspiracy' as of considerable importance for assessing Eliot's overall significance and for understanding some aspects of English cultural history, but on re-reading my own research I rapidly recognised that my interest in Eliot's social and political thought and his activities in that domain had dwindled to the point of almost complete boredom. I have therefore largely avoided imposing that one-time preoccupation upon any reader of the present volume.

However, by that time I had cheerfully but somewhat foolishly promised to dedicate my intended little book on Eliot to two good friends, Gabriel Josipovici and Tamar Wang, which rather prevented me from simply abandoning the book entirely. So the familiar formula of gratitude in my dedication is intended with some mild degree of affectionate irony, not least because I recognise that a great deal of the book in its finished form may stray very far from their own interest in T. S. Eliot.

What also saved the book from simply being put back in the filing cabinet was the publication, while I was drafting it, of the long-awaited enormous new edition of *The Poems of T. S. Eliot*, edited by Christopher Ricks and Jim McCue, which provoked me into thinking that I might still have something useful to say. It prompted a letter to the *TLS* (16th October 2015) briefly indicating one of the several problems I had, not merely with the new edition but with some central tenets of so much Eliot criticism and scholarship. This book is in part an expansion of that letter.

Nevertheless, this is still not the book on Eliot which I wanted to write. Ideally, I would offer what I regard as appropriate literary criticism: detailed arguments based upon close critical analyses of Eliot's work, using extensive quotation as the very substance of any such criticism. For reasons which the book considers, this has not seemed possible. Instead, I have resorted to combining paraphrase with reference, and I ask that you consult those references in lieu of the indispensable but sadly absent quotations. I also dislike some of the conclusions about Eliot towards which I have been led, but since parts of the book might be characterised as merely hints followed by guesses, I would be more than content to see my case disputed.

I record my gratitude, without assigning any blame, to several ex-colleagues at the University of Kent who, over many years, contributed to my shifting responses to Eliot, including Ian Gregor, Michael Grant, Graham Clarke, and, particularly for a generously illuminating recent exchange, David Ellis. The work of two students in particular contributed to one section, Howard Williams and Eldad Druks. I thank other friends who have also helped shape the book, including Kevin Davey for several exchanges in the past few weeks, Terry Eagleton for conversations which have now spanned over fifty years, and Marion O'Connor, who has enjoyed (a most felicitous error by the dictation program for 'endured') my preoccupation with Eliot over the past months.

This book is the last in a batch of self-published titles under the imprint 'New Crisis Quarterly', which has itself prompted some reflections within the book. I might suggest that it be read alongside two other NCQ titles, *Literary Conversions* and *Eliotics*, were I not only too aware that they might constitute further embarrassing evidence of the continuing inadequacy of my response to Eliot's work.

B.S.
January 2016

# Acknowledgements

Parts of this book have been previously published.

'Eliot: Modernism, Postmodernism, and after',
in *The Cambridge Companion to T. S. Eliot*,
edited by A. David Moody, 1994.
© Cambridge University Press 1994
Reprinted with permission.

'*Dayadhvam* : Looking for the Key' appeared in
'DA/*Datta* : Teaching *The Waste Land*', a special issue of
*CIEFL Bulletin*, (New Series) Vol. XI, Nos. 1 & 2,
December 2001, pp. 33-47, Hyderabad, India..
I am warmly grateful to the editor for its publication.

I am also genuinely grateful to the Permissions Department
of Faber and Faber for very helpfully clarifying the
provisions of their fair use policy. If I have still inflicted
substantial damage upon anybody's intellectual property I
will of course promptly withdraw this book from the
extremely limited circulation it is likely to have.

1

# *Prelude* : RED

*.. I read much of the night...*

Yesterday, I came across a somewhat curious website. Its purpose seems to be to assemble what it calls 'evidences' concerning the history of reading. Let me quote its rationale:

*Welcome to UK RED*
*The Reading Experience Database*

What did United Kingdom residents and British subjects living or travelling abroad read between the invention of the printing press in 1450 and the end of the Second World War in 1945? How, and in what circumstances did they read?
Search or browse our database to find out...

UK RED captures the reading tastes and habits of the famous and the ordinary, the young and the old, men and women. The texts range from books and newspapers to ephemera such as playbills and tickets, and from illuminated manuscripts, novels and poetry to tombstone inscriptions and graffiti.

Entries in UK RED illustrate the diversity of reading experience and practice as well as patterns within particular periods and across time. The evidence of reading is drawn from a multitude of sources, including diaries, memoirs, commonplace books, marginalia, sociological surveys, and criminal court and prison records.

Ambitious. But puzzling. Though I can only speculate, not having seen the justifications and explanations which presumably supported the application for what must have been a considerable research grant, the project seems to be a curious conflation of a crowd-sourced Wikipedia-type assemblage and a compilation modelled in part on the original Oxford English Dictionary.

The ambition of the *OED* – a dictionary 'compiled upon historical principles' – was to record the first use and subsequent senses of every word in the English language, thereby enabling a tracing of the changing and multifarious meanings and usages for each word. To do so, it appealed to a world-wide range of contributors, who were asked to send in to the editor small slips of paper giving a sentence or phrase in which a particular word occurred, with a precise specification of the source and date. The slips of paper flooded in and the children of James Murray, the general editor, were daily enlisted in the tedious task of sorting and filing the accumulating slips. There is a pleasant anecdote to the effect that one of Murray's younger children, on being invited to a friend's house, after being shown around, said inquiringly: "And where does your Daddy do his slips?"

In a somewhat similar fashion to the *OED*'s procedure, potential helpers to *UK RED* are invited to send in or add directly to the website short excerpts from accounts of somebody reading some book or text at some time, and to specify the source and date. The assumption underpinning the *OED* enterprise was that it would be possible to distinguish the various senses of a word from the recorded contexts, albeit brief, and that though there might be many nuances of meaning, or even individually idiosyncratic uses, nevertheless the accumulating historical changes in common usage could be securely established.

It is less clear what the overall aim of the RED website might be. Is it envisaged that one might somehow track overall changes in habits or practices of reading? Or trace the shifting evaluations of certain kinds of text or even of specific authors? Or compile statistically significant analyses of some aspects of reading? But what then is the status and reliability of the recorded 'evidences'? Though the *OED* could never record every instance of a particular word, there was some plausibility to the notion that one could establish, more or less, the first usage of a word or the appearance of a particular sense of a word, with subsequently dated instances being assimilable to, and perhaps made intelligible by reference to, that changing history. But what might be the equivalent in relation to the general reading of texts? Even if one leaves aside the surely undeniable fact that most people's reading of most texts has itself not been recorded, has left no 'evidences' to be excerpted, it might be implausible to regard those instances which have left some record as being reliably representative – and of what? Is there a sufficiently shared or common experience or practice of what we, or the *OED*, call "reading"?

A compilation of historical 'evidences' might indeed help to clarify some differences between a mediaeval monk meditatively chewing his way through an assigned Lenten text in the cloisters of Canterbury Cathedral and a modern commuter swiping her tablet screen while riding the Metro to work. But this evening, when you jot down in your intimate diary, or perhaps broadcast on your world-wide blog, that today you read Bernard Sharratt's book on T. S. Eliot, will you make it clear to your own ardent future readers, if any, whether they should imagine you gently browsing on a bright sunny morning under an apple tree or fiercely concentrated in a studious library hunched in silence?

Will you take care to inform a RED website of the future whether you read (past and present tenses) these words with a superior smile or a suppressed yawn – and why? Without such contexts, clarifications, responses, and elaborations (and they are far from easy to record) the mere 'evidence' that you once 'read' this book, or any other, must seem of a somewhat limited value. Incidentally, how long after my writing it (2015) are you reading this book now, anyway, and what difference might that make?

I don't want to pursue much further the several intriguing questions raised by this website, except to suggest that it seems indicative of a wider development in the 'study of literature' and indeed in the academic Humanities generally. Insofar as the current (2015) mantra is 'big data' and the current *desideratum*, or even necessity, is big research grants, one can see how the notion of such a website might once have appealed.

In apparently trying to treat 'evidences' of reading experiences as some form of raw data, the project has an affinity with other recent tendencies, including for example the work of Franco Moretti and his collaborators in attempting to arrive at statistically based analyses of networks and affiliations, ostensibly diagrammatising the relations between texts, a form of comparative literary studies which at times seems to involve no actual reading of the texts themselves but can apparently operate its procedures quite contentedly by relying upon summaries and descriptions of texts.[1]

---

[1] See for example: *Atlas of the European Novel, 1800–1900* (1998), *Graphs, Maps, Trees: Abstract Models for a Literary History* (2005), *Distant Reading* (2013)

4

It might be worth exploring – if, of course, a sufficiently lucrative research grant were available – the relations between these academic tendencies and the assumptions, presumptions, and requirements of a changing publishing industry, in which Amazon.com can prompt me with a score of 'personal recommendations' at every purchasing click and authors can now be paid at a rate based upon the precise number of pages actually perused on an e-book reader.

But what has all this to do with T. S. Eliot? I want to suggest that Eliot and his works might indeed be considered in relation to such developments, but I shall do so only in the course of demonstrating that my own 'reading' of Eliot has been far from a single unified experience, to be summarised in an 'evidence' or two. I want to explore how the various ways, times, and even places, in which I have read Eliot have been shaped not only by broad cultural developments, but by factors that some of my own readers might want to categorise as personal, or merely accidental, or indeed as irrelevant.

It was, we can recall, a dictum of the early Eliot, which deeply influenced a generation or more of his readers, that the activity of the poet 'as poet' should be curiously 'impersonal', that one could and should separate the man who suffers from the poet who creates. There was surely a corresponding implication that the activity of the critic was also to be in a certain sense 'impersonal', that indeed – one might say – the person who reads the poem 'as a poem reader' can and should be distinguished from the person who turns the pages. But in allowing and endorsing any such distinction, do we already find ourselves treading a path that leads towards treating 'literature' as providing the depersonalised data of large research grants and as primarily catering to the financial calculations of large publishing corporations?

Rather than accept Eliot's use of the term 'impersonal', one might perhaps speak more appropriately of 'de-personalised' – as, for example, in my use just now of the impersonal phrase 'one might perhaps...'. I might indeed, but since I assume that any reading of a poem (or of any text) is a personal one, by which I mean that it is the act of an individual of a certain age, class, gender, with a more or less specific range of political and cultural beliefs, and a particular set of experiences, including previous reading experiences, I am intrigued by the notion that one should, or even can, somehow leave these personal factors out of the account, though it obviously depends upon what 'the account' is taken to be. There is, to be sure, a difference between my reading Eliot's poems and an actor on stage speaking Shakespeare's verse in *persona* for a paying audience, and it might be argued that a critic is essentially 'staging' a performance, but this doesn't entirely clarify the issue.

I can readily accept that an investigative scholar should endeavour not to falsify or mis-report the results of their investigation, and, somewhat more cautiously, that she or he should try to be aware of, make due allowance for, and indeed make explicit, their personal biases, limitations, perspectives, preferences, and prejudices, though even in the case of impartially-minded scholarship the premises and frameworks of the very questions posed for investigation may be considerably less 'impersonal' than the apparently impersonal tone and conventions of much scholarly writing would imply – as, for example, feminist critiques of a great deal of received scholarship have frequently indicated.

Lurking, or looming, here are some old disputes concerning the relations between literary scholarship and literary criticism, and between the professional and the common reader.

The ways in which those disputes have been formulated have often owed something to Eliot's various contentions, including his campaign against attenuated Romantic notions of literature as expressive or even confessional, and his related insistence upon the quasi-professional commitment of, and demands upon, those who would wish to remain poets after the age of twenty-five. I won't rehearse those debates directly, though I will be tussling with them somewhat obliquely.

Close to the core of Eliot's position was his insistence that a work of art 'cannot be interpreted': that it can only be criticised according to 'standards', in comparison with other works of art, and that any "interpretation" (the scare quotation marks are his) should take the form of presenting "relevant historical facts" which the reader is not assumed to know. Yet in his own case he also insisted that no biography be permitted, thereby implying that details of a writer's life were not among the relevant historical facts. One of the problems I do want to explore is how far we – or I – might now think again about Eliot's position, and its influence, given that a great many apparently relevant historical facts concerning Eliot's life have by now become more easily available.

As I write, there are five volumes published – so far – of *The Letters of T. S. Eliot*, a total of some 4,600 printed pages of correspondence, only up to 1931. The new 'annotated text' of the *Poems of T.S. Eliot* has been published in two volumes totalling over 2,000 pages. In a recent issue of the *TLS* there was a full-page advertisement for the next swathe of *The Complete Prose of T.S. Eliot,* comprising, thus far, four substantial volumes of everything he published up to 1933. Highlighted in the advert was the following comment :

WILL SET IN MOTION A GOLDEN ERA OF ELIOT
SCHOLARSHIP (*Chronicle of Higher Education*).

Possibly so. But are these projects, impressive as they may
appear to be, another instance of a 'big data' mentality and
primarily shaped by a convergence of large research grant
criteria and publishing industry calculations?

Perhaps it is now time to recall – or at least to record –
what it was once like actually to read Eliot's poems. On the
RED website I find the following 'evidences' concerning
Eliot, both excerpts taken from Jonathan Rose, *The
Intellectual Life of the British Working Classes*, (2001):

> Coachman's daughter Anne Tibble was enraged by
> "The Waste Land", which she read as a scholarship
> student at a redbrick university: "Eliot's neurosis of
> disillusion was horrifying ... almost utterly invalid ...
> almost entirely without feeling for others. Eliot showed
> people as ugly, stupid, shabby, vulgarian, squalid,
> somehow indecent ... the 'broken fingernails of dirty
> hands' ... Weren't these my father's and my mother's
> hands?" The experience of reading it plunged her into
> depression, but in the late 1920s it was difficult to
> express her real feelings about one of the greatest
> living poets ... Instead, she channelled her scholarly
> energies toward the poetry of John Clare, whose work
> affirmed the literacy of working people.

And:

> Bernard Kops, the son of an immigrant leather worker,
> had a special understanding of the transition from
> autodidact culture to Bohemia to youth culture,
> because he experienced all three. He grew up in the
> ferment of the Jewish East End ... read "The Tempest"
> at school, and cried over "The Forsaken Merman". At

fifteen he became a cook at a hotel, where the staff gave him Karl Marx, Henry Miller and "Ten Days that Shook the World". A neighbour presented him with the poems of Rupert Brooke, and "Grantchester" so resonated with the Jewish slum boy that he went to the library to find another volume from the same publisher, Faber and Faber. Thus he stumbled upon T. S. Eliot. "This book changed my life", he remembered. "It struck me straight in the eye like a bolt of lightning ... I had no preconceived ideas about poetry and read 'The Waste Land' and 'Prufrock' as if they were the most acceptable and common forms in existence. The poems spoke to me directly, for they were bound up with the wasteland of the East End, and the desolation and loneliness of people and landscape. Accidentally I had entered the mainstream of literature".'

Does anybody still read T. S. Eliot with reactions like those? Can anyone?

Capturing a momentary snapshot of a person reading might indeed tell us something interesting, as here, but how we read a major poet changes over time, over a life-time. Yet trying to recount or recapture a lifetime's reading of Eliot is not easy. So, let us go then...

*

# Readings

I first read Eliot when I was fifteen. By accident. Looking
in the school library for something on classical music,
about which I knew absolutely nothing, I came across a
slender volume entitled *Four Quartets*. The book seemed
slim enough to select, as probably sufficiently basic and
introductory. I started to read it. And could not stop. That
calm opening voice from nowhere and from no-one moved
me with its quiet confiding authority. Neither proclaiming
nor persuading. Stating the obvious yet enigmatic. Inviting.
Echoing in my mind. But to what purpose I did not know.
With what meaning I did not even think to ask. The words
held me as I followed. Into a garden I did not quite know
how to imagine. Those lucid words, taken individually, the
phrases read one at a time, were not mysterious, yet the
sentences somehow eluded any clear overall sense.
Tentative, yet involved upon themselves. Composed, like
music. Softly entangling me, quietly embaffling me. I did
not try to explain. I did relish the mood, the effect. I read
right through to the end of the short volume without
stopping. And then went back to the beginning...

At that time, as a believing Catholic teenager, I had no
difficulty understanding, or at least recognising, such
elements in the poem as: 'Lady, whose shrine stands on the
promontory...', or 'The wounded surgeon plies the steel',
or even 'The hint half-guessed, the gift half-understood, is
Incarnation...'. I thought I knew already what those
passages, and that crucial term, indicated. Later, I acted
the role of Thomas Becket in a school production of Eliot's
*Murder In The Cathedral*. I also wrote a piece for the
school magazine comparing those two Anglo-American
winners of the Nobel Prize for Literature, T. S. Eliot in

1948 and Winston Churchill in 1953. I must also have read more Eliot when I 'did' A-Level English Literature, but I have no clear memory of my responses to specific poems, though I do have one 'evidence' of my overall reaction to his poetry at around that time.

I was taught by a good Leavisite, Bill Maxwell, who steadfastly refused throughout the year to tell us what to think. Even to tell us what he thought. He would ask, repeatedly: "Well, what do *you* think?" And one of us would be encouraged to read out a few lines or a short passage from the 'set' text, and try to say, haltingly or confidently, what we thought of it. "So," Bill would then say, turning to someone else in the class, "what do *you* think about that?" – about what the other of us had just said. Bill constantly deployed only a handful of other repeated questions, always posed with a kind of attentive hesitation, and an endless variation of tone: "Oh, I see. And, mm, *why* do *you* say that?" "So, erm, and *where* do you find *that*?" And so the discussion went around the class. Each of us quoting. And counter-quoting. Commenting upon each other. Arguing with each other. "Yes, but...."

By collusive preparation, we once tried to persuade Bill that we all really preferred Mickey Spillane to whichever A-level assigned text we were supposed to be discussing that day. Initially he was genuinely shocked, and did not really believe us, but it went against his fundamental stance for him explicitly to argue us out of our apparent critical consensus. He simply persisted, turning from one to another, a little desperately:   "So, er, what do *you* think about *that*?"

At the end of the academic year, as the exams approached, Bill set aside a couple of sessions of 'revision'. To our amazement, he remembered what we had variously and collectively said about each of the set texts, and systematically summarised our opinions and reactions in brief bullet points on the blackboard, reminding us. And then asked: "So, *now* what you think about *that*?"

We also wrote occasional essays for him. I have one essay I wrote about that time with the title: 'The merits and limitations of T. S. Eliot's "impersonal" conception of art.' To anticipate some later themes: the essay was six pages long, 3,700 words, of which 1,350 were quoted from Eliot. Thirty separate quotations. It was the way Bill had taught us to read, and to write. I still quite like the final page or so, though I will spare you the rest of the 'evidence':

> <... The fourth and last front upon which Eliot seems to be waging a war with the prevailing opinion of the 1920's is in theorising about the act of poetic creation. I have already indicated that perhaps here Eliot was relying too much upon his own experience of creation, and his formulation seems to hover between a conception of the poet as a medium, almost in the Spiritualist sense (like his own Madame Sosostris!) and a medium in some other sense, related to that in which we might talk about one language as being a better medium for expression in certain fields than another language. At the same time, it seems to me, Eliot is deeply influenced by the Aristotelian idea of 'co-principles' in any 'substance' - of form and matter: he seems to see the poet as giving a new 'form' to the material of ordinary life. I can only sketch the elements I consider important in any consideration of the worth of Eliot's conception: to do more would take us eventually to a critique of the philosophical psychology underlying Eliot's idea of the human intellect - it would, for example, have to decide according to whose terminology Eliot is distinguishing between 'emotion' and 'feeling', and probably have to take up and examine

the interesting hint dropped by Eliot when he remarked:

The point of view I am struggling to attack is perhaps related to the metaphysical theory of the substantial unity of the soul.

My own feeling, for what it is worth, is that Eliot's account in this sphere rests upon suspect premisses, and that he had a philosophically misleading notion of the relation between thought and word.

One could summarise the above consideration of four aspects of 'impersonality' by saying that Eliot's view is immensely beneficial in the practical sphere, for the aspiring poet and for the critic, while in the more far-reaching spheres it is by no means easy to dismiss him as unimportant, irrelevant, wrong, or even as outdated. But if one is to make a decision as to whether one is going to adopt Eliot's view as a guiding light to one's appreciation of art, it might be relevant, as a final point, to consider one's reactions to two quotations from Eliot:

Anyone who has observed one of the great dancers of the Russian ballet school will have observed that the man or woman whom we admire is a being who exists only during the performances, that is a personality, a vital flame which appears from nowhere, disappears into nothing, and is complete and sufficient in its appearance. ... A ballet is a development of several centuries into a strict form. In the ballet only that is left to the actor which is properly the actor's part. There are only limited movements he can make, only a limited degree of emotion he can express. He is not called upon for his personality. The differences between a great dancer and a merely competent dancer is in the vital flame, that impersonal, and, if you like, inhuman force which transpires between each of the great dancer's movements. So it would be in a strict form of drama.

The second is an aside in *After Strange Gods*:

It is characteristic of the more interesting heretics ... that they have an exceptionally acute perception, or profound insight, of some part of the truth.

Does one prefer ballet-dancers or heretics? >

So I ended the essay, with a question, of course. It should perhaps be made clear that my school was a somewhat unusual one: it was a Roman Catholic junior seminary, for intending priests, where we were taught – whatever our previous educational background – Greek, Latin, Hebrew, logic and philosophy. It had a good library, and I read, much of the time. I had clearly read a fair amount of Eliot, but it is the style or tone of the essay which now strikes me as most indebted to Eliot, with the continual resort to that impersonal 'one' and the very Eliotic formulation: 'it would, for example, have to decide according to whose terminology Eliot is distinguishing between 'emotion' and 'feeling'...'

The essay title was, I think, indicative of the time: though the classroom discussion had been largely conducted through close reading of individual poems, the more formal written essay was to be concerned with what was, in effect, a theory of literature – though, of course, any explicit notion that we were dealing with 'theory' would still have been regarded as an alien intrusion into the pragmatic practices of English literary criticism.

As it happens, Eliot the person died the year I went to Cambridge to 'read English'. And as it also happens, if that is an appropriate way of putting it, I was the first of my working-class Liverpool family to go to university. Away from my Catholic seminary, I was soon to prefer both ballet dancers and heretics, and, of course, it made a difference to how I read Eliot.

*ii: ... the poetry does .. matter...*

My first year at university. I was in the foyer of my college, just going out. A small hunchback bounced in from outside. Perhaps seventy years old. He could have been a goblin. Startlingly direct, abrupt: "Who are you? What are you reading?" "Er, Undergraduate. English." "Humph. Do you know my friend Leavis?" "Well, I know *of.. .*" "Wait here." The alarming figure went immediately to the phone in the hallway. I heard: "Leavis. Yes. I'm bringing a young friend round to see you. Now." The phone clanged. Ten minutes later I stood on Leavis's doorstep, my arm gripped by (he had now told me) "Corboy" (I vaguely knew the name – a previous master of my college). Confused, I only hoped I would soon be sitting quietly in some invisible corner, just listening. The door was opened by the unmistakable figure. "In you go," said Corboy, thrusting me forward. And then he left.

It was, I suppose you might say, satisfactory. If being caught in a non-stop verbal cross-fire between FRL and QDL for an hour or so can be regarded as satisfactory. But I was invited again. And Leavis would sometimes even come to tea. And again and again he would probe the same question: where precisely, when precisely, does *Four Quartets* go *wrong*? At what point does it begin to fail? From memory, or with the text before us, again and again. Insistent. It mattered.

On one occasion, after a sparse tea, by the sheer intensity and probingly exact intelligence of his pursuit, he silenced an eminent, normally highly voluble and very rationalist philosopher of science who had no particular interest in literature. And after Leavis left, Ernan conceded to me that he now saw that it really did *matter* if and where *Four Quartets* failed.

So, was 'The dove descending...' deliberately unsuccessful? Perhaps 'There are three conditions...' was somehow intended to be slack? Or did it all still work even up to: 'With the drawing of this love...'? As an aside, once, Leavis jabbed at: 'Then fools' approval stings' – "That's me, y'know. The fool." A nasal snarl. "But he sent me a postcard, finally, y'know – he said : I was right, y'know." At that point I had no idea what he was talking about. But it clearly mattered.

After several such exchanges, I tentatively suggested that perhaps *Four Quartets* 'fails' because of us. Because of how we read it, them. Eliot had so written the poem, I argued, that the ' failure' was that of the  reader of the poem – not, as I hastened to make clear, some reprehensible defect on Leavis's own part, but rather that Eliot had so composed the overall sequence of all four quartets as to make it simply beyond the capacity of *any* reader, however dedicated and seriously attentive, to sustain the critical and emotional responses demanded by the poems, to the point where a completely satisfactory reading from the beginning of *Burnt Norton* right through to the end of *Little Gidding* was  actually impossible...

Of course, my 'case' would have required – as Leavis always insistently demanded – a close critical analysis of all four poems: to show in detail how they worked as a single self-echoing 'long poem', such that the more intensely we read, and the more we register and try to take into account the multiply enveloping chains of allusion and intra-referential connections, the less we can honestly credit ourselves with sustaining the appropriate intensity of attention adequate to the task of fully reading the entire work as a whole...

Thus, I tried to argue, it was not so much a question of *where* the *poem* failed, but that at some individually variable point we have to recognise and admit  that our attention and emotional engagement has now lapsed, rather as – to echo the musical analogy or parallel which Eliot himself deploys – we can often recognise ourselves as no longer listening with adequate attention to the final movements of a Beethoven late quartet, let alone if we attempted to listen to all Beethoven's late quartets, one after the other...

Thus, *Four Quartets* taken as a single whole poem can at times seem like an ever-deepening cluster of endless associations whose significance is to be explored and discovered only within the poem itself, by repeated re-readings, and any critical account would at best consist of a re-weaving of *all* the resonant phrases which make up the poems themselves. 'These words echo thus in your mind...'

But even the most fully engaged reader has at some point, which might vary with each repeated reading, either to put the volume down, or to start again, or to continue by a kind of abandonment – or surrender – of critical response in favour of an on-going acquiescence in what the poem is claiming to be able to tell us, culminating in the final reassurances which take us into a territory akin to the closure of the *Divina commedia,* but by that stage of the reading process supported only by the self-sustaining movement of the whole poem itself and not by any scaffolding either derived from an explicit and articulate Christian philosophy or based upon any authoritative declaration of dogmatic certitudes. The poem as a whole thereby attempts to succeed eventually (if it does) as an act of quasi-religious conversion upon the reader...

Thus I rabbitted on, trying out various formulations. Years later, I elaborated this position to sketch what I then more generally called the process of 'literary conversion'.

But Leavis was not persuaded. Not only because it was obviously quite impossible to sustain my case by the kind of detailed 'close reading' that might have convinced him – it was indeed almost self-cancelling to attempt it. I don't recall whether this ongoing but intermittent exchange was before or after Leavis gave the Clark lectures in 1967. I know I went to hear them, and I do remember Leavis, in the course of one lecture, starting to quote, to recite, in that strangely compelling nasal voice, from some way into one of the Quartets – and not being able to stop. I recognised the temptation. So he simply continued quoting, right to the end of the Quartet. And then apologised for not leaving enough time to finish his lecture as he had intended.

He had written in 1932, some thirty-five years earlier:

Poetry matters because of the kind of poet who is more alive than other people, more alive in his own age. He is, as it were, at the most conscious point of the race in his time. ('He is the point at which the growth of the mind shows itself,' says Mr I. A. Richards.) The potentialities of human experience in any age are realized only by a tiny minority, and the important poet is important because he belongs to this (and has also, of course, the power of communication). Indeed, his capacity for experiencing and his power of communicating are indistinguishable; not merely because we should not know of the one without the other, but because his power of making words express what he feels is indistinguishable from his awareness of what he feels. He is unusually sensitive, unusually aware, more sincere and more himself than the ordinary man can be. He knows what he feels and knows what he is interested in. He is a poet because his interest in his experience is not separable from his interest in words; because, that is, of his habit of seeking by the evocative use of words to sharpen his awareness of his ways of feeling, so making these communicable. And poetry can communicate the actual quality of experience with a subtlety and precision unapproachable by any other means. But if the poetry and the intelligence of the age lose touch with each other, poetry will cease to matter much, and the age will be lacking in finer awareness. What this last prognostication means it is perhaps impossible to bring home to anyone who is not already convinced of the importance of poetry. So that it is indeed deplorable that poetry should so widely have ceased to interest the intelligent.

Perhaps by now I was lacking in finer awareness, but for me the poetry was slowly ceasing to matter quite so much. By 1968 politics had certainly replaced poetry as my most immediate concern. Nevertheless, it seemed, Eliot remained, if now a different aspect of Eliot...

*iii : ... yes, but...*

For three years, out of touch with the Faculty, I had been officially supervised only by postgraduates. So in 1968 I asked Leavis to provide a reference for my postgraduate research application. Learning that my other referee was to be Raymond Williams, he huffily declined: "He never *says* anything." He might have relented, but Queenie Leavis stepped in anyway, hoping – vainly – that I might write a Ph.D. on Richard Jefferies. Leavis did agree that I might, one day, write a book on him – "Yes, you can have access to all the papers" – but not, assuredly not, as a Ph.D topic. In Cambridge! It was only some years later that I read Leavis's comments on the appropriate criteria for postgraduate research in English, an acerbic appendix in his *English Literature in our time and the unvesity*, 1969, and was retrospectively terrified at my temerity in asking him for a reference.

My intended, if undeclared, topic at that point was the Moot Group, the self-declared 'conspiracy' of which Eliot had been a central member in the late 1930s and 1940s, and out of which had developed his *The Idea of a Christian Society* and *Notes Towards the Definition of Culture.*

But then a phrase intervened. Reading, again, Raymond Williams's *Culture and Society* I was struck by three passages, indeed three lists, linking Eliot, Leavis, and Williams himself. Williams had written, in 1958, ten years earlier:

> Eliot's emphasis of culture as a whole way of life is useful and significant. It is also significant that, having taken the emphasis, he plays with it. For example:

> > Culture ... includes all the characteristic activities and interests of a people: Derby Day, Henley Regatta, Cowes, the twelfth of August, a cup final, the dog races, the pin table, the dart board, Wensleydale cheese, boiled cabbage cut into sections, beetroot in vinegar, nineteenth-century Gothic churches, and the music of Elgar.

Then, a few pages later, Williams on Leavis, including a long quotation from Leavis himself:

The basis of [Leavis's] case, and of the essential connexion with literary studies, appears in the opening pages of *Mass Civilization and Minority Culture:*

In any period it is upon a very small minority that the discerning appreciation of art and literature depends: it is (apart from cases of the simple and familiar) only a few who are capable of unprompted, first-hand judgment. They are still a small minority, though a larger one, who are capable of endorsing such first-hand judgment by genuine personal response. The accepted valuations are a kind of paper currency based upon a very small proportion of gold. To the state of such a currency the possibilities of fine living at any time bear a close relation. . . . The minority capable not only of appreciating Dante, Shakespeare, Donne, Baudelaire, Hardy (to take major instances) but of recognizing their latest successors constitute the consciousness of the race (or of a branch of it) at a given time. For such capacity does not belong merely to an isolated aesthetic realm: it implies responsiveness to theory as well as to art, to science and philosophy in so far as these may affect the sense of the human situation and of the nature of life. Upon this minority depends our power of profiting by the finest human experience of the past; they keep alive the subtlest and most perishable parts of tradition. Upon them depend the implicit standards that order the finer living of an age, the sense that this is worth more than that, this rather than that is the direction in which to go, that the centre is here rather than there. In their keeping ... is the language, the changing idiom, upon which fine living depends, and without which distinction of spirit is thwarted and incoherent. By 'culture' I mean the use of such a language.

And then the measured but also characteristically muffled response by Williams:

In certain respects this is a new position in the development of the idea of Culture. Yet it mainly derives from Arnold whom Leavis quite properly acknowledges as his starting point. What goes back to Arnold goes back also to Coleridge but there are significant changes on the way. For Coleridge the minority was to be a class, an endowed order of clerisy whose business was general cultivation, and whose allegiance was to the whole body of sciences. For Arnold, the minority was a remnant, composed of individuals to be found in all social classes, whose principal distinction was that they escaped the limitations of habitual class-feeling. For Leavis, the minority is, essentially, a literary minority, which keeps alive the literary tradition and the finest capacities of the language. This development is instructive, for the tenuity of the claim to be a 'centre' is, unfortunately, increasingly obvious. ' "Civilization" and "culture" are coming to be antithetical terms,' Leavis writes a little later. This is the famous distinction made by Coleridge, and the whole development of this idea of culture rests on it. Culture was made into an entity, a positive body of achievements and habits, precisely to express a mode of living superior to that being brought about by the 'progress of civilization'. For Coleridge the defence of this standard was to be in the hands of a National Church, including 'the learned of all denominations'. Since this could not in fact be instituted, the nature of the defending minority had continually, by the successors of Coleridge, to be redefined. The process which Arnold began, when he virtually equated 'culture' with 'criticism', is completed by Leavis....

Finally, Williams moves to specific critique:

> To put upon literature, or more accurately upon criticism, the responsibility of controlling the quality of the whole range of personal and social experience, is to expose a vital case to damaging misunderstanding. English is properly a central matter of all education, but it is not, clearly, a whole education ... the damaging formulation of the nature of the minority remains. Leavis might have written:

> > The minority capable not only of appreciating Shakespeare, the English common law, Lincoln Cathedral, committee procedure, Purcell, the nature of wage-labour, Hogarth, Hooker, genetic theory, Hume (to take major instances) but of recognizing, either their successors, or their contemporary changes and implications, constitute the consciousness of the race (or of a branch of it) at a given time.

> If he had done so (while apologizing for the arbitrariness of the selection), his claim that 'upon this minority depends our power of profiting by the finest human experience of the past' would have been, in some degree, more substantial. It is a matter not so much of theory as of emphasis. If, however he had entered such dangerous lists, the whole question of the nature of the minority, of its position in society, and of its relations with other human beings, might have been forced more clearly into the open.

I am reasonably certain that Leavis would not have accepted that Williams was *saying* anything at all in this passage. Certainly it is a more convoluted, complex, and cautious formulation than Leavis's own emphatic claim that the poet is 'at the most conscious point of the race in his time.' But, beyond the respectfully reticent phrasing, the divergence runs in the end very deep indeed. And, of course, the criticism of Leavis's list also takes us back critically to Eliot's earlier list of 'cultural' activities.

It was in another, related, passage, directly on Eliot, that I then came across the phrase I was to spent some three years more or less trying to understand. At stake, indeed, was the very notion of 'consciousness', but this I did not fully realise until some time later. Williams did not emphasise the phrase, but I have italicised it:

> In thinking of culture as 'a whole way of life' Eliot emphasizes that a large part of a way of life is necessarily unconscious. A large part of our common beliefs is our common behaviour, and this is the main point of difference between the two meanings of 'culture'. What we sometimes call 'culture' – a religion, a moral code, a system of law, a body of work in the arts – is to be seen as only a part – the conscious part – of that 'culture' which is the whole way of life. This, evidently, is an illuminating way of thinking about culture, although the difficulties which it at once exposes are severe. For, just as we could not assume a correspondence between function and class, so we can not assume a correspondence between conscious culture and the whole way of life. If we think of a simple, and stable, society, the correspondence is usually evident; but where there is complication, and tension, and change, the matter is no longer one of levels, a given percentage of a uniform whole. *The consciousness can be a false consciousness, or partly false,* as I think Eliot showed in *The Idea of a Christian Society.* . . . In theory, the metaphor of 'levels' may be illuminating; in practice, because it derives from observation not only of a culture but of a system of social classes, and, further, because the

degree of conscious culture is so easily confused with the degree of social privilege, it is misleading.

When he first published this in 1958, Williams had not yet read Lukacs but in 1968 that phrase 'a false consciousness' was bound to lead me not only to Eliot's *The Idea of a Christian Society* but more critically to Lukacs's *History and Class Consciousness*. If only because I was by then beginning to see that there were several lurking parallels between Eliot's position and certain motifs within Lukacs.

Thanks to the promptings of Adrian Cunningham I had been reading Eliot's unpublished paper to the Moot Group on Coleridge and the clerisy, alongside my faltering attempts to understand Lukacs, in an almost daily dialogue with Paul Connerton. I had also recently joined the editorial team of a 'little magazine' called *Slant* which was attempting an eclectic combination or syncretism between Christian theology and Marxism, religious faith and political commitment, and I was beginning to wonder, again, if I really did comprehend or believe in such notions as 'Incarnation', while being increasingly convinced that I did indeed believe in, and could clearly encounter in Cambridge, the political connections between culture and class.

Much of 'Western Marxism', I was beginning to register, can be derived from the book of essays, *History and Class Consciousness*, published by Lukacs in 1923, the year after *The Waste Land* appeared. The core argument of the book as a whole rested upon a distinction between the actual (and allegedly 'false') consciousness of the European working class and the 'imputed' consciousness fully appropriate to their actual situation. For Lukacs in 1923 the crucial task of the Communist Party was to articulate that imputed consciousness on behalf of those who could not articulate it for themselves. And I could see that Eliot's very Anglo-Catholic notion of the Christian church as embodying a shared culture which was to be understood and appreciated at different 'levels' of intellectual understanding thus had a certain parallel with Lukacs's notion of the different levels, or indeed hierarchies, of 'consciousness' which supposedly characterised the communist movement – and it was then no surprise to find Thomas Mann drawing upon Lukacs for his model of a Jesuit in *The Magic Mountain*. The programme of several Communist parties in Western Europe, especially during the Popular Front period, had once reflected this emphasis, in seeking to provide a 'popular culture' as almost a total way of life, a Party-shaped environment for such activities as sport and recreation, holiday-making and adult education – a short-lived flourishing given memorable filmic expression in Brecht's film *Kuhle Wampe*. And not unlike, as I well knew, the 'total culture' which the Catholic Church attempted to provide for its followers.

Arguably, however, it was not in fact 'levels' of a shared but differently articulated consciousness which constituted either the Christian church or the classic Communist party, but rather the often bureaucratic imposition of a hierarchy of alleged Truths, and in both cases the lower echelons, the lay believers or ordinary party members, were expected not so much to express that belief or culture in their own assuredly limited ways, but rather to acquiesce in what their superiors informed them were the orthodox criteria for genuine faith or correct commitment. The baseline of both institutions was in practice a certain dogmatic definition of the truths which were claimed to underpin the organisation itself and its objectives. It was only within that framework that ordinary members or followers were expected to affirm their faith and commitment, by obedience, discipline, and loyalty. There was therefore a certain circularity in the relation between dogma and institution, in that it was upon the basis of a particular version of Christian theological dogma that the function of the church hierarchy in defining that dogma was justified, just as it was through a certain reading of Marx that the authority of the Party to determine the orthodox interpretation of Marx was itself founded.

The long decline of the Christian church, in both membership and its hegemonic function within the state and society, had left any version of Coleridge's proposal for the 'clerisy' as 'carriers' of 'culture' increasingly without a clear social basis. Eliot inherited that *impasse* and his notion of a conscious clique of dedicated Christians, percolating the society with their example and commitment, as partly exemplified by the Moot Group, was a somewhat forlorn revival and revision of Coleridge's project. In a similar, but somewhat more rapid development, the discrediting of the Soviet Communist Party model, from the Stalinist moment onwards and most dramatically in the 1956 Twentieth Congress 'secret speech' finally admitting Stalin's crimes – followed by the Soviet intervention in Hungary – left many erstwhile Communists in a similar dilemma: how to implement any notion of a left-orientated 'common culture' with neither an organised party allegiance to achieve it nor a clear theoretical consensus to sustain it, while in addition 'orthodox' Marxist economic theory suffered almost as sharp and total a decline in credibility as Christian theology once had. The problem of recruitment was also shared: even if church membership could at least be temporarily regenerated by the process of simply having children born into a believing or at least practising christian family, for the considerable number of post-1956 ex-communists who were no longer a Party the constant issue was not only how to continue to recruit new adherents but also to delineate what it was that such recruits were being encouraged to join or even to support.

If Raymond Williams was a focal figure for the articulation of these post-1956 problems within the first British New Left, it was no suprise that his emerging successor, Terry Eagleton, had already found himself – as, like myself, a New Left Catholic – confronting both versions of the dilemma, with Eliot for a time as a major reference point for Eagleton. It was in that Catholic Marxist journal *Slant* and in, for example the 1968 *Slant* symposium *From Culture To Revolution* that Eagleton first began to sketch out the terrain on which his future influential readings of Eliot and of post-Leavis approaches to 'literature' more generally would be traced. In 1970 I reviewed Eagleton's *Exiles and Emigrés* in the *Cambridge Review*. It was sandwiched between reviews of *Dickens the Novelist* by F. R. & Q. D. Leavis on one side and of *Prisms* by Theodore W. Adorno on the other. The times they were a-changing.  A few fragments from my review at the time can conveniently indicate the coming direction.

< Terry Eagleton's earlier critical work, *Shakespeare and Society*, clearly referred back to Raymond Williams's *Culture and Society*. In *The Long Revolution* Williams at one point discussed the terms 'exile,' 'vagrant,' 'rebel,' etc.: the various distinct ways in which an 'outsider' can relate to a society. Recently, Perry Anderson, in *New Left Review*, sketched a map of inter-war English culture in which 'exile' was a key-word, and demonstrated the dominance in most sectors of an emigrant – only literary criticism really escaped.

This apparently accidental feature was placed, persuasively, within a wider pattern: the absence in this country of both classical sociology and marxism, ways of grasping a society in its totality. Anderson's analysis omitted creative literature and the physical sciences. Eagleton, in his new book, extends the map, starting from the familiar dominance even in the English literature of the period of emigrants: James, Conrad, Eliot, Pound, and others oblique to specifically English society, Joyce, Yeats, Shaw, etc. But the actual emigrants are not (except Eliot) his main concern: other writers too, he argues, were in various ways outsiders to the society of which they were members. That tension offered them a stance – that fine line between inwardness to and detachment from the experience which is the artist's subject – from which they might have been expected to produce a 'totalizing' account. Yet none of them – Bennett, Galsworthy, Wells, Forster, Woolf, Huxley, Waugh, Orwell, Greene, Auden – managed more than a partial, limited, restricted view. Eagleton's essays probe their failures, the gap they left to be filled, if at all, by exiles in a different sense.

Anderson highlighted the phenomenon, but never satisfactorily uncovered its roots; Eagleton digs, wielding 'class' as the basic tool. Yet it is never entirely clear what he is looking for: perhaps one can accept that some 19th century novelists (Dickens, George Eliot) embraced a wider span, presented more permeating structures; perhaps, today, elsewhere, Solzhenitsyn is a candidate (see Lukacs' recent essay). However, one seeks 'totalization' partly to disclose contradictions, the clash of partial perspectives assumed to be compatible. Here Eagleton is on firmer ground: he is adept at exposing paradoxes, ambiguities, in the value-systems of these various authors – the tension in Waugh between morality and style as criteria of adequate living, the deadlock in Green's simultaneous critique of humanism and orthodox catholicism, each a premise to erode the other, the linguistic reproduction in Bennett of the social mode from which he recoils....

[Above all,] the essay on 'Eliot and the uses of myth' shows what Eagleton is relevantly capable of: his tracing of the absence of 'objective correlative' in early Eliot, the fine delineation of Eliot's later, connected, attempt to find a 'relation between an existential present and the sense of a totalized historical pattern.' This is the real focus of the book, and the argument convinces, even convicts: 'the truth seems to be that the thin texture of social reality with which we are left is all that Eliot is in any case capable of imagining.' That radical incapacity in the major English poet of the period needs social, cultural, political, as well as 'literary' or 'psychological,' explanation.

[Such an account] might well come from Dr Eagleton himself, for though the overall thesis remains elusive, the basis from which it might be substantiated is present. Literary criticism, according to the Anderson sketch, usurped the function of a totalizing discipline, in Leavis's and then Williams's work. But Lit. Crit. has had a schizophrenic status, simultaneously marginal and central, 'at once the most intense and most peripheral' discipline, to adapt Eagleton's phrase for poetry. Eagleton himself once analyzed the failings of Lit. Crit. in a memorable article in *Spartacus*: its tension between genteel amateurism and technocratic professionalism, its minority vigilance posing as humanely central, its withered pragmatism – 'a reverent concern for the *texture* of living experience combined with a complacent unconcern for its *structure*, its informing social reality.' This methodological unease is particularly acute in novel criticism: both 'character-study' approaches and 'close-reading' techniques seem to limp. Eagleton's analyses in this book advance an intermediate possibility: a kind of phenomenological grasp, of character as gesture; Eagleton has, one remembers, even written a (theological) book entitled *Body as Language*.

[After a characteristic excerpt fom Eagleton on Greene] ... This is to grasp both texture and structure, and the technique interlocks with two other features of the book likely to provoke: 'class' for Eagleton is not an abstract matter of income-levels nor a question of vulgarity versus decency, but a current, colour, texture, feel, sense, present within every facet of a life, embodied, incarnate; a creative work cannot be free of that permeation; criticism cannot refuse its relevance. Secondly, Eagleton's own language is itself a gesture, sometimes rudely forceful, more often a successful re-enactment, an alert fusion of metaphorical, descriptive energy and dialectical logic. [For example:]

Encompassing these local unevennesses [in *Prufrock*] is a pervasive variation of texture: stumbling, chloroformed lines are suddenly sharpened by transient aperçus, dramatic but ephemeral crystallizations in material fragments – butt-ends, coffee-spoons transfixing pins – which are always inert images: discrete physical objects marooned in a tremulous wash of consciousness.

Only a criticism which attempts, as this does, to be simultaneously descriptive and clearly evaluative, sensitive yet committed, phenomenological and marxist, spanning – indeed fusing – philosophical, theological, aesthetic, political options, can approach the necessary mode for cultural criticism, surpassing a narrowly 'literary' criticism. Perhaps we can still aim for that elusive 'totalization' – and Eagleton is at least a step ahead of most English critics on the way. >
Meanwhile I had abandoned the proposal to work on Eliot's Christian conspiracy, the Moot Group, and embarked instead on a research thesis on 'autobiography and class consciousness', trying to combine historical and literary inquiry, through an almost Leavisian 'close reading' of texts not normally thought of as 'literature' – the auto-biographies of several British 19th-century working-class political activists – within an overall approach influenced by Lukacs, by E. P. Thompson, and, slightly bizarrely, by Jacques Lacan. T. S. Eliot was receding from my reading – though, as it turned out, not entirely.

*iv : ... on or about May 1968...*

In the immediate aftermath of the 1956 debacle, the early British New Left tried to construct a mild imitation of that earlier attempt to provide an all-embracing political and cultural way of life, with its Partisan coffee-houses, local discussion groups, and emphasis on the role of new forms of popular culture. The focus and agency was provided by the periodical *New Left Review,* a merger in 1958 of *The New Reasoner* edited by ex-Communists and *Universities & Left Review* edited by Oxford students. But in 1962/3 that overall approach of the journal was in effect swept aside with the emergence of a younger cohort who took editorial control and changed the direction of the periodical. The article by Perry Anderson in *New Left Review* to which I referred in my review of Eagleton had not only offered a comprehensive intellectual critique of the English academic terrain but also implied a programme, almost an manifesto, for the new New Left. It is worth spending some more time on Anderson's account.

Before publication, Anderson's article had been delivered as a paper to the Tawney group in Cambridge and it seemed appropriate that after the paper was given a small group, hosted by Terry Eagleton, gathered in Raymond Williams's rooms in Jesus College, Cambridge, not least since those rooms had once been occupied by Coleridge. Had Coleridge or even Williams himself been present perhaps the late-night discussion would have developed rather differently. As it was, the critical disagreement amongst this distinctly younger generation actually revolved that night around the respective political implications of the Beatles versus the Rolling Stones, with Anderson lucidly arguing the case for the Stones. Perhaps a mild harbinger of further developments to come...

As, later that summer, *les événements* unfolded in Paris, Anderson's article offered this concluding précis of his thesis:

The results of this survey may now be briefly summated. The culture of British bourgeois society is organized about an absent centre – a total theory of itself, that should have been either a classical sociology or a national Marxism. The trajectory of English social structure – above all, the non-emergence of a powerful revolutionary movement of the working-class – is the explanation of this arrested development. Two anomalous results followed, the visible index of a vacuum. A White emigration rolled across the flat expanse of English intellectual life, capturing sector after sector, until this traditionally insular culture became dominated by expatriates, of heterogeneous calibre. Simultaneously, the absence of a centre produced a series of structural distortions in the character and connections of the inherited disciplines. Philosophy was restricted to a technical inventory of language. Political theory was thereby cut off from history. History was divorced from the exploration of political ideas. Psychology was counterposed to them. Economics was dissociated from both political theory and history. Aesthetics was reduced to psychology. The congruence of each sector with its neighbour is circular: together they form something like a closed system. The quarantine of psychoanalysis is an example: it was incompatible with this pattern. Suppressed in every obvious sector at home, the idea of the totality was painlessly exported abroad, producing the paradox of an anthropology where there was no sociology. In the general vacuum thus created, literary criticism usurps ethics and insinuates a philosophy of history. It was logical that it should finally be the one sector capable of producing a synthetic socialist theory.

The void at the centre of this culture generated a pseudo-centre – the timeless ego whose metempsychosis in discipline after discipline has been encountered in this survey. The price of missing sociology, let alone Marxism, was the prevalence of psychologism. A culture which lacks the instruments to conceive the social totality inevitably falls back on the nuclear psyche, as First Cause of society and history. This invariant substitute is explicit in Malinowski, Namier, Eysenck and Gombrich. It has a logical consequence. Time exists only as intermittence (Keynes), decline (Leavis) or oblivion (Wittgenstein). Ultimately (Namier, Leavis or Gombrich), the twentieth century itself becomes the impossible object. The era of revolutions is, necessarily, unthinkable.

The consequences of this total constellation for the Left need no emphasis. The chloroforming effect of such cultural configuration, its silent and constant underpinning of the social status quo, are deadly. British culture, as it is now constituted, is a deeply damaging and stifling force, operating against the growth of any revolutionary Left. It quite literally deprives the Left of any source of concepts and categories with which to analyze its own society, and thereby attain a fundamental precondition for changing it. History has tied this knot; only history will ultimately undo it. A revolutionary culture is not for tomorrow. But a revolutionary practice within culture is possible and necessary today. The student struggle is its initial form.

The only British locus for an emergent counter-current had, argued Anderson, been literary criticism:

Suppressed and denied in every other sector of thought, the second, displaced home of the totality became literary criticism. Here, no expatriate influence ever became dominant. Leavis commanded his subject, within his own generation. With him, English literary criticism conceived the ambition to become the vaulting centre of 'humane studies and of the university'. English was 'the chief of the humanities'. This claim was unique to England: no other country has ever produced a critical discipline with these pretentions. They should be seen, not as a reflection of megalomania on the part of Leavis, but as a symptom of the objective vacuum at the centre of the culture. Driven out of any obvious habitats, the notion of the totality found refuge in the least expected of studies. ...

Lacking any sociological formation, registering a decline but unable to provide a theory of it, Leavis was ultimately trapped in the cultural nexus he hated. His empiricism become banally reactionary in old age. Like many thinkers, he survived himself to his detriment. But the importance of his achievements remains. It is no accident that in the fifties, the one serious work of socialist theory in Britain—Raymond Williams's *The Long Revolution*—should have emerged from literary criticism, of all disciplines. This paradox was not a mere quirk: in a culture which everywhere repressed the notion of totality, and the idea of critical reason, literary criticism represented a refuge. The mystified form they took in Leavis's work, which prevented him ever finding answers to his questions, may be obvious today. But it was from within this tradition that Williams was able to develop a systematic socialist thought, which was a critique of all forms of utilitarianism and fabianism – the political avatars of empiricism in the labour movement. The detour Williams had to make through English literary criticism is the appropriate tribute to it.

The conclusion Perry Anderson drew from his extraordinarily ambitious analysis and scintillating taxonomy of the contours of almost the entire range of academic disciplines, was that the primary task of the new New Left was now to develop the totalising approach so singularly absent – and this could best be enabled by making available to English readers the accumulated resources of European continental theory, which would supply that disabling lack in the English intellectual landscape. The new publishing house New Left Books, later Verso, therefore embarked upon an impressive programme of translation and distribution of the high points of European intellectual culture. The sought-after totalising framework or perspective was presumably supposed to enable – at some point in the future – a more decisive and effective strategic intervention in the socialist cause. . . .

Some parallels with Eliot's earlier cultural-political project are immediately striking, if odd. Though the choice of imported European theorists might be different, the notion that therein lay the remedy for England's intellectual poverty was shared. It had, after all, been a prime ambition of *The Criterion* under Eliot's editorial direction from 1922 to 1939 to make available to its parochial English readers the full scope of continental thought. And though the kind of totalising account which Anderson postulated was clearly intended to lead to rather different political outcomes from those favoured by Eliot, nevertheless the *kind* of socio-cultural analysis offered in Eliot's *The Idea of a Christian Society* and *Notes Towards the Definition of Culture* had clearly been one of the direct influences against which Raymond Williams had originally initiated his own critical trajectory: Eliot's work had, after all, been the immediate precursor to, as well as the target of, Williams's *Culture and Society*.

Yet Eliot receives no mention or acknowledgement in Anderson's argument: in literary criticism, apparently, 'no expatriate influence ever became dominant' – despite the obvious sense in which Leavis' whole project was shaped not only by the centrality for him of Eliot's poetry but also by the contours of his literary-critical judgements and historical interpretation having been so considerably influenced by Eliot's critical essays. Nor was Eliot ever mentioned in that discussion in Williams's rooms the evening after Anderson's paper.

Since Anderson's programmatic analysis, now half a century ago, the British New Left has valiantly absorbed wave after wave of translated contributions towards a theoretical consolidation, intellectual transformation, and putative totalisation – which has never, somehow, actually emerged. More significantly perhaps, no overall strategic conception of the originally desired transition towards 'socialism' has clearly emerged either. Indeed, faithful readers of the tenaciously long-running *New Left Review* have effectively been subscribers to an editorial objective the content of which was procrastinatedly undefined and the strategy for achieving which remained frustratingly opaque – and in such circumstances the temptation to re-label one's intellectual efforts, whether as author or reader, as 'theoretical practice' was understandably alluring, if perhaps somewhat unconvincing. It is therefore with a sense of disappointed *déjà vu* that one is now inclined to put some recent Verso volumes on *The Idea of Communism* on the shelf alongside *The Idea of a Christian Society*.

Looking back, some decades later, at his original analysis Anderson re-surveyed the intellectual scene. Commenting on Terry Eagleton's prolific intervening work, Anderson offered a summary of what he saw as Eagleton's account of the trajectory of literary criticism:

The meaning of criticism now became redefined. For Arnold it was the uplift of great works of literature alone that could redeem the lower orders. This conception of literary value passed down to Leavis, who attempted to reconcile Augustan and Romantic stances by emphasizing both the sociability of literature and the arduousness of understanding it—in opposition to either academic isolation, or amateur appreciation of its abiding tradition. In fact, *Scrutiny* merely became one more embattled minority. Its failure paved the way for ever more technical conceptions of criticism as a professional discipline without civilizing pretensions. Their sway was in due course overthrown by the vocally anti-objectivist 'literary theory' of the most recent period. Yet this too is only another avatar of the shrinking of the critical project itself. Latter-day criticism, Eagleton concluded, serves no wider interest than itself. Williams's greatness was to escape its horizons, in a radical and unclassifiable *oeuvre*. But this work was in effect addressed to a counter-public that was missing—a politically organized, class readership, such as had once existed in Weimar Germany or Britain in the thirties. In the eighties, under the stifling weight of the mass media, feminism has come nearest to creating such an alternative public sphere.

The logic of this paradigm-shift allegedly entailed that:

Literature as such was an illusion: it was that segment of writing  socially valued at any given time—such valuations being always imbued with the dominant relations of ideology and power. Literary criticism, or theory, was therefore no more than a branch of such ideologies, without unity or identity, to be buried unceremoniously.  What was required instead was a cultural theory equivalent to the older science of rhetoric—that is, a typology of the different forms and functions of signifying practices at large. Liberated from any canonical incubus, such a rhetoric could then freely mine every available methodological resource for particular ends, in the general service of a socialism giving substance to the liberal ideals of human betterment.

There was perhaps a further entailment:

This obsequy for literary criticism left one ambiguity unresolved. Was it just literature that had been laid to rest, or the critical attitude as well? Williams had repudiated the very term criticism, as too contaminated by invidious judgement. But the strict logic of this position undermines the very politics it is designed to advance: for if texts are not to be criticized, on what grounds can societies? (*NLR*, 180 & 182, 1990)

Since, it seemed, 'literature as such' 'had been laid to rest', Anderson does not directly discuss any 'literature' at all and again, as in the earlier analysis, does not even register the once-pervasive impact of Eliot as both critic and poet, and, indeed, as cultural theorist.

However, as a postscript to this phase of my own engagement with Eliot, I want to recall the last lecture I heard Raymond Williams give in Cambridge, a tribute to the recently dead Lucien Goldmann, in 1971. By then Williams had indeed read Lukacs. I have added the italics:

Goldmann, following Lukács, distinguishes between actual consciousness and possible consciousness: the actual, with its rich multiplicity; the possible, with its degree of maximum adequacy and coherence. A social group is ordinarily limited to its actual consciousness, and this will include many kinds of misunderstanding and illusion: elements of false consciousness which will often, of course, be used and reflected in ordinary literature. But there is also a maximum of possible consciousness: that view of the world raised to its highest and most coherent level, limited only by the fact that to go further would mean that the group would have to surpass itself, to change into or be replaced by a new social group. Most sociology of literature, Goldmann then argues, is concerned with the relatively apparent relations between ordinary literature and *actual consciousness*: relations which show themselves at the level of content, or in conventional elaboration of its common illusions. The new sociology of literature—that of genetic structuralism—will be concerned with *the more fundamental relations of possible consciousness, for it is at the centre of his case that the greatest literary works are precisely those which realize a world-view at its most coherent and most adequate, its highest possible level.* We should not then mainly study peripheral relations: correspondences of content and background; overt social relations between writers and readers. We should study, in the greatest literature, the organizing categories, the essential structures, which give such works their unity, their specific aesthetic character, their strictly literary quality; and which at the same time reveal to us the maximum possible consciousness of the social group—in real terms, the social class—

(*NLR* 1/67, May-June 1971)

There had been a shift, certainly, between the 'case' put by Leavis and the position argued by Williams, but also a continuity: ' it is at the centre of his [Goldmann's] case that the greatest literary works are precisely those which realize a world-view at its most coherent and most adequate, its highest possible level' . This might even seem not so very distant, after all, from Leavis in 1932:

Poetry matters because of the kind of poet who is more alive than other people, more alive in his own age. He is, as it were, at the most conscious point of the race in his time. ('He is the point at which the growth of the mind shows itself,' says Mr I. A. Richards. )

And:

To invent techniques that shall be adequate to the ways of feeling, or modes of experience, of adult, sensitive moderns is difficult in the extreme. Until it has been once done it is so difficult as to seem impossible. One success makes others more probable because less difficult. . . . That is the peculiar importance of Mr. T. S. Eliot. ... he has solved his own problem as a poet, and so done more than solve the problem for himself.

Perhaps there was, after all, a strategic or at least rhetorical need, in contention with this persisting continuity, for a sharp 'epistemological break', soon to be undertaken by Eagleton.

But what, then, was one to make of the 'literature' still so crowded upon the bookshelves and proliferating on the reading lists – for example, that once unprecedented poem *The Waste Land,* which had indeed in its own time acted almost as the paradigmatic analysis and manifesto for an earlier generation and for an earlier ambitious periodical, *The Criterion?*

\*

# *Lecturing* : on *The Waste Land*

*...hypocrite lecteur..?*

By 1971 I had written my PhD and had even found a job, teaching 'English Literature'. But was English Literature now just an illusion? Eliot, certainly, was not going to go away. At the University of Kent in the early 1970s there was a whole course on Eliot. There was even an Eliot College and an annual series of Eliot Lectures, financed by Faber & Faber, and attended by Mrs Valerie Eliot. Various colleagues were 'working on' Eliot: Michael Grant was shortly to edit *Eliot: The Critical Heritage*, Graham Clarke to compile four substantial volumes, 1858 pages, of *Eliot: Critical Assessments*, Martin Scofield to publish *T.S. Eliot: The Poems*, and so on. I gave lectures on Eliot and language, on Eliot and drama, even on Eliot and the Moot Group - at some point I had borrowed Alec Vidler's set of the unpublished papers from the meetings of the Moot Group, though I conscientiously honoured my undertaking not to make copies of them, and even resisted (it was easy to do in those days) any temptation to publish articles using them.

The University of Kent at Canterbury in the 1970s was multi-disciplinary in a way that tried partly to counteract the state of affairs which Anderson had analysed. Not only did every student in the Humanities Faculty have to take an integrated overall programme in the first year, which combined cross-disciplinary core courses with co-disciplinary options in 20th century European philosophy, literature, and history, but Kent was also at that time rapidly developing a variety of quite new interdisciplinary degree programmes, including the first Film Studies degree in the UK, the first Women's Studies program, and even the first MA in Socialist Studies.

Within this context, however, Eliot continued to be discussed in fairly traditional seminars and lectures. I gave a short series of lectures in which I tried to assess the significance of the then-recently published facsimile edition of the material that became *The Waste Land*. That material raised for me again some of the issues around 'impersonality', including very directly the relationship between the work and the writer, the poem and the poet. My thinking about it even seemed to offer a somewhat mischievous way into an account of the work of 'T. S. Eliot' as indeed a kind of 'illusion'.

What follows is not, however, a reconstruction of those lectures, as given at the time, but rather a layering of the overall argument which I then constructed, from my initial reading of the facsimile of *The Waste Land* material, together with some more recent responses to the relevant letters and other material which have since become available. Time past and time present, therefore, are both perhaps contained in this version.

The lecture format itself, of course, allowed the provision of handouts to the audience, reproducing some of the material discussed, and it also allowed considerable amounts of oral quotation. Given the copyright restrictions on quoting Eliot – a topic to be considered later – I can only suggest that, if possible, you have that facsimile edition to hand. Since the two-volume edition of the annotated text of the poems published in 2015 now includes a great deal of the material relevant to my argument, I have tried in this writtten version simply to summarise that material where relevant and to give references to where it can be found in that new edition. So, shall we follow...

## i : composing

A close reading of the assemblage of typescripts and manuscripts published as *T.S. Eliot: The Waste Land: a facsimile and transcript of the original drafts including the annotations of Ezra Pound edited by Valerie Eliot* (Faber and Faber, 1971) – hereafter referred to as 'the facsimile' – can lead to confirmation of what was previously only suspected or known in rather general terms: that the poem, or indeed the collection of poems, which Eliot originally envisaged as comprising what was to become *The Waste Land* and had given to Pound for comment, suggestions, and correction, was radically different from the version eventually printed in 1922 and now so familiar.

When Ezra Pound died in 1972, a year after the facsimile edition had finally appeared, the suggestion by *The Times* obituarist that the structure and success of *The Waste Land* owed more to Pound's editorial reshaping than to Eliot's initial assemblage of draft fragments, aroused some instant indignation. The obituarist wrote (2 November 1972):

[Pound] arranged for the publication of Mr T. S. Eliot's earliest poems; and helped him with the recension of a somewhat, originally, inchoate assemblage of verse that ultimately became *The Waste Land*. . . . The recent publication by Mrs Valerie Eliot of the original draft of *The Waste Land* with Pound's suggestions for excision and for improvement of the writing of particular passages reveals Pound's extraordinary flair as a physician for other people's sick poems – 'There and there thou ailest!' – and his staunchness and loyalty as a friend. ... The original version of the famous episode of the typist and the carbuncular young man was much longer and, as the final draft is not, nasty. ... A whole section in heroic couplets about a lady of fashion called Fresca, is not only a poor parody of Pope – Pound was right in telling Eliot that you cannot write a parody of Pope unless you can write better than Pope in his own form, which no poet of this century can do – but also peculiarly nasty. ... If The Waste Land had been published in its first draft, it would have been a document of, not exactly madness, but very distressing psychological instability. Pound was the main instrument in turning it into an enigmatic near-masterpiece.

This prompted an irate letter to the editor from a Mr Michael Rose (9 November 1972):

Sir, I am not qualified to comment on the larger issues which your obituary of Ezra Pound, by its oddly fragmented mixture of criticism, history and gossip, will raise; so I restrict myself to this: I find it extraordinary that the occasion should have been used to attempt a demonstration that Pound was more important to the completion of The Waste Land than Eliot...

However, if one tries now – and it takes a considerable effort of deliberate amnesia – to read the material of the poem as Eliot initially offered it to Pound, one can readily conclude that it was indeed an unimpressive performance and that it desperately needed Pound's intervention.

What looms large in the material are several sections of verse narrative or description: a caustically satirical but rather limp account of a drunken night-out in Boston ; a set of stanzas devoted to Fresca, a would-be poet(ess); the tepid sexual encounter, which partly survives now as the typist/Tiresias episode; an extended account of a sea voyage, which ends in the familiar lines about Phlebas. In addition, Eliot seems to have envisaged some inclusion of a lengthy piece entitled 'The Death of the Duchess' and perhaps a long poem about Saint Narcissus, only a few modified lines of either being eventually incorporated into the final version of the poem. All these various materials, in my view – and Pound's – were very unsatisfactory, indeed largely failures. As well as the typed pages, there are several passages of apparently very rapidly drafted later lines, and some pages of handwritten fair copies of various sections.

Since this facsimile material appeared in 1971 scholars have pored over the problems it presents. In particular, the question of the chronology of Pound's engagement with the material was something of a puzzle. In some still influential accounts (which remain available in print and on-line), it had been assumed that the sequence of events was roughly as follows: Eliot wrote some passages of Part III of his intended 'long poem' in Margate during his convalescent stay in October 1921; he then went to Lausanne in November 1921, meeting Pound briefly in Paris *en route*; in Lausanne he wrote more of the poem, which in some form he showed to Pound; then, according to a letter dated 24th of December 1921, Pound wrote to him saying how much the poem had been improved; in January 1922 Eliot returned to London, again seeing Pound briefly in Paris, and there was a further exchange of letters between Pound and Eliot late in January 1922 discussing some minor details of Pound's response.

This account is however very misleading. The crucial letter apparently dated 24th of December 1921, first published in 1950 in the *Selected Letters* of Pound, and still so dated in volume 1 of the 1988 edition of Eliot's letters,[2] is in fact

---

[2] Edited by D.D. Paige, Faber and Faber, 1950, p.169; *The Letters of T. S. Eliot*, edited by Valerie Eliot, Volume I 1989-

mis-dated in this narrative. Pound dated it himself as '24 Saturnus, An 1', which we know from his design of a new calendar (celebrating the completion of *Ulysses*) published in *The Little Review*, was for him 24th January 1922.[3] The corrected date implies that Pound's enthusiast phrase 'MUCH improved' refers to a version of *The Waste Land* sent to him in Paris *after* Eliot had returned to London, and the subsequent exchange of letters is a follow-up to that response. It seems possible from Pound's second letter – the third in the exchange – that Pound himself no longer had a copy of the poem in front of him by the end of January 1922, since he remarks to Eliot that he 'thought' he had 'crossed out' a query from Dorothy Pound, which implies that he no longer had a typescript to check.[4]

The sequence of Eliot's own composition of the material has also been subjected to considerable academic scrutiny. It is perhaps appropriate that a poem which has been praised for introducing a typist into modern poetry has eventually yielded some of its compositional history through an examination of the three typewriters involved.

---

1922, Faber and Faber, 1988, [henceforth: *L I, 1988*], p. 497. This edition was corrected and supplemented in 2009. References to this revised edition are simply to *L1* and subsequent volumes of the letters are referenced as *L2, L3*.
[3] The mis-dating was first corrected by Hugh Kenner, in *Eliot in his Time*, ed. A. Walton Litz, Princeton University Press, 1973, p. 44, n.7.
[4] *L I*, p. 504: Eliot to Pound [24? January 1922]; p. 505: Pound to Eliot [27? January 1922]; see also p. 506: Eliot to Pound 12 March 1922. The 2015 edition of the poems includes extracts from these letters in the extended notes on *The Waste Land, I,* p.547ff.

A number of the pages of material included in the package of *Waste Land* drafts have been dated to as early as 1914 or even October 1913, and some perhaps to 1916 or possibly 1919. It seems probable that Eliot (re-)typed much of the newer material which now survives as Parts I and II of the published poem on his long-serving typewriter before late August 1921, at which point – as we know from Vivien's letter of 23 August 1921 (*L1*, p. 575) – Eliot's brother Harry, on a visit to London, gifted his own better typewriter in exchange for Eliot's old one. Some parts of *The Waste Land* materials were then typed, on this second typewriter, before Eliot went to Margate in October 1921, though he probably did not take the typewriter with him, and he only typed up some of the further material written in Margate in the interval between returning to London and then going off to Paris and Lausanne. Eliot almost certainly did not have a typewriter with him in Lausanne, and both the fair copies and the scribbled drafts of Parts IV and V were hand-written there. Eliot spent a fortnight in Paris on his way back to London in the first weeks of January 1922, at which point he borrowed a third typewriter, Pound's own machine, to provide typewritten versions of part IV and V.[5]

Whatever scholarly consensus might one day be arrived at concerning this possible sequence of composition, there still remains – it seems to me – a widespread and major misinterpretation of the implications of Pound's interventions. My own suggestions are relatively independent of the precise details of the disputed chronology.

---

[5] The most determined attempt to give a full account is now in Lawrence Rainey, *Revisiting The Waste Land*, Yale University Press, 2005. Rainey carefully tabulated several years of Eliot's typewritten material, including the paper used. See p. 34f for Rainey's dating.

The usual account assumes that Pound excised the whole of two of the longer descriptive sequences – the stanzas concerning Fresca and those entitled 'The Death of the Duchess' – while Eliot himself removed the opening Boston night-out episode. Most critics also see Pound as having so severely mauled the account of the sea voyage in Part IV that Eliot was appropriately following Pound's response by removing the whole of it.

However, if one looks more closely at Pound's treatment of the sea voyage in Part IV it is clear that he was in fact salvaging a much shorter and far more compressed poem from Eliot's somewhat slack and sprawling lines. Pound reduced the three opening quatrains from 12 lines to perhaps 8 and the following 69 lines to approximately 22 half-lines. One can easily reconstruct what would have been the resulting passage, which moves rapidly and succinctly, eliding and cutting the action in recognisably Poundian fashion (*Facsimile*, pp. 62, 64, 66, 68):

> With a light fair breeze
> We beat around the cape
> From the Dry Salvages
> A porpoise snored on the swell astern.
> Opened, a water-cask smelt of oil
> The garboard strake began to leak
> The canned beans were stench
> Two men came down with gleet;
> "Eat!" they said, [*etc.*]

This seems to me also the case if one examines in detail Pound's editorial changes and deletions in both the Fresca and the Hampstead / Duchess sequences. Of the 36 rhyming couplets concerned with Fresca, Pound initially cut a mere 4 lines, and commented critically in the margin, but, presumably on a second reading, he cut more severely, leaving only about 22 lines of the original 71 —to which

Eliot at some point still thought of adding about 15 new lines in draft.[6] The opening 45 lines of Fresca, reduced to 9, would then have run, in Pound's cut version:

Admonished by the sun's inclining ray,
White-armed Fresca blinks, and yawns, and gapes,
Her hands caress the egg's well rounded dome,
She sinks in revery, till the letters come.
Fresca! In other time or place had been
A meek and weeping Magdalene;
More sinned against than sinning, bruised and marred,
The lazy laughing Jenny of the bard.
Now autumn's favourite in a furnished flat.

And so on.

The opening section of "The Death of the Duchess", in three segments of 9, 5 and 2 lines, was reduced simply to:

The inhabitants of Hampstead
Know what to think and what to feel
The inhabitants of Hampstead are bound
                    forever on the wheel.

But what is there
For me and you
What is there for us to do?

The remaining 58 or so lines had several whole and half-lines cut, and others marked with negative comments, but there is no vigorous scoring through of whole passages.[7] Again, it would be possible to retrieve a much reduced, and

---

[6] *Facsimile*, pp. 38 & 40, pp. 22 & 26, p. 29.
[7] *Facsimile*, pp. 104, 106.

admittedly still not very impressive, poem from Pound's apparently scattered corrections and excisions.

As an indicative comparison, the Tiresias / typist episode takes up lines 121-188 in the version Eliot gave to Pound, but in the published poem these 67 lines are compressed into 41, lines 215-256.[8] In this case, Eliot simply accepted Pound's emendations and we are now so familiar with the compressed version that we can find it almost unthinkable that the poem once included Eliot's original version.

It is not therefore, in my view, the case that Pound wished totally to exclude either the Fresca or the Hampstead and Duchess components from the poem which he saw Eliot as still in the process of composing. I would even make a more tentative argument for Pound  not at first totally excluding the short poem entitled 'Dirge' ('Full fathom five..') which Eliot at some stage might have intended for insertion into Part IV (Pound merely marked it: '?? doubtful'), and also perhaps some part at least of the poem on Saint Narcissus, the name evoking another kind of death by water. In all these various cases, Eliot seems to have made, or brought with him, a handwritten fair copy to work on in Lausanne, presumably at least to consider for inclusion in the final poem.

Whether Eliot himself cancelled the 54 lines of the Boston sequence, the typed page of which open the draft of the poem, before or after Pound saw the draft materials, is unclear, but certainly Pound offered no comment on this typescript page as we have it.

---

[8] *Facsimile*, pp. 42-47,  140-41

These mildly tedious detailed considerations are of some importance because they raise several related questions.

What overall shape for the poem did Eliot have in mind when he assembled this body of material to take with him to Lausanne? And what shape did Pound perhaps propose, assume, or intend, when he made his various editorial interventions?

As to the first, it is at least plausible to suggest that prior to both Pound's interventions and Eliot's own drafting of Part V in Lausanne, the overall poem may well have had something like the following rough shape, scale, and perhaps order. Using a shorthand hopefully clear from the facsimile edition, one could suggest that the poem was somehow to consist of:

Part I: Boston (54 lines); April (18 lines); roots/ rock (12 lines); hyacinth girl (12 lines); Sosostris (18 lines); unreal city / Stetson (18 lines). [total c. 130 lines?]

Part II: 'The chair she sat in' (35 lines); 'my nerves are bad' (18 lines); perhaps (re-)conflated with some of 'The Death of the Duchess' material: the Hampstead passage (15 lines) and 'In the evening' (58 lines); the pub scene (35 lines). [total c.160??]

Part III: Fresca (72 lines); rats / king (16 lines); unreal city / Eugenides (12 lines); London swarming (16 lines); typist (68 lines); Margate / Hampstead / Richmond, etc. (? 16 lines). [total c. 200?]

Part IV: sailors (12 lines); sea voyage (70 lines); Phlebas (8-10 lines); and possibly some part of Saint Narcissus (34 lines); and perhaps Dirge (17 lines). [total c. 140?]

It would be helpful to have a new edition of the facsimile material which would make it easier to register such possibilities, though it is at least an informative exercise to re-arrange photocopied pages from the facsimile into some such order. Unfortunately, the 2015 edition of the poems makes any such alternative original arrangements even harder to grasp.[9]

On my tentative suggested overall arrangement, each Part of the poem (still retaining its working title 'He Do the Police in Different Voices') would have had a broad consonance of both scale and content with the other Parts, each comprising an alternation between quasi-descriptive or narrative verse sections, focused on 'characters', and shorter much more compressed or 'poetic' passages of both comment and intense imagery, punctuated with intermittent strategic placings of clearly marked brief quotation fragments (those eventually italicised in print).

In a short article published in April 1921, 'Prose And Verse', Eliot had written: 'I see no reason why a considerable variety of verse forms may not be employed within the limits of single poem'.[10] Much later, in the overall composition of *Four Quartets* Eliot was to deploy an arrangement alternating longer and shorter verse forms as the most obvious structural parallel between the respective five parts of each Quartet.

---

[9] Unfortunately, I find the overall arrangement of the 2015 edition wholly unsatisfactory and the suggestion concerning 'interlude' sections in the original *The Waste Land* unconvincing, but a footnote is not the place to dispute these matters.

[10] *Chapbook*, 22, April 1921, pp. 3-10. Now available on-line : http://muse.jhu.edu : *The Complete Prose of T.S.Eliot: The Critical Edition*, published by Johns Hopkins Press and Faber and Faber Ltd.

In a *Waste Land* modelled in a similar way, as schematically outlined above, the overall scale of each Part and the organisation of its constituent components would have had a certain consistency, more or less immediately visible on the printed pages.

Each Part, moreover, would have had a somewhat similar distribution of 'voices' from clearly differentiated social backgrounds, and at least four of the Parts also included some version of an 'unreal' encounter (Stetson, Mr Eugenides, the hallucinated three women in the sea voyage, and the mysterious third who walks beside us) – figures perhaps not entirely to be assimilated into normal social categories or situations. There is also an element of triple patternings, both of content and of verse, echoing across each Part. Most obviously, the distribution of a larger cast of 'characters' gives the poem a much broader canvas and a wider range of 'different voices' than in the familiar published version.

Following this highly tentative suggestion, we can further outline what the overall arrangement of the poem might have looked like *after* Pound's *initial* local interventions. It would have retained compressed but still substantial versions of the 'Hampstead' and 'evening' segments in Part II, the cut-down versions of both 'Fresca' and the typist in Part III, the compacted version of the sea voyage, and possibly the 17-line 'Dirge' in Part IV. Added to this would have been the draft of Part V which Eliot had typed on Pound's typewriter from his handwritten drafts composed in Lausanne, and which Pound approved for inclusion almost without comment. It is possible that Pound would have seen some such provisionally assembled overall version before Eliot finally left Paris for London in January 1922, perhaps when Eliot returned Pound's typewriter to him.

This, I am suggesting, would have been roughly the overall shape and state which the poem had when Eliot returned to London with it, to ponder Pound's detailed interventions and annotations. It would then have been Eliot's decision not only to omit the long opening Boston episode but also to excise most of the Duchess section (leaving from that material only a reduced and re-written 'my nerves' passage), to leave out the whole of Fresca, and to remove the entirety of Part IV apart from Phlebas – a set of decisions which, taken together, could well have prompted Pound's emphatic reaction when this new configuration (now retyped into only 19 pages?) was sent to him from London towards the end of January 1922: 'MUCH improved' was his immediate comment. But it was no longer the poem which Pound had seen in Paris only a week or so before: the new version was not at all what Pound had been expecting.

Thus, primarily by (in my reconstructed sequence) wholly deleting rather than retaining the several compressed versions of segments which Pound had amended but nevertheless intended to be left in, Eliot had not only considerably reduced the poem but also radically altered its overall compositional character, almost removing the broadly comparable patterning and scale of each Part. This is most drastically apparent in the now very odd reduction of Part IV to a mere eight or ten lines. But what remains unclear is whether Eliot in that rapid revision was consciously striving to arrive at a definite alternative overall structure, and if so what it was. Such a comprehensive reduction would still, however, have left Eliot querying in his reply to Pound precisely the various specific and local elements he was unsure about in Pound's detailed response to the new version and which he therefore raised in his follow-up letter to Pound.

What is apparent from the original annotated materials is that Pound had previously offered only very local interventions, a matter of improving individual lines, excising bad lines or passages, deleting some short segments, but mainly compressing rather than excising several of the longer sequences. Pound himself seems to have suggested, at least on the evidence of the facsimile materials themselves, no overall re-shaping or basic re-structuring of the materials into another organization or order. Indeed, the only substantial mark on the typescripts indicating a possible, and rather minor, re-ordering change of that kind is a pencilled arrow by Eliot himself, moving the hyacinth girl lines to *before* the 'roots that flourish' passage – though he did not implement this alteration of sequence in the end. But the structural changes Eliot had now made, probably in only a week or so of drastic revision in London, were very considerable indeed.

It is of course possible that when they met in Paris in early January 1922 Pound and Eliot directly discussed and considered possible re-shapings of the whole poem and the rationale for its eventual overall organisation. However, when Pound responded to the revamped version on 24th of January 1922, Eliot seemed still to be wanting to include what Pound referred to as 'the remaining superfluities', but Eliot remained uncertain where to place them, perhaps as elements within the poem or as short ancillary poems. Pound firmly advised that though these might possibly go at the beginning of the poem, or perhaps before it as separate items, the poem itself definitely ended with 'Shantih'. It is worth emphasising that the only evidence that Pound clearly perceived an overall shape or structure for the poem was in his second letter in late January 1922, replying to Eliot's query as to whether or not wholly to excise even the Phlebas lines. It's also perhaps worth noting that a complete excision of 'Part IV' at that stage might have left the remaining four Parts still to some extent consonant in overall parallel structure, and Eliot in a letter on 20th January 1922 to Scofield Thayer even spoke of the poem as being 'in four parts' (*L1*, p. 263)

It was Eliot's query concerning Phlebas which provoked from Pound his clearest, and indeed the only, extant indication that Pound had by then a definite conception of the structure of the poem as a whole, as distinct from the local corrections and comments he had previously offered on the typescripts. He emphatically advised Eliot not to print *Gerontion* as some kind of prelude or prologue and then added:

> I DO advise keeping Phlebas. I more'n advise. Phlebas is an integral part of the poem; the card pack introduces him, the drowned phoen. sailor, and he is needed ABSoloootly where he is. Must stay in. (*L1*, p. 630)

Pound remarked in the same letter, 'I thought I had crossed out her queery' (*sic*) – a question from Dorothy Pound about the use of 'wash' in connection with 'barges' – which indicates that Pound no longer had his own annotations in front of him and therefore could not be sure. This also implies that he had already sent back the retyped (carbon?) copy of the poem itself and was responding to Eliot's other queries only from his memory of the text.

Eliot had thus, it is worth repeating, sent the new 'MUCH improved' version of the poem, which he had finished re-assembling and revising in London, to Pound around the third week of January, after returning from Paris with the still partly unresolved material only a few days before. The crucial process of re-casting and re-typing might only have taken the week or so between returning on January 16th and the weekend of the 24th by which date Pound had already received the new version in Paris.

Whether by the time he posted this probably still-provisional new version to Pound even Eliot himself had any settled grasp of a firm overall pattern or structure in the revised poem can therefore be questioned, since not only was he still hesitating over 'the remaining superfluities', but – as we have seen – his follow-up letter to Pound had tentatively suggested adding *Gerontion* and deleting Phlebas. It is only during this follow-up exchange of letters in late January that Pound at last so emphatically characterised the poem as running from April to Shantih, and as 'the longest poem in the language'.

Nevertheless, at various times much later into 1922 Eliot himself was still considering a possible two-part publication of the poem, to be spread across the first two issues of *The Criterion*.[11] The notion that Parts I and II might be published separately from, and therefore read some three months in advance of, Parts III, IV and V might well indicate a continuing preparedness on Eliot's part to regard the poem as far from the fully integrated and complexly unified masterpiece it has since often been taken to be.

The tentative conclusion which therefore emerges would be that Eliot himself had no more secure a grasp of any overall cohesion and final unity of the poem than Pound's memory of it would have provided him with, even when Pound was trying, also at various times later in 1922, to persuade Quinn, Liveright, and *The Dial* to accept it as a unified achievement rather than as the assemblage of fragments or perhaps even as a volume of single poems

---

[11] E.g. *L I*, p. 537 : to Richard Aldington, 30th June 1922; p. 569 : to Richard Cobden-Sanderson, 10th September 1922.

which it most obviously by then would still have appeared to be.

I might put this more bluntly or emphatically: it is plausible that by late January 1922 neither Eliot nor Pound 'understood' the poem fully as a structured whole, or if they did so, they quite possibly understood it rather differently from each other. Insofar as Pound was still expecting the final version to include all the sections he had so radically compressed, and Eliot had misunderstood Pound as intending them to be excised completely, each had to some extent mistaken the other's conception of the overall form of the poem. And if Eliot had finally decided that the total excision of these considerable elements was now preferable, it was a late and perhaps very rapid decision taken after, and despite, the considerable effort Pound had already expended on the original intended components of the poem.

Put another way: what is especially odd, even unique, about *The Waste Land* is that its process of dual composition, combining the interventions of Pound's local corrections and detailed revisions with Eliot's own overall last-minute reshaping of what was previously a semi-structured collage or bricolage, meant that neither Pound nor Eliot necessarily grasped, even to each other's satisfaction, what any overall formal organisation of the poem, as finally published, actually was – and is.

The character of Pound's localised annotations and the jointly but differently intended overall reduction of the poem from a thousand lines to about 450, coupled with Eliot's continuing uncertainties as to what was to be included or excluded, plus the hesitation over the status of part IV, the possible function of *Gerontion* as a kind of curtain-raiser, and Eliot's readiness to publish the poem in separate parts across two issues of *The Criterion*, all tend to suggest that Eliot himself may well have been, and remained, almost as puzzled by any overall unity the work may have seemed to possess as subsequent critics have been.

Which is perhaps where the provision of the notorious Notes is especially relevant. Eliot later claimed that they were merely the factitious result of the poem proving to be several pages too short for the volume envisaged by Boni and Liveright. Yet this is at best disingenuous, since it would appear that he had begun to consider, and even perhaps compose, some form of Notes to the poem as early as February 1922, well before any definite publishing contract.[12] It is in the Notes that Eliot comes closest to claiming, or implying, that he had at least intended, and even achieved, an articulated overall composition.

The first Note speaks of the 'plan' of the poem and its 'incidental' symbolism as being derived from Jesse Weston's book – 'incidental' implying that some other but unspecified symbols in the poem are somehow more central or integral. But which are which? The claim that Tiresias somehow unifies the whole poem also deliberately leads the reader to look for a definite organising principle or some structuring architectonic motifs or devices as the way in which the poem is intentionally orchestrated. Yet the most Eliot offers in the way of any formal bonding is the notion of personal 'association', while the editorial character of the Notes seems to endow even these 'associations' with a merely supplementary character, as if the poem already enjoyed a structural or formal cogency

---

[12] See Eliot's letter to Maurice Firuski on 26th February 1922, proposing a possible *de luxe* edition, including 'some notes I intend to add'. This letter is mentioned in *L I*, p. 515 n.3 but not included. It is quoted in Rainey, *Revisiting*, p. 97.

and consistency to which – as with the 'incidental' symbolism – any such further personal associations might then be attached as merely ancillary or even accidental.

Of course, the one thing the Notes do *not* provide by way of assisting the reader towards understanding the nature of the poem is any reference whatsoever to the work of Ezra Pound, still less any acknowledgement of Pound's role in its composition. Even the phrase *il miglior fabbro* was at first only an inscription in the single complimentary copy sent to Pound himself, until it was added as late as 1925 to the printed UK editions of the poem, and then not till 1932 in any American edition.

Pound too, it can be noted, still seemed at times during 1922 to be undecided as to whether 'The Waste Land' referred to one poem or to a series of poems, the title perhaps of an overall volume rather than of a single poem. On 12th March 1922, pursuing his scheme of providing some form of collective financial assistance for Eliot, Pound referred to 'the most interesting 19 page poem in the language', but in an article published on 30th March 1922 he refers to Eliot as having produced 'a very important sequence of poems'. In a reported but perhaps reliable comment by John Peale Bishop, as late as August 1922 Pound apparently referred to *The Waste Land* as 'the new series of lyrics'.[13] After its publication, as David Moody has pointed out, Pound referred in print to *The Waste Land* on only two occasions: in that article of 30th March 1922 and in a letter to a little magazine in 1924. Unlike his emphatic public propaganda on behalf of Joyce's *Ulysses*, Pound for the rest of his life was almost

---

[13] See A. David Moody, *Ezra Pound : Poet*, volume 2, Oxford University Press, 2014, pp. 35, 33, and Rainey, *Revisiting*, p.74.

silent in print concerning *The Waste Land*.[14] Quite possibly, Pound too remained uncertain as to quite what kind of composition he had helped to produce.

There is, however, one indirectly recorded comment by Pound which may indicate what Pound himself had perhaps intended in his initial editorial interventions upon Eliot's material.

In the week after Pound's death, Basil Bunting also published an obituary article in *The Times*, in which he wrote (12th November 1972):

> When Mauberley and Homage to Propertius and the earliest Cantos were published, before The Waste Land and before Ulysses, Pound had set a standard capable of lasting. ... I, very young and presumptuous, thought I had found in Pound's Propertius most, or at least much, of what I had wanted to do with verse, but had lacked the skill. However, most poets and critics found it less difficult to understand what Joyce and Eliot were up to, and to expound or imitate them. Joyce and Eliot had taken a shorter journey through rather easier country.
>
> Besides, in 1922 when The Waste Land and Ulysses first reached beyond the coteries to something that might be called the public, very few people had any idea how much their authors owed to Ezra Pound ... Even his friends did not notice it.

A poet as alert to words as Bunting presumably registered that the verb 'notice' here could have also the sense of 'notifying': that nobody, including the 'loyal' Pound, ever

---

[14] Moody, *op.cit.*, p.33.

said in public quite how much the poem was indebted to Pound, even when Eliot received constant adulation for it. Bunting went on:

It took the critics a long time to forgive Ezra for puzzling them with new, misleading, complex, endless poetry. He said in the Thirties that Eliot had got stuck because he could not understand *Propertius*, and all the rest had got stuck a few books earlier still.

This reported comment concerning Eliot's alleged incomprehension of Pound's *Homage to Sextus Propertius* suggests at least one direction in which we might look for what Pound was perhaps aiming at in his re-working of *The Waste Land* material. And even what Eliot himself was reacting to in composing or compiling his original version.

Some critics have traced the genesis of *The Waste Land* to Eliot's New Year resolution in January 1920 to begin the process of composing a 'long poem'. A few months earlier, in October 1919, Eliot had written for *The Athenaeum* a review of Pound's *Quia Pauper Amavi*, published in England that month. The contents of that volume were listed as: Langue d'Oc I-V, Moeurs contemporaines, I-VIII, Three Cantos, Homage to Sextus Propertius I-XII.

In his review Eliot wrote that the new volume, Pound's 'best formed', 'is probably the most significant book that he has published' since it showed that Pound had 'pursued a constant aim with a deliberate and conscious method.' Eliot is fairly sharply dismissive of the poems grouped as 'contemporaneous', being unconvinced that they are good poems or that, 'even with Martial behind it, the modern satirical vein is of permanent importance.' But: 'the Propertius ... is one of the best things Mr. Pound has done. It is a new persona, a creation of a new character, recreating Propertius in himself, and himself in Propertius'.

He noted that: 'Parts of one elegy are joined to another, parts are omitted, the order is changed, and the series of twelve is extracted from all of the four books of elegies.' However, Pound in a letter to *The Athenaeum* responded to the review by complaining that Eliot had not made it clear whether he actually liked or approved of the *Propertius*. Eliot's reply somewhat evaded the question: 'As for his suspicion that I did not enjoy his Propertius, I did not think the question of public interest: *his non plebecula gaudet.*' [The plebs do not delight in these things.][15]

Eliot's own second volume of poems had quite recently been published by the Hogarth Press, on June 20, 1919, comprising a mere seven poems. This was expanded to twenty-three poems in the limited edition of *Ara Vus Prec* (*sic*) completed in December 1919, and published by John Rodker in February 1920, by reprinting most of the 1917 *Prufrock* volume. A variant of that volume was published in America as *Poems* in February 1920. Between then and the first appearance of *The Waste Land*, Eliot published only one short poem[16] and was presumably mainly preoccupied in assembling materials for and drafts of his 'long poem'. The ever-productive Pound meanwhile had published several ur-Cantos, including the Ovid Press volume *The Fourth Canto*, as well as the Ovid Press *Hugh Selwyn Mauberley*, and the more commercial collected volume *Umbra*.

---

[15] Now available at http://muse.jhu.edu : *The Complete Prose of T.S.Eliot.*

[16] 'Song to the Opherian', in *Tyro* I, 1922, p. 6 under the pseudonym Gus Krutzsch. A typed version of the 12-line poem is included in the facsimile material, p. 99, with Pound's amendments.

On 8th December 1921, just before Eliot passed through Paris on his way to Lausanne, Pound's latest collection *Poems 1918-21* was published by Boni & Liveright, which included most of *Quia Pauper Amavi*. But the contents list was now divided into two subtitled sections: 'Portraits' and 'Cantos'. 'Portraits' consisted of the following: 1. Homage To Sextus Propertius i-xii; 2. Langue D'oc i-v, Moeurs Contemporaines i-viii; 3. Hugh Selwyn Mauberley, Part I, Envoi 1919, Part II 1920 (Mauberley). The section 'Cantos', instead of the ur-Cantos 1 to 3 as in *Quia Pauper Amavi*, now contained four Cantos simply entitled 'The Fourth Canto' to 'The Seventh Canto'. The contents list itself is elaborately laid out, with the titles of each Part and of the individual poems variously aligned and indented.

As it happened, Horace Liveright was in Paris from 30th December 1921 to 4th January 1922, visiting Pound just as Eliot came back from Lausanne. One can assume that Liveright delivered Pound's own author's copy or copies of the just-published *Poems 1918-21* to him in Paris, and one might even fairly confidently assume that Eliot was given a complimentary copy of Pound's new volume. Certainly, Liveright had dinner with Pound, Joyce, and Eliot on 3rd January 1922, the day after Eliot's return from Lausanne, probably just at the time when Eliot was borrowing Pound's typewriter to work on the hand-written Lausanne material.

Though almost all of the separate elements which have survived into *The Waste Land* were already composed by this point, it is worth asking whether the final revision and re-assemblage of that material in Paris and then, rapidly, in London may have been influenced by the complex arrangement of Parts, grouped sections, and individual poems in Pound's newly published *Poems 1918-21* and whether indeed Eliot's ongoing consideration of the finally appropriate form for his own 'long poem' might have been shaped, or re-shaped, by his renewed response to much the same material, though now rather differently re-organised, as he had previously reviewed in *Quia Pauper Amavi*.

Eliot once remarked of one of Pound's earlier volumes that 'in *Lustra* are many voices'.[17] Eliot's own second book, though published anonymously, had been the short essay *Ezra Pound : His Metric and Poetry* commissioned by the publisher Knopf to accompany the controversial American appearance of *Lustra* in 1917 – which had first included 'Three Cantos' in their original form, very different versions from the later Cantos now numbered I-III, but already envisaged as beginning Pound's own 'poem of some length'. In choosing to work towards his own 'long poem' under the provisional title 'He Do the Police in Different Voices' Eliot may initially have had in mind more a set of various kinds of poem which would nevertheless, as 'different voices', have been unified as an overall orchestrated collection, a single cohesive volume rather than a single poem. And he may have envisaged at that stage a volume in imitative response to Pound's deliberately ordered and complex construction of *Quia Pauper Amavi* and, later, *Poems 1918-21*. Both these volumes had a much more explicit overall arrangement than *Lustra* and also incorporated, as their constitutive 'Parts', far more elaborately constructed sequences of individual poems.

Moreover, despite the fact that Eliot's Notes to *The Waste Land* make no reference whatsoever to Pound's work, it is patently the case that many phrases, motifs and metric forms which appear in the facsimile material can indeed be

---

[17] Introduction to *Ezra Pound Selected Poems*, Faber & Gwyer, 1928, p. xv

traced back to Pound's poems included in *Lustra, Quia Pauper Amavi,* and *Poems 1918-21.* One striking example might be indicated by a comparison between the sea voyage in Pound's original 'Canto III' in *Lustra* and Pound's compressed version of Eliot's sea voyage section in Part IV of *The Waste Land* material. But even without such Poundian intervention, one can trace distinct verbal echoes from, for example, 'Canto Four' as published in *The Dial* for June 1920 (pp. 689–692), only a few dozen pages away from E. E. Cummings's review of Eliot's own *Prufrock* volume in the same issue (pp. 781–4). In that Canto we encounter smoky light and torches melting in the glare, silver mirrors and swallows crying, a black cock crowing and the carvèd foot of a couch, leaves and petals in water and barges scraping, Terreus and someone waiting for golden rain, a questioning of the wind in a palace, 'what wind is the king's?'[18] And so on.

However, even though Eliot had obviously read all Pound's recent poems carefully, and numerous local echoes can be traced, nonetheless – as Basil Bunting's remark suggests – it is neither the *Sextus Propertius* nor the Cantos included in these volumes which seem to have shaped Eliot's conception of a possible overall form or structure for his own projected 'long poem' as a single work, but rather perhaps the looser but nevertheless carefully orchestrated relationships between separate poems which is offered within the other sections of *Quia Pauper Amavi* and of *Poems 1918-21* and in the overall organisation of those volumes.

---

[18] I suspect that this Canto stayed long in Eliot's working memory: on p. 691 'the camel drivers sit in the turn of the stairs' and there are 'three steps in an open field'.

Just as *Langue D'oc, Moeurs Contemporaines* and the *Mauberley* sections in *Poems 1918-21* offer period-shaped composites, precisely as 'Portraits', which in the one case gives us an indicative sampling of the sensibility of mediaeval Provence, and in the other a satirical portrait of the contemporary cultural-aesthetic landscape of London, so the collection of material which Eliot initially took with him to Lausanne and then presented to Pound could well have been intended as a somewhat similar survey, collage, or 'Portrait' of what in Eliot's view constituted the social, sexual, and cultural 'waste land' which he was attempting to delineate. This may have been envisaged as a set of apparently separate poems which, when assembled together as a 'long poem', would form a coherent work, but one perhaps still planned as basically a thematic volume consisting of 'Parts', as Pound's *Quia Pauper Amavi* had been. Eliot's revised overall title perhaps signalled a shift towards a different conception of the work, though it is not clear when the intended title was changed.

David Moody has argued, though not all critics would agree, that most of Pound's early volumes collecting individual poems were indeed carefully ordered and orchestrated, so that the poems formed a deliberate sequence. Certainly, the structure of *Hugh Selwyn Mauberley*, in particular, has long been argued over in ways reminiscent of critics offering their differing accounts of the problematic organisation of *The Waste Land*.[19] That *Hugh Selwyn Mauberley*'s collocation of short poems had an overall patterning and deliberate order was clear, if only from the nested arrangement of the contents list, even if critics continue to disagree as to quite what Pound intended

---

[19] See for example John Espey, *Ezra Pound's Mauberley*, University of California Press, 1955, 2nd edition 1974.

by the indicated arrangement, whether a single 'long poem' or not.

When reviewing *Quia Pauper Amavi*, in October 1919, Eliot had himself more less dismissed the satirical verse forms which had comprised the bulk of his own output thus far. Nevertheless, in envisaging an appropriate form for his own 'long poem' it was perhaps more specifically in imitation of the kind of overall structure of the *Moeurs Contemporaines* or *Mauberley* that Eliot had begun to assemble his new work throughout 1920-21, and it was still with some such form in mind that he was intending to reshape the material he took with him to Lausanne: somewhere between a collection of individual poems and a single poem constituting a unified volume.[20]

On the other hand, however, what Pound – when he set to work on this collection of typewritten and handwritten pages – was arguably seeking to re-configure Eliot's material *into* was formally something much more like the *Sextus Propertius* or even the *Cantos* sections of his *Poems 1918-21,* with their rather different forms of organisation. These were, after all, for the Pound who read Eliot's materials in Paris in late 1921 and early 1922, what he had recently regarded as the cutting edge and potential future of his own explorations in ambitious poetic form. Though he was clearly still content to see much of his earlier material in the *Quia Pauper Amavi* volume re-issued, he had already moved beyond them towards the formal

---

[20] A comparison might also be pursued with the complex arrangement of individual poems in Yeats's 1921 volume, *Michael Robartes and the Dancer* – ten poems from which had appeared in *The Dial*. See my *On Yeats: Upon A House* (NCQ 2015).

.

developments of the Cantos, with *Sextus Propertius* as the crucial intermediate stage.

So, although Pound mainly concentrated on improving Eliot's local metrical technique and phrasing, the accumulated impact of his various excisions and compressions was in effect – whether deliberately and consciously or not – to produce something very much closer in shape to his own recent work in progress and much more in accordance with his own formal preoccupations. Indeed, one might compare the detailed cutting and splicing which he performed on *The Waste Land* material with the procedures which Pound had previously applied to the poems of Propertius. One might even suggest that Pound was thereby constructing a new 'portrait', a *Homage to Sextus Possum*, not so much a new *persona* for Pound himself as a distilled and compact 'portrait' of the current best work of 'T. S. Eliot', as Pound saw and judged it.[21]

One connected consideration is that Eliot seems to have envisaged each Part of *The Waste Land* as clearly demarcated, with a numeral and a separate subtitle, each perhaps beginning on a new page – if only for reasons of filling out printed space in a slim single volume – whereas Pound in the Cantos tended towards a more run-on flow of verse passages. To read *The Waste Land*, even in its present published version, while leaving out the numbering and the sub-headings of the divisions is to bring it

---

[21] It is worth comparing what Pound did to Eliot's material with the detailed account of Pound's work on Propertius in J.P. Sullivan, *Ezra Pound and Sextus Propertius*, University of Texas Press, 1964, especially the useful summarising table on p. 112 and pp. 138-141 detailing the disparate sources of Part VI of Pound's *Homage*.

considerably closer in feel and flow to Pound's early Cantos, with their sudden transitions of speaker, time, and place, their medley of shifting multiple voices and explicitly marked quotations.

But there is a still further element we might take into account in considering this complex interaction between Eliot's and Pound's respective notions of what was being (differently) aimed at in the various revisions of the *Waste Land* material. In late 1921 the *Propertius* and the *Mauberley* poems, and even the Cantos, were not Pound's immediate preoccupation. When Eliot saw him in Paris, in December 1921, Pound had just completed several months of intense work on another 'portrait', but one this time in the form of a staged opera: his *Testament of Villon.*

As with the *Propertius*, Pound's working procedure had been to select and assemble passages from Villon's *oeuvre* in order to construct a kind of composite portrait of the poet. Unlike Pound's previous *personae*, even those in the form of dramatic monologues, the *Testament* opera was indeed a fully dramatic work, intended for performance on the stage and therefore composed, even more than Pound's previous work, to be heard in all its ambitious aural complexity. But while Pound's music may have been successful in some respects, the opera was drastically limited in terms of stage action: for much of the time the central character, Villon himself, simply stands immobile while Pound's various characters take up positions around him, singing in different voices. [22]

---

[22] There is a partial recording of the opera, currently available on *Ego Scriptor Cantilenae: the music of Ezra Pound*, Other Minds,, OM 1005-2 CD, with excellent textual material.

Eliot too had recently been experimenting with a form of quasi-dramatic composition: *Sweeney among the Nightingales* clearly anticipates elements of the later Aristophanic drama fragment *Sweeney Agonistes* to which Eliot promptly returned after *The Waste Land* had finally appeared. [23] But it too was primarily only a sound drama, lacking in anything that might provide compelling dramatic action on stage. Even ten years later, in *Murder in the Cathedral*, Eliot still tended merely to place his central protagonist on stage with almost nothing to do, while the Chorus, Tempters, and Knights mainly take up positions around him. That static concentration upon the isolated character of his main protagonist is distinctly reminiscent of how Pound's opera had treated Villon. In a somewhat confused way, Eliot may even have envisaged Tiresias as having a similar quasi-dramatic centrality, and though there is no clear sense of the kind of stage upon which they might be played, there are obvious 'dramatic' elements in *The Waste Land* material: the recounted conversation in the pub and the neurotic exchange in Part II, 'In the Cage' or 'A Game of Chess' – which, incidentally, may well be indebted to the first scene of John Rodker's experimental *Theatre Muet,* in which a neurotic couple, Pierrot and Columbine, try to play chess in a bare room but are distracted by menacing steps upon the stairs.[24]

Here Eliot's original title for *The Waste Land*, 'He Do the Police in Different Voices', might be recalled once again,

---

[23] In November 1920 he had published 'The Possibility of a Poetic Drama', *Dial* , lxix, 5, pp. 441-447.

[24] This scene was published in Pound's *Catholic Anthology*, 1915, alongside the first appearance in book form of any of Eliot's verse, including *Prufrock* and, interestingly, *Hysteria.* Rodker's strange drama is included in *Poems & Adolphe 1920*, edited by Andrew Crozier, Carcanet, 1996.

though now with a somewhat different emphasis. It would be interesting to know if – for example, during his stay in Munich – Eliot had encountered Karl Kraus's one-man performances of Shakespeare, in which Kraus, merely sitting behind a table on a bare stage, 'did' the whole of a Shakespeare play 'in different voices'. In his *The Last Days of Mankind,* serially published between 1915 and 1922, Kraus had also composed a formidably ambitious drama shaped as a collage of many different 'voices' largely excerpted from the daily press of wartime Vienna. The published opening lines of *The Waste Land*, partly evoking memories of Munich, could almost be the script of a typically short scene from *Last Days.*

In somewhat the same way as Strindberg's later chamber plays can be seen as proleptically reaching for the formal possibilities soon to be developed in early cinema, so the dramatic experiments of Karl Kraus and of both Pound and Eliot at this time might be regarded as almost anticipating the possibilities of what was soon to emerge as a quite new artistic form: that of radio drama. Pound wrote to his father on 29th November 1924, concerning the form of the Cantos: 'Simplest parallel I can give is radio where you tell who is talking by the noise they make.'[25] Eliot might have said much the same of *The Waste Land.*

The first radio drama on the BBC is dated to late 1922.[26] Pound's Villon opera was to be impressively broadcast by the BBC in 1931 purely as a radio production, while in December 1972 BBC Radio 3 memorably transformed

---

[25] This unpublished letter is quoted in Margaret Fisher, *Ezra Pound's Radio Operas, the BBC Radio Experiments 1931-1933, MIT Press*, 2002, p. 40. See especially the whole of Chapter 2.
[26] I owe this information to my erstwhile colleague Alan Beck. See http://www.savoyhill.co.uk/invisibleplay/.

*The Waste Land* into a radio production simply by assigning lines and passages to different actors' voices and adding some sound effects, including the appropriate musical quotations – almost no other editorial interventions were required.[27] Eliot of course later returned several times to the possibilities of a staged 'poetic' drama, and in 1923 had even considered composing a puppet play, but it might be suggested that it was Samuel Beckett who eventually gained most from these early modernist gesturings towards a form of radio drama.[28]

We can now step back from these various intertwining strands of argument and suggestion concerning the influence of Pound's work and preoccupations upon Eliot's conception of what became *The Waste Land*.

Overall, I am proposing that Pound's attempts to turn Eliot's materials into something much more locally Poundian, when combined with Eliot's over-reacting reductions and partial re-organisation, unexpectedly and almost accidentally resulted in a quite new structure and formal shape for the poem as a whole which not only was not 'authored' by either, or indeed both, but actually constituted a kind of suspended compromise between the diverging formal intentions of these closely collaborating, but actually very different poets, while together they – almost – invented a novel form of dramatic polylogue, the appropriate medium for which had not yet been formally developed.

---

[27] Produced by Terence Tiller. See *Radio Times* entry on http://genome.ch.bbc.co.uk. Kraus's *Last Days* was also broadcast as a radio drama by the BBC, on 11th December 1999.
[28] Note also that Eliot's very earliest poems featured 'marionettes'. Alfred Kreymborg, who had included Eliot in *Others* in 1916, published his *Puppet Plays* in 1923.

Thus, *The Waste Land* was not so much jointly authored as jointly authorised: in January 1922 Eliot and Pound ratified to and for each other the shared decision to allow the poem to appear in an unpredicted form which neither had fully intended, or expected, or possibly even comprehended. Except, perhaps, retrospectively, when the deed was done.

Pound was perhaps the first to grasp that what had almost accidentally been created as *The Waste Land* was indeed a possible new form, one to be further explored and developed. It was in 1923, after his intermittent but year-long engagement with *The Waste Land,* from incohate collection to acclaimed publication, that Pound radically revised his own earlier Cantos for publication in *A Draft of XVI Cantos*. But that is another story.

How all this impinges upon notions of the poet as 'impersonal' might be considered further. But it was not surprising that readers and critics faced with this almost incomprehensible composite work would seek to situate the overall finished product in terms of their own preferred ways of reading contemporary poetry, yet with most of them nevertheless concurring – quite correctly – that this was indeed a new and radical departure.

However, it therefore followed for most readers, and for subsequent critics, that this bafflingly innovative work had somehow necessarily to be attributed to the deliberate and consciously intended formal ambition of its apparently single author. That *The Criterion* and *The Dial*, even before its actual publication, both gave the work and its presumed sole author their prominent endorsement would have reinforced the challenge offered to its first readers: to understand and to approve the judgement which had already, it seemed, been so authoritatively passed upon this strange poem. But that endorsement had already had its own complexities.

## ii : publishing

When Eliot passed through Paris on his way back from Lausanne and was introduced to Horace Liveright, Liveright promptly offered a contract to publish the poem which he almost certainly had by then seen, if at all, only in an incoherent and unfinished state. He was meeting Pound every day during the six days he spent in Paris and it is possible that Pound showed him some of the as yet unrestructured material, and Pound would certainly have enthusiastically prompted any such publishing offer. However, that Liveright offered to publish the poem 'sight unseen' is perhaps not so surprising. Eliot's reputation was rapidly growing, not least because he had published so very little poetry up to now. Liveright would understandably have been excited – and commercially attracted – by the prospect of securing a work which looked as if it might suddenly double Eliot's slim published output thus far.

That Liveright offered to publish a volume which was not yet even finished was symptomatic of the subsequent publishing history of *The Waste Land*, which has been almost as well-trodden a terrain for scholarly investigation as the chronology of the poem's composition. The narrative that has slowly emerged is by now reasonably clear, and need not be repeated here in detail. [29]

Two points are salient however. Eventually, Eliot sent a fair copy of the revised *The Waste Land*, without the Notes, to John Quinn in New York with instructions that Liveright would only be given the poem *after* the contract to publish

---

[29] Again, Lawrence Rainey has provided a usefully detailed account though much of the tale is told in the now-published letters and usefully summarised in the 2015 edition, I, p. 557ff.

it was concluded. Quinn was later to tell Eliot that Liveright had almost gotten 'cold feet' about publishing the work at all, until the commercial deal with *The Dial* to take 350 copies of the Boni & Liveright edition was concluded a mere month or so before it was to be published. It might be a reasonable assumption that the cold feet arose when Liveright finally had his first sight of the poem *after* he had already signed the contract to publish it.

One might assume, perhaps, that this was because the poem was too adventurous for Liveright, but it should be remembered that it was Boni & Liveright who had published Pound's *1918-21* volume and their temporary 'cold feet' may even have been because the single 'long poem' Eliot finally presented to them did not after all seem to represent a coherent advance upon, or even a successful assimilation of, Pound's more innovative recent work.

Meanwhile, *The Dial* had also been attempting to buy, or just to see, the poem. Like Liveright, *The Dial* had obvious commercial motives. If one looks through the issues of *The Dial* from the point at which Thayer and Watson took it over in January 1920 there is a remarkable rising curve of interest in the work of Eliot. Between January 1920 and December 1920 only a couple of possible references appear, whereas by the issues of late 1921 Eliot is being mentioned or alluded to in roughly half the individual articles. Clearly, Eliot's work – slender as it was at that point – had roused considerable interest among *The Dial*'s readers. However, when the co-owners and editors Thayer and Watson were both in Europe in July 1922 neither had as yet seen the poem, so Watson prompted Pound to ask Eliot for a copy.

In a letter dated 28th July 1922, Eliot promised Pound that he would let him have a copy 'for confidential use' as soon as he could make one, but of 'the two available copies' one had gone to Quinn to present to Liveright 'on completion of the contract', and 'the other is the only one I possess.' Eliot added that he had no objection to Watson or Thayer 'seeing the manuscript' (*L I*, p.552.) Certainly, this 'manuscript' cannot be the copy of the poem which Eliot had by then sent to Quinn, but rather a copy Eliot was now promising to send to Pound. Nor, obviously, was this 'manuscript' the hand-written and typescript pages which Eliot later sent to Quinn: the facsimile materials.

Eventually, in August a copy did indeed reach Thayer and Watson, but only after the suggestion had already been floated, and implicitly accepted, that the poem should be given *The Dial* award – worth the considerable sum of $2000. It was an expensive deal: the award had been established only the year before and was intended to be generous enough to enable a writer to live for a whole year.[30]

Which meant that Liveright had undertaken to publish the poem before he had read it, and Thayer and Watson had in effect promised to give it the *Dial* award before the editors had seen it, both decisions taken primarily, or largely, upon the basis of Pound's no doubt forceful recommendation – which was itself, however, after the postal exchange with Eliot in late January 1922, almost certainly based only upon Pound's memory of the extensively amended materials and of the 'much improved' version he had only briefly seen when it was sent to him in Paris, perhaps just for a day or two, since Pound himself had not had any

---

[30] Rainey estimated its value as the equivalent of $83,000 in 2003.

continuing access to a subsequent copy of any revised version(s).

The complicated negotiations concerning the triple publication of the poem, by Boni & Liveright as a book in America in December 1922, by Watson and Thayer in *The Dial* for November 1922, and by Eliot himself in the first issue of *The Criterion* in October 1922, were only finally agreed on 7th September 1922: Quinn invited Gilbert Seldes, acting for *The Dial,* and Horace Liveright to his office that morning and formally concluded the legal contract whereby *The Dial* would publish the poem without the Notes and buy 350 copies of Liveright's edition with the Notes, and in addition formally undertake to give Eliot the annual award of $2000.

So, it is arguably the case that none of the participants in that three-way 7th September negotiation – including John Quinn, who had not yet received Eliot's package of the draft material – were fully in a position to have made a considered critical judgement on the poem independent of the influence of Pound's proselytising and his insistently authoritative previous pronouncements to them upon its worth. In any case, the main consideration even of *The Dial* owners may have been commercial rather than critical: their primary concern was to secure the kudos of a growing reputation, above all for the success of their periodical.[31]

---

[31] When Watson was finally able to read the poem in August 1922, he wrote to Thayer: 'I found the poem disappointing on first reading but after a third shot I think it is up to his usual - all the styles are there..' Quoted in Rainey, *Revisiting*, p. 83.

In any case, it is certain that none of the negotiators (or even Pound himself?) had at that stage seen or understood the extent to which the poem as it was to be finally published might be regarded as having a dual composition, so oddly shared between Eliot and Pound.

In a curious way, however, Boni & Liveright's American edition of the poem did indeed have a kind of dual authorship: that of the poet and that of the voice responsible for the Notes added to the poem. Pound did not see, or perhaps even know about, the Notes until they were published in the December book edition. Pound had himself of course added brief indicative notes to several of the poems in his own previous volumes, but the extent and character of Eliot's notes upon his own poem was almost unprecedented: a variant upon editions of classical or canonical texts intended for pedagogical scrutiny. By mock-humbly offering this ancillary apparatus of quasi-scholarly notation and clarification upon his own work, Eliot was thereby deliberately placing himself not only within the European canon summoned up by his range of quoted references, but also ostentatiously enlisting himself in the elite literary ranks of such as Shakespeare and Milton whose works had already entered the restricted pantheon of footnoted school editions, alongside the traditionally revered Greek and Latin corpus. The adding of the Notes to the Boni & Liveright *The Waste Land* thereby anticipated and prompted the later proliferation of endless pedagogical explication while endowing its author with a form of self-awarded instant classic status.

But crucially, in addition to any such considerations, the provision of the Notes was perhaps primarily intended to camouflage by their obfuscation the awkward possibility that Eliot himself still had no firm confidence in or secure grasp of any overall structure of the peculiar poem which had eventually emerged.

## iii: reviewing & assessing

It is then noticeable that the initial American reviewers (who had access to the Notes in the Liveright edition, which were not available to its first British readers) shaped their responses far more by considerations of the apparent form of unity suggested by the Notes than by any convincing critical assessments of the poem's specific formal character as a whole. [32]

One explanation for its overall 'unity' was that it was some kind of expressionist mono-drama, though nobody made an explicit connection with Pound's unpublished opera or with radio drama. When Edmund Wilson first saw the poem his reaction had been far from favourable but once he had seen the Notes, in advance of publication, he had modified his stance. His early and influential review in *The New York Evening Post Literary Review* on November 25th 1922 put the suggestion of a 'monodrama' into circulation, linking Yevreynov's term with the role of Tiresias:

> What I called monodrama (wrote Yevreynov) is a kind of dramatic representation which endeavours with the greatest fullness to communicate to the spectator the soul state of the acting character and presents on the stage the world surrounding him as he conceives it at any moment in his stage experience ... only with him do I identify myself, only from his point of view do I perceive the world surrounding him, the people surrounding him.

---

[32] I am here indebted to Michael Grant's *Eliot: The Critical Heritage* (1982) and Graham Clarke's *Eliot: Critical Assessments* (1990).

But even Wilson's review, like many others, attempted to map onto the poem a coherence drawn from the mythic materials of Jesse Weston and Fraser's *Golden Bough,* towards which Eliot's notes had so (un)helpfully pointed.

Other early American reviews of the Boni & Liveright edition, which did not attempt to match it primarily with the Notes, managed nevertheless to speak approvingly but only somewhat vaguely or evasively of its alleged unified structure and form. Others bypassed the critical issue by simply summarising its postulated sources outside the poem: ' rather than commenting on the poem itself, Jepson preferred to discuss *From Ritual to Romance, The Golden Bough* and Cabell's *Jurgen* ' (*L I, 1988*, p. 45n) —a strategy not unfamiliar to later lecturers upon the poem.

Even Gilbert Seldes in his review in *The Nation* resorted to such elliptical phrases as its 'alternation between the visionary... and the actual' and its 'hidden form'. Since Seldes had been one of those who had negotiated the publication of the poem in *The Dial,* on 7th September, perhaps he knew what that 'hidden form' was when he bought it, but declined to clarify or disclose it to his readers when he reviewed the poem two months later. He also claimed to see in the poem 'the inversion and complement of *Ulysses*' – whatever that meant – and here he was in line with Eliot's own elucidatory lure by his later reference to the underpinning mythic structure of *Ulysses*. But how any 'mythic structure' was realised in Eliot's own poem was not precisely elucidated by any American reviewer.

The earliest English readers of the poem as published in the October 1922 issue of *The Criterion* were in a slightly different position from their American counterparts, not having the Notes to guide them. But while Eliot's editorship of *The Criterion* was known to a small band of invited contributors (indeed this was let slip in one of the early American reviews) the fact that Eliot's editorship was anonymous would undoubtedly have helped further to reinforce the impression for its first readers that this strange and almost imperviously puzzling poem had already been firmly endorsed by those most competent to judge it. The readers of *The Criterion* were not to know that those involved in its American publication and in *The Dial*'s prestigious award had barely seen it before signing contracts to publish it, and that the author himself was responsible for anonymously endorsing its status in his undeclared role as judicious editor.

Whereas some forty American reviews were largely positive, of the dozen or so English contemporary reviews at least ten were unimpressed. The Hogarth Press edition of less than five hundred copies took over two years to sell in England, whereas the Boni & Liveright edition went quickly into its third thousand. English critics eventually matched American academics in elevating the poem's status and in attempting to make coherent or at least comprehensible the structure of the poem. In particular, F. R. Leavis's essay in *New Bearings in English Poetry,* published in 1932, did as much for such attempted readings of the poem as Cleanth Brooks' 1937 essay did in America. Thereafter, the notion persisted that the poem was somehow planned and profoundly organised.

A year before the draft materials became available, Ian Hamilton, at that time the influential poetry editor for the *TLS*, wrote (my emphasis):[33]

---

[33] *Eliot in Perspective,* ed. Graham Martin, 1970, p.102, 110.

*Of course, Eliot wanted the poem to be difficult and no doubt conceived of its difficulty as an important aspect of its total meaning.* There is the practical difficulty of the poem's wealth of cultural allusion and there is the deeper, but related difficulty of its general structure; the difficulty of detail and of plan. Dozens of attempts have been made to provide plausible solutions, to document the allusions, to guess Eliot's structural intentions, and the assumption has invariably been that a poem which flourishes so many interesting signposts must know where it is going, and that all the critic needs is to be more learned and ingenious in his interpretations than the next man. Eliot's knotty seriousness of aim has hardly been called in question— although when lines here and there have not fitted into the explicator's explication there have been nervous mumblings of discontent.

And:

Most studies of *The Waste Land* have *taken it for granted that it is written to a marvellously intricate plan,* that Eliot is godlike in his remote, clandestine machinations. Typical of much academic criticism is the assumption that whatever *is* in a poem belongs in it, as by divine law. Eliot's notes, the information that Pound sub-edited the poem, the opinion of Eliot's close friend Conrad Aitken that the whole was made up fairly arbitrarily of bits and pieces which had been around for years, the tediously demonstrated fact that none of the interpretations is finally more convincing than the others and that all have been obliged to embrace suspect ingenuities; none of this has deterred the true disciple from his conviction that the work is some kind of dense, elaborate miracle of form which it is the poetry lover's humble, lengthy duty to attempt to document. But the mysteries remain…

Hamilton does not quite take the next step, though he gets close.

However, even before the facsimile edition was published in 1971 there were partial exceptions to the widely shared assumptions which Hamilton somewhat sceptically recounts. Characteristically, the ever-perceptive Hugh Kenner, in his *The Invisible Poet* (first published in 1959, reprinted 1969) offered, on the one hand, some fairly typical and persuasively appreciative critical comments on the impressive technical assurance of the poem, such as:

> The typist passage is the great *tour de force* of the poem; its gentle lyric melancholy, its repeatedly disrupted rhythms, the automatism of its cadences, in alternate lines aspiring and falling nervously ... constitute Eliot's most perfect liaison between the self-sustaining gesture of the verse and the presented fact. Some twenty-five lines in flawlessly traditional iambic pentameter, alternately rhymed, sustain with their cadenced gravity a moral context in which the dreary business is played out; the texture is lyric rather than dramatic because there is neither doing nor suffering here but rather the mutual compliance of a ritual scene. The section initiates its flow with a sure and perfect line composed according to the best 18th-century models. (p. 142-43)

— which hardly squares at all with what we can now see of Pound's dismissive and drastic changes in the original verse of the typist passage. But Kenner also wrote (my emphasis) :

> ... the wholeness, *not at first foreseen by the author*, which the greater part of *The Waste Land* at length assumed. That wholeness, since it never did incorporate everything the author wanted it to, was to

some extent a compromise, got by permuting (*sic*) with another's assistance materials he no longer had it in him to rethink; and finally, after Pound, by simply eliminating everything not of the first intensity, had revealed an unexpected corporate (*sic*) substantiality in what survived, Eliot's impulse was to 'explain' the poem as 'thoughts of a dry brain in a dry season' by pre-fixing *Gerontion*.

That is to say, the first quality of *The Waste Land* to catch a newcomer's attention, its self-sufficient juxtaposition without copulae of themes and passages in a dense mosaic, *had at first a novelty which troubled even the author*. It was a quality arrived at by Pound's cutting; it did not trouble Pound, who had already begun work on *The Cantos*. But Eliot, preoccupied as always with the seventeenth-century drama and no doubt tacitly encouraged by the example of Browning, naturally conceived a long poem as somebody's spoken or unspoken monologue, its shifts of direction and transition from scene to scene psychologically justified by the workings of the speaker's brain. ...

... But a five-parted work of 434 lines entitled *The Waste Land*, with sudden wrenching juxtapositions, thematic links between section and section, fragments quoted from several languages with no one present to whose mind they can occur: this dense textural unity, as queer as *Le Sacré du Printemps*, must have *seemed to Eliot a little factitious until he had got used to the poem in its final form; which, as everyone who has encountered it knows, must take some time.* (pp.127-8)

Kenner's insight was, I think, confirmed when the working materials were finally published. In 1922 neither Pound nor Eliot, in my view, had actually comprehended or would have agreed upon the structural or formal coherence later attributed to *The Waste Land* as published. But Eliot now – in Kenner's phrase – had to 'get used' to it.

## iv : dilemmas

The publication, and the immediate American and growing international success, of *The Waste Land* in its published form(s) posed a number of dilemmas for its author. One was whether or not publicly to acknowledge the role played by Pound. Neither the front cover of *The Criterion* nor – unthinkably – the title pages of the two book versions attributed the poem to joint authorship, and the laconic, but very accurate, dedication — *il miglior fabbro* —was first added only in Eliot's *Poems 1909-1925*, published by Faber in 1926. Eliot had in the January 1922 exchange of letters with Pound proposed to make the contribution explicit by prefacing the poem with Pound's own somewhat burlesque verses claiming his part in a 'caesarean operation' and delivery. But the loyal Pound had demurred at that option (*L I*, p. 625).

When, on 25th June 1922 (*L I,* p. 681) Eliot wrote to John Quinn, he allowed Pound only a post-parturition role, saying that he had written, 'mostly when I was at Lausanne for treatment last winter', a long poem of about 450 lines and added 'I think it is the best I have ever done, and Pound thinks so too'. No mention of midwifery here. After the complex publishing contract was safely signed by Quinn on 7th September, with Eliot as sole legal author, Eliot was slightly more forthcoming. Writing to Quinn on 21st September 1922 (*L I*, p. 748) he admitted that his 'only regret (which may seem in the circumstances either ungracious or hypocritical)' was that the *Dial* award had come to him before Pound, but Quinn would find in the manuscript of *The Waste Land* 'the evidences of his work' so that the manuscript was worth preserving 'in its present form' only because it is 'the only evidence of the difference which his criticism has made to this poem'. While declaring that he was 'glad' that Quinn would be able to judge this for himself, Eliot then made it perfectly clear that these 'only copies' of 'the portions which I have suppressed' should never appear in print.

Eliot's declaration that Pound should have been awarded *The Dial* award before, and instead of, himself at least registered a degree of embarrassment, but it was surely a gesture of considerable moral ambivalence to give the surviving *The Waste Land* materials to Quinn, with the explicit comment that they were the only record or evidence of Pound's editorial and critical interventions, while at the same time enjoining Quinn to keep the material wholly confidential. Eliot must surely have registered, albeit with some relief, that without access to that very material no-one else could possibly know the extent of Pound's involvement.

When in July 1923 Pound sent the sequence of Malatesta Cantos to Eliot for publication in *The Criterion*, Eliot in a quite extraordinary editorial move simply deleted the opening line of Canto VIII:

'These fragments' you 'have shelved' (shored) against your ruin.

– and justified himself in a somewhat curt letter to Pound on the grounds that people were already claiming that they wrote each other's poems. A draft version of that very Canto had included a passage recalling the meeting between Pound and Eliot in Verona in June 1922 when Eliot had already finalised the text of *The Waste Land* but – it seems – had not brought a copy for Pound to see. Pound's letter asking for a copy to show Thayer and Watson is subsequent to that meeting.

In his *Introduction* to Pound's *Selected Poems* published by Faber in 1928 Eliot did mention (p. xxi), presumably from memory, Pound's comments on the Fresca episode, warning Eliot not to try to pastiche Pope, but though this is almost the only detailed acknowledgement of Pound's specific interventions, Eliot merely refers to 'an excellent set of couplets' without indicating in any way that the couplets in question were originally in *The Waste Land* draft.

It may also be relevant to some of the suggestions made earlier that Eliot, as its editor and publisher, omitted from that 1928 Faber *Selected Poems* of Pound the very poem which Basil Bunting claimed Eliot had failed to grasp, assimilate, or surpass: *Homage to Sextus Propertius*. Eliot justified that decision on the grounds that he was 'doubtful of its effect upon the uninstructed reader, even with my instructions'. And that it 'would give difficulty to many readers: because it is not enough a 'translation', and because it is, on the other hand, too much of a 'translation', to be intelligible to any but the most accomplished student of Pound's poetry....'

When *Propertius* was finally published separately by Faber and Faber in 1934, the blurb – surely by Eliot – has an intriguing tone:

> When we published some years ago the *Selected Poems of Ezra Pound*, Mr Eliot considered that 'Homage to Sextus Propertius' should be omitted, being a rather more advanced work of considerable length, demanding separate study. But now that the selected poems has become a popular member of the *Faber Library*, and the *XXX Cantos* are proceeding with the conversion of England, there cannot be many readers left who will commit the mistake of taking *Propertius* to be a jumbled translation of the Elegies of the Latin

Poet. It will now be recognised as the last, and most important *persona* through which the modern poet spoke before the immense undertaking of the Cantos.

The sly crack concerning 'the conversion of England' is a delicious Eliotic touch.

Subsequently, Eliot seemed uneasily aware that Pound's contribution merited rather more recognition than he was prepared to allow it to have, but for another decade he nevertheless did not offer any clear public acknowledgement, or apparently consider it appropriate ever to rectify that lack of full recognition.

In 1938 Eliot did make a mildly more explicit comment, in a short note replying to an article in the small circulation periodical *Purpose* questioning the basis of Pound's reputation. Referring to his use of the phrase '*il miglior fabbro*' Eliot said that he wished to honour Pound's 'technical mastery and critical ability in his own work, which had also done so much to turn *The Waste Land* from a jumble of good passages into a poem'.[34] The ambiguity as to whether it was simply the general influence of Pound's 'own work' allows the comment to stop short of any explicit acknowledgement of direct intervention. Eventually, in the *Paris Review* interview in 1959, another two decades later, in response to a direct question concerning Pound's contribution, Eliot formulated the interesting response: that the poem was as 'unstructured' when it left Pound as it had been when it reached him.

---

[34] 'On a recent Piece of Criticism' *Purpose*, 10.2, April-June 1938, p.92-3.

*v : more dilemmas – as critic*

In his Introduction to Pound's *Selected Poems* Eliot had emphasised the 'logical development' of Pound as a poet. However, the question which persistently lay in wait for Eliot himself, once *The Waste Land* had appeared, was his own development as a poet. This involved somewhat more complex issues than simply how far to acknowledge Pound as almost co-responsible for the famous poem, and thereby perhaps undermine his own growing reputation as 'the author of *The Waste Land'*. Indeed, Eliot's problems as the author (it seemed) of *The Waste Land* were threefold: as critic, as poet, and as editor-publisher.

His dilemma as critic was one for which Eliot was well prepared. Even before *The Waste Land*, Eliot's critical edicts, frequently gnomic or apodictic in formulation, were often disdainfully, authoritatively, and anonymously delivered in the prescriptive mode, as guiding principles for the correct and proper pursuit of poetic excellence: to dissever the poet as man from the poem as art, to construct an *objective* correlative, to overcome the dissociation of sensibility, to pursue a combination of impersonality and erudition whereby the whole history of European literature from Homer onwards – and so on.

From a different perspective, however, these operative demands can be seen as disguised defensive devices. If a poem was somehow the product of an impersonal and wholly objective construction, no more the expression of a singular personality than an item of craftsmen-like joinery, such as the turning of the leg of a table, then *The Waste Land* also could be registered as an almost objectively predetermined paradigm shift consonant with an emergent poetic generation. If the new, the genuinely new, were to take its place in and to mutate or modify the entire previous literary tradition, then this was primarily a matter of mastering inherited compositional techniques (to be anthologised in Pound's selection of technical innovations in his *ABC of Reading* ) and then surpassing them in a practised and hard-won professional dedication (admittedly, with the contribution of some suitably self-deprecating 'individual talent'). Thus the poet's work was not to be accounted for as a romantic expression of one's subjectively suffering self or as the mere recording and formulation of personal experience.

Moreover, if the very style of the new work was primarily due to the rediscovery and resuscitation of the true and once-dominant (though oddly and temporarily displaced and almost forgotten) mainstream articulation of the correct creative relationship between emotion and intellect in a properly associated sensibility, running from Donne through Laforgue to, well, Eliot himself, but by-passing Milton, Shelley, *et al.*, then surely the individual modern poet was more of a cultural medium for what the age truly demanded than a merely idiosyncratic agent – and it therefore followed that any biography of the poet would be irrelevant as well as impertinent.

In all these respects, then, any critic who followed Eliot's prescriptive pronouncements would in effect be dissuaded from reading Eliot's poems as anything more individually expressive than the conjuncture of the smell of cooking and reading Spinoza, of falling in love and the sound of the typewriter, and not at all as the almost shattering and barely controlled overflow of extremely powerful personal emotions and devastating individual experiences.

It was thereby, in effect, the task of criticism to shield the real sources of *The Waste Land* – not indeed the Tarot pack or even Jesse Weston, but – well, what? Whereas, in the acutely difficult period leading up to *The Waste Land* the private agonies of the relationship with Vivien may have been what most needed to be shielded from prying inquiries, after *The Waste Land* was published a further factor, the compositional genesis of the poem itself, had now also to be kept protectively undeclared. And both Pound and Eliot kept firmly quiet about that, if perhaps for different reasons.

So, as the privileged critic of, or at least commentator upon, his own work Eliot was happy to accept the notion that *The Waste Land* was indeed a single unified poem and that it was somehow inexplicably, and perhaps even mysteriously, composed and organised. In 1930 he remarked:[35]

> ... the possibilities of 'meaning' in poetry are so extensive, that one is quite aware that one's knowledge of the meaning even of what oneself has written is extremely limited, and that its meaning to others, at least so far as there is some consensus of interpretation among persons apparently qualified to interpret, is quite as much a part of it as what it means to oneself.

And in 1942: [36]

> ... a poem may appear to mean very different things to different readers, and all of these meanings may be

---

[35] The quotation is from Eliot's introduction to Wilson Knigh*t, The Wheel of Fire,* Oxford 1930, p. xiv as given in Rossell Hope Robbins, *The T. S. Eliot Myth*, NewYork, 1951, p. 127 – an unusually acerbic and negative reading of Eliot, still well worth reading.
[36] Quoted in *The Eliot Myth* p.130 from 'The Music of Poetry', Glasgow, 1942, p. 15, concerning *The Waste Land*.

different from what the author thought he meant. ... The reader's interpretation may differ from the author's and be equally valid – it may even be better. There may be much more in the poem than the author was aware of.

In 1971 the facsimile edition prominently quoted a comment attributed to Eliot:

Various critics have done me the honour to interpret the poem in terms of criticism of the contemporary world, have considered it, indeed, as an important bit of social criticism. To me it was only the relief of a personal and wholly insignificant grouse against life; it is just a piece of rhythmical grumbling.[37]

Eliot's critical stance obviously meant that at least during his lifetime any approach to the biographical sources of that 'rhythmical grumbling' was to be firmly protected, given its highly personal and acutely painful character. But in addition to protecting his private troubles with Vivien, which had undoubtedly contributed to the emotional content of the poem, the same evasive accounts now also served to avoid or occlude a full explanation of how the formal structure of this paradigm-shifting poem had been generated.

Thus one continuing undeclared influence of *The Waste Land* upon Eliot himself may well have been to shape his critical contributions in an even more defensive direction: his continued insistence that we should not seek to disclose

---

[37] Recorded by Henry Eliot, whose criticisms of *The Waste Land* in his letter to Eliot, March 1923, *L2*, p.74, are worth noting.

the poet through the poem, or adduce biographical information to illuminate the poetry, but rather to treat the poem itself, the words on the page, as the object of our enquiry, without assistance from the poet's own glosses, interpretation, or commentary, all served Eliot very well in allowing him never to disclose the odd and almost fortuitous concatenation which had cooperatively engendered this particular poem, one which had so significantly transformed his reputation and career.

His own metaphor or simile of the catalyst which initiates a chemical reaction while itself remaining unchanged may have had a somewhat ironic resonance for one to whom had been attributed a crucial transformation in the very nature of modern poetry-making — but which he himself was unable to explicate.

### vi : dilemmas – as poet

If Pound had not intervened as he did, Eliot's somewhat hapless montage of materials would perhaps have emerged in an overall form which would have been much more accessible and acceptable to conventional readers. Apart from the 29 lines dashed off as the water passage of Part V (which Eliot later claimed were the only good lines in the poem), there is little in the original components taken separately to worry the cautious reader (and still less anyone who had read Pound's *1918-21* volume). But the poem as published was decidedly seen as innovative and radical by many of its early readers – and applauded (or dismissed) for that reason.

Yet, crucially, for Eliot as a poet, there were to be no later circumstances in which that unique and almost fortuitous conjuncture of his own and Pound's disparate inter-weavings would or could ever be repeated. Which meant that the Eliot who had assembled the original materials was never again to be in a position to envisage developing or even emulating the apparently intended formal innovations attributed to the published poem. And probably he had no interest in trying to. In a perhaps consciously defensive move, he very quickly informed Richard Aldington that *The Waste Land* was behind him and that he was seeking a new form and style (*L1*, p.786). However, it may be that Eliot – like everyone else who has since read and been influenced by *The Waste Land* – was himself faced with both assimilating its influence and resisting its example. And perhaps failing.

Eventually, Eliot did indeed find his own voice and mode, but it was very different from the poem which had established his transformative reputation. If one now carefully reads through all the poems published in the 1996 volume *Inventions of the March Hare,* and then the *Collected Poems 1909-1935,* but *without* re-reading *The Waste Land* in its published form, there is arguably a 'logical' development from, say, *Gerontion* in the 1920 volume to the separately published short poems grouped as 'Ariel Poems', which were among the few poems he published in the decade after 1922: *Journey of the Magi* in 1927, *A Song for Simeon* in 1928, *Animula* in 1929 and *Marina* in 1930 — though it is worth noting that the order of contents in the *Collected Poems* somewhat obscures this chronological publishing sequence. The Ariel poems are shaped, metrically and even thematically, in ways that link back very readily to *Gerontion* and even to *Prufrock*. In particular, the almost colloquial cadences and easy enjambement which had characterised Eliot's way of composing, even in the Boston, Fresca, and Duchess materials omitted from *The Waste Land*, are here noticeable again. It was, arguably, that recognisable Eliotic voice which Pound's local interventions had partially dislodged from *The Waste Land*.

The 'Unfinished Poems' concerned with Sweeney and Coriolanus can also be read alongside both the earlier satirical verse from before 1922 and the material which was rejected from the *Waste Land* drafts. Certainly, the continuity between the final two poems of *Poems 1920* and the *Sweeney Agonistes* fragments written in the immediate wake of *The Waste Land* and finally published separately in 1932 is clear. One might compare the telephone conversation of Dusty (1932 edition, p. 13) with the deleted Fresca's chatty tones (Facsimile p. 38), while Klipstein and Krumpacker's night out in London can immediately recalls the excised Boston sequence. One suspects that Madam Sosostris may even have migrated from some early version of Doris and Dusty's preoccupation with the fortune-telling cards, while the motifs of 'I'd be bored' (p. 24) or not knowing if one is alive or dead (p. 29) clearly chime with much of the *Waste Land* material. And though the *Fragments of an Agon* may also be akin to radio drama, neither the Ariel nor the unfinished poems share any of the much puzzled-over formal characteristics of *The Waste Land*.

Two of the poems included in later *Collected Poems* editions in fact recycle lines left out of *The Waste Land* material, but Eliot's attempts during this period to write 'major' poems in *The Hollow Men* and *Ash Wednesday* seem to me interestingly unsuccessful attempts to return to what may have been the original formal intention for his 'long poem', that of sequencing or constellating a set of connected but relatively independent short poems. It would take me far beyond the scope of my present argument to explore this suggestion.

However, just as it is now in practice difficult to read the original materials (and we do not have them all, even in the facsimile edition) which Eliot initially attempted to weld into his intended 'long poem' without involuntarily allowing our knowledge of the actual published version of *The Waste Land* to intrude, so it is a difficult but instructive exercise to try to read Eliot's entire sequence of poetic composition *without* including one's almost unavoidable awareness of *The Waste Land*, removing as far as possible from one's consideration and memory the finally published version. The trajectory which would emerge if one could successfully omit awareness of the published *The Waste Land* from a reading of the total *oeuvre* of T. S. Eliot would arguably have a much clearer and more consistent direction of travel than is apparent if we do include what can even now, as we read through the entire collected works, seem a strangely anomalous item in his overall output, not in terms of its personal material but as regards its overall form.

We might then go back and attempt another read-through, but this time including in our alternative chronological construction the materials which Pound partly rejected and which Eliot himself then wholly excised from the published poem, those materials which quite considerably constituted *The Waste Land* as Eliot alone might independently have completed it. What is then arguably apparent is a much less impressive but rather more consistent development than one which includes *The Waste Land* as published. Of course, to justify or even exemplify either of these suggested read-throughs in an adequately persuasive printed critical argument would require very extensive quotation — and therefore not only the tolerant patience of my reader but also hideously expensive copyright fees.

At least, this overall suggestion might be reinforced by the implication that it was not, after all, the radical Eliot of *The Waste Land* who later abandoned its avant-garde aspects – a complaint often registered against him – but rather that the earlier Eliot eventually recovered his own trajectory, with *The Waste Land* as an almost accidental formal cul-de-sac. But it was of course unthinkable after 1922 for 'T. S. Eliot' to omit from his public *curriculum vitae* the one poem which had most decisively given him his growing reputation and was indeed for a long time the persistent justification for repeatedly publishing his *Collected Poems* in the first place.

Such tentative suggestions concerning Eliot's overall poetic development are not to be developed here, though I would argue that Eliot did finally achieve a quite different form for his 'long poem' in *Four Quartets*. Certainly, my argument so far does not lead me to deny the objective achievement of *The Waste Land* itself, not only its many impressive lines, passages, and sections but above all – on my account – Eliot's extraordinary and courageous (or desperate?) decision to publish it in the form it had unexpectedly taken, a form which thenceforth provided the criteria upon which its own 'success' was to be critically based. The subsequent development of modern English literature is indeed unthinkable without *The Waste Land* – whatever its remarkable genesis.

*vii : dilemmas – as editor*

The launch issue of *The Criterion* in October 1922 included *The Waste Land* but without the Notes. Its publication in the periodical posed a further dilemma for Eliot, this time primarily as editor.

The poem was not the lead item in the contents list, nor was it given any particular editorial prominence, but several reviewers predictably focussed their response to the launch of *The Criterion* by highlighting *The Waste Land*. Since Eliot's dual role as editor of the periodical and as author of the poem was undeclared, the publication of the poem, whole and austere, in that first issue of *The Criterion* had given the poem a further instant status, in combination with its award from *The Dial*, as almost a manifesto and exemplar for the programme not merely of some poetic coterie but of a self-confidently affirmative cultural intervention, the new periodical itself (whatever the behind-the-scenes improvisations and uncertainties in actually getting *The Criterion* off the ground).

Eliot made it clear in a number of letters that he did not want his role as editor of *The Criterion* to be publicly acknowledged and thereby known to his employers at Lloyds bank, since even as an unpaid job it may have contravened his employment conditions, and this may be understandable. But the relationship between his editorial role and his authorship of *The Waste Land* was not merely accidental. It is surely a legitimate suggestion that the poem was effectively offered in that first issue almost in lieu of an editorial by Eliot. And in particular his decision not to publish the Notes in the periodical was significant.

Without doubt the poem could be, and was, read as offering an implicit diagnosis of the state of European culture and sensibility in the wake of the 1914-18 war, a cultural condition for which the launching of *The Criterion* was intended in part to provide a remedy. Whereas European culture is presented in the poem as a fragile assemblage of fragments from previous moments, and the present state of culture is regarded with gloom and pessimism, the declared aim of *The Criterion* was to seek to make available to its readers those contributions to European culture which its editor regarded as possibly enabling the development of a more healthy cultural situation across the continent, including even provincial or even parochial England. Publishing *The Waste Land* in the first issue of the periodical was then a gesture of both diagnosis and possible redemption: that this poem could be written at all meant that the considerable challenge put before its readers was therefore not perhaps entirely hopeless.

It is worth citing the advance flyer for the launch of the Criterion :

THE CRITERION is not designed to occupy the place of any other literary periodical. The work of reviewing new books, exhibitions, theatres and concerts is performed by periodicals appearing weekly or monthly. On the other hand, THE CRITERION will not be a literary or artistic miscellany; it will have more in common with the critical quarterlies of a hundred years ago. Its contents will consist for the most part of essays longer and more considered than arc possible in reviews which appear at shorter intervals.
THE CRITERION aims at the maintenance of international standards. In the belief that the intellectual life of Europe, like its economic life, depends upon communication and exchange, it will present in translation writings of foreign men of letters, whose work should be better known in England.
THE CRITERION aims also at the constant revision of the critical opinions of literature, at historical as well as comparative criticism.

Thus the explicit function of *The Criterion* was to operate as a common forum for the best creative and critical writing in Europe, to mediate and to help create a common European culture. However much Eliot might later have come clean (or otherwise) in claiming that *The Waste Land* was little more than a piece of personal grumbling, it is undoubtedly the case that it was taken much more widely to be a representative expression of and for a whole cultural moment, and Eliot's placing of it in that first issue of *The Criterion* was surely a decision made in conscious awareness that this was indeed one way of regarding the poem. Even if he declined to include any 'manifestoe' in the first issue[38] he clearly offered the poem as, and quickly saw it received as, something more than a mere personal cry: it was a 'Portrait' of the age. But what then did the age demand? And how far was Eliot qualified to provide it? Indeed, did his readers need him to provide it – if not, what was the point of *The Criterion*?

The first readers of the new periodical were – it seemed – expected not to need any condescendingly helpful Notes to the poem, but by including them in the Hogarth Press edition of 1923 it was implied that others (including even the sophisticated Bloomsbury set themselves?) did indeed require such assistance. The Boni & Liveright and Hogarth Press editions reinforced the poem's presentation as a complete yet deliberately fractured work of art: the Notes which speak airily of the 'plan' that in some unstated way united the poem comprised almost an anthology of footnoted references to an impressive range of European canonical literary texts, the force of which was implicitly to insinuate *The Waste Land* itself into their select number.
All of which had the undoubtedly desired effect of impressing upon its first *Criterion* readers that it was now up to them, perhaps in some awe and humility, not only to discover the cohesion and significance of *The Waste Land* itself, but also to respond to its elusively *almost* explicit –

---

[38] Eliot to Pound, 19th July 1922: 'I have decided not to put any manifestoe in the 1st number, but adopt a protective colour for a time until suspicion is lulled. What do you think of 'The Possum' for a title?' (*L1,* p. 708)

yet strangely unclear or even inaccessibly 'deep' – diagnosis of the cultural, and indeed moral, sterility to which it pointed. Any putative reader's most immediate task was presumably to equip themselves with sufficient erudition, or at least secondary acquaintance with the references indicated, to qualify as those at whom the poem and the periodical were aimed : that select band who might even begin to irrigate the dire cultural drought. Especially perhaps those who, having read the un-annotated version in *The Criterion*, might have been encouraged to buy the annotated Hogarth Press edition, or who, conversely, having bought the limited editions on either side of the Atlantic might see themselves as suitable apprentice subscribers to *The Criterion*.

In addition, the strange style of notation and reference in the Notes was not only a matter of Eliot's somewhat tongue-in-cheek or mock scholarship. Such apparently helpful yet curt notes as that on line 202 ('V. Verlaine, Parsifal') deliciously combined a covertly patronising condescension with a flattering attribution of shared cultural reference, while the lordly admission of imperfect knowledge concerning the exact constitution of the Tarot pack of cards, or the precise source of an Antarctic expedition allusion, went hand in fashionable glove with the ostentatious presumption that one's readers could as readily tackle Dante's Italian or Hesse's German as Ovid's Latin or Baudelaire's French, while – of course – conceding that some lesser readers might need helpful pointers to a translation of the Buddha's Fire Sermon or a brief elucidation of how a Upanishad should formally conclude.

It should perhaps be noted that *The Dial* was quite prepared to publish poems and short reviews in French and that it assumed some minimal competence in German – though *The Dial* itself (Jan-June, 1920, p. 409) also noted that in some American states it was illegal to buy or sell a book in a foreign tongue. That Pound's *Cantos* were increasingly characterised by the inclusion of untranslated phrases and sentences from a variety of languages, but without the assistance of any notes or references, may even have prompted Eliot (reading for example the 'Eighth Canto' in the May 1922 issue of *The Dial*) to take steps to make his own work more rather than less accessible, or even perhaps *vice versa*.

The overall oddity of the Notes is that, while they do provide local references, they simultaneously dangle a 'plan' in front of the reader and yet withhold any specificity as to what that plan is. Implicitly, therefore, only one reader – the author – was actually privy to the complete secret, the full requisite range of cultural knowledge. For those in the know, that Eliot was indeed both author and editor, this might have reinforced the notion that the desired cultural salvation was to be sought in the pages of his new periodical, and that they should promptly take out a subscription. At the same time, however, it was a stern warning to any naive subscribers that if they wished to keep up, they had much further work to do, and that *The Criterion* (the title was eloquent) was to provide the required syllabus. (Of course, this high-minded ideal notion was scarcely to be matched by what often reads merely as the Higher Literary Gossip in the actual numbers of the periodical over the following years.)

Yet what qualified the semi-anonymous editor himself to provide that remedial syllabus? Who indeed could, if European culture was in as dire a state as the poem was taken to imply? Except perhaps the author of the poem?

It was therefore tactically appropriate that Eliot's role as editor of *The Criterion* was not declared, thereby crediting the whole operation, as well as the appearance of the poem itself, with an air of authoritative, and indeed impersonal, editorial endorsement and validation, which might not have been quite so persuasive if Eliot's dual function had been openly acknowledged. After all, Eliot was in effect acting as a self-publisher, proclaiming and enhancing his own poetic status. But what editorial programme was actually to be followed after this opening poetic salvo?

In fact, Eliot himself – as he well knew – was also one of those readers facing a demanding course in self-education. He had previously had an extra-ordinary mentor in the irrepressibe pedagogical enthusiasms and alert antennae of Ezra Pound, but Eliot had also known what it meant to be something of a hard-pressed auto-didact, even while concealing the fact. Sometimes not very successfully: the notorious mistake in the title *Ara Vus Prec* was due to his knowing no Provençal and relying, as he later ruefully admitted, upon an editor of Dante who also didn't know the language.

The immediately visible but perhaps misleadingly displayed erudition of Eliot's Notes to *The Waste Land* might be contrasted with his self-deprecating account of the somewhat spurious basis upon which he had been appointed to Lloyd's Bank, his linguistic competence at the time stretching not nearly as comprehensively as his employers assumed. One could add his frequent references to his less than secure grasp of contemporary German and Italian in his editorial correspondence for *The Criterion*: Dante's 13th century idiom was hardly that of either trans-national currency drafts or contemporary Italian essayists.

Somewhat earlier, in Eliot's frantically busy days as a hack reviewer, the impersonal tone of many of his hurried reviews, often aided by his anonymity in accordance with the practices of many English periodicals of the time, to some extent camouflaged the extent to which Eliot may well – like many fellow reviewers – have been learning from the volume under review the very field upon which he was ostensibly exercising expert judgement.

Moreover, Eliot had previously tried several times to organise a syllabus of required reading for the inadequately educated. His immediately impressive outlines for various courses of lectures, or the syllabi and reading lists for his extramural classes (now available online in the *Complete Prose*) can be put alongside his comments concerning the extent to which he was often in the situation of having himself to mug up those very texts only barely in advance of his class or audience. Fortunately for him perhaps, his adult education classes were subject to somewhat less rigorous external monitoring of the tutor's competence or qualifications than would have been the case for, say, a University junior lecturer. Eliot's lofty assertion concerning the sweated labour required in the Reading Room of the British Museum was a prescription both cloaking and confirming his own sense of considerable inadequacy. And the apparent erudition of both the reviews and the poems themselves may often have been the accidental bye-product of his almost random but multiple and simultaneous reviewing commissions.

In the correspondence concerning *The Criterion* there is a further element of autodidactic training on the job. Eliot frequently appeals to his widening circle of contributors for suggestions and judgements to complement his initially uncertain acquaintance with European reputations: he asks about the status of Pirandello, or seeks guidance on Thomas Mann, or notes his own possession of works by potential contributors while admitting to not having read them, as in the case of Stefan George. It is indeed a familiar feature of the editorial role that one learns rapidly from one's own publication and its remorseless deadlines what is to be selected or sought after as significant.

Though it was partly upon the basis of his experience as a banker that Eliot was appointed as a director of Faber & Gwyer in 1925 it was clearly also because of his growing reputation as a critic and poet, and as part of Faber's decision to bring *The Criterion* into the fold of the publishing house. From that point onwards, whatever his actual achievement or even competence, Eliot was in the strange and perhaps enviable position of being his own self-publisher, and indeed self-publicist, so that in his capacity both as editor at *The Criterion* and director at Faber and Faber, he enjoyed a position not dissimilar to that of his role as adult education tutor: able to both assess and advertise his own self-approved accomplishments. One suspects that in Eliot's later publishing career he might well have enjoyed the unusual privilege of choosing his own candidates, if any, to supply readers' reports on his own work. And the decision to keep reprinting his own poems, in varying collected combinations and in well-publicised single booklets, was presumably largely his own. Few authors have been in a position so to further their own reputations, including indirectly by enhancing and furthering those of others such as Pound and Joyce who provided the context for his own comparative appreciation.

It was precisely those circumstances that made possible :radical innovations and revisionary explorations: the mutually supporting company of the Modernist musketeers was a crucial enabling condition for 'Modernism'. Without T. S. Eliot at Faber & Faber one wonders how much of the *Cantos* or *Finnegans Wake* would have been published, if at all, at least in England.

Taking on the editorship of *The Criterion* in the first instance as an unpaid and exhaustingly demanding chore might seem a selfless dedication to converting a dullard English readership into a well-informed constituency of an emerging pan-European cultural avant-garde. But it can also be seen as a calculated (and nearly mis-calculated) tactic of self-promotion which actually paid off in his appointment in 1925 as a director of Faber. From that perspective, his multifarious activities, rather than dispersing his strained resources, were more or less deliberately aligned and co-ordinated to become interconnectedly supportive of what he constantly proclaimed to be his primary self-definition – as a poet.

Eliot thereby implemented a circular strategy in which the criticism created the taste by which he was to be enjoyed, or – perhaps formulated more tightly – the critical framework and criteria by which his own creative work was to be positively assessed. The periodical provided the platform from which he was regularly to articulate a cultural agenda; the publishing house constructed a growing community of other writers among whom he would be acknowledged and even enthroned; and the periodical recruited such chosen authors into the Faber publishing list. Yet in that very process, Eliot risked the undermining dissipation of his capacity to produce the poetry which was allegedly his primary objective. If he still really believed it was. What happened increasingly was that 'T. S. Eliot' became a celebrity icon within an emerging culture industry, endlessly invited, and often willing, to pronounce upon much outside his own competence.

Eliot's whole career trajectory may thus be seen as the slow construction of a self-supporting system, founded upon the continual re-production of its commercial and critical value by his role as self-publisher, simultaneously Faber & Faber's commissioning literary editor and their star performer, with his growing list of volumes of criticism, and the regular *Collected Poems* but above all *The Waste Land* in variously revamped editions being consistently reprinted.

Whether that entire structure rested in fact upon a somewhat shaky and possibly even hollow foundation in the undisclosed crucial role of Pound in the genesis of *The Waste Land* may occasionally have troubled Eliot's own partly suppressed awareness of the serendipity of the whole achievement.

### *viii : situating?*

However, if we step back from sketching these various inter-supporting practices or aspects of Eliot's efforts, the question which emerges might be whether an account – including this one – which credits Eliot with some such overall programme of attempted cultural hegemony is not itself a kind of misleading camouflage for what was in practice mainly, and certainly initially, a desperately dispersed series of attempts to keep his drowning head above financial flood waters and for that reason to conceal his own insecure foundations.

For example, Terry Eagleton in a brilliantly compressed account of Eliot's entire *oeuvre* almost constructs for Eliot both a deliberate aesthetic coherence underpinning *The Waste Land* and a decisively devised political-cultural programme, down to the details of his poetic practice:[39]

> Eliot came to Europe with the historic mission of redefining the organic unity of its cultural traditions, and reinserting a culturally provincial England into that totality. He was, indeed, to become himself the focal-point of the organic consciousness of the 'European mind', that rich, unruptured entity mystically inherent

---

[39] Terry Eagleton, *Criticism and Ideology*, NLB, 1976. p.146f.

in its complex simultaneity in every artist nourished by it. English literary culture, still in the grip of ideologically exhausted forms of liberal humanism and late Romanticism, was to be radically reconstructed into a classicism which would eradicate the last vestiges of 'Whiggism' (protestantism, liberalism, Romanticism, humanism). It would do so in the name of a higher, corporate ideological formation, defined by the surrender of 'personality' to order, reason, authority and tradition.

The wholesale demolition and salvage job which it was Eliot's historical task to carry out in the aesthetic region of English ideology was one for which he was historically peculiarly well-equipped, as an expatriate with a privileged, panoramic vantage-point on that area. . . . Confronted with world imperialist crisis, severe economic depression and intensifying working-class militancy, English society in the early years of Eliot's career as poet and critic stood in urgent ideological need of precisely the values his literary classicism encapsulated. Yet the ideological potency of that classicism rested in its refusal of static, rationalist forms for an empiricist, historicist mould – rested, indeed, in the production of a classicism contradictorily united with the evolutionary organicism of the Romantic tradition. . . .

By framing his classicist doctrine in the organicist terms of the Romantic tradition, Eliot is able to combine an idealist totality with the sensuous empiricism which is its other aspect. If the aesthetic region of ideology is to be effectively refashioned, poetic language must clutch and penetrate the turbulent, fragmentary character of contemporary experience, sinking its tentacular roots into the primordial structures of the collective unconscious-ness. As such, poetry offers a paradigm of ideological affectivity in general: Eliot's ideal of the organic society is one in which a finely conscious elite transmits its values through rhythm, habit and resonance to the largely unconscious masses, infiltrating the nervous system rather than engaging the mind. Hence the radical anti-intellectualism of the scholarly, esoteric Eliot: the nervous distrust of abstract ideas, the insistence on the poetic transmutation of thought into sense-experience, the imagist emphasis on the hard, precise image as 'containing' its concept, yoked to the symbolist preoccupation with poetry as music.

But, despite this fluently persuasive account, was there really such a clear-cut 'mission' being pursued across the range of Eliot's work? One might attempt to answer that query in relation to the editorial direction of *The Criterion*, by examining the eventual scope of Eliot's proffered 'syllabus' for his readers. One could list the contributors and even attempt to summarise the contents of those seventeen years of issues.

That would surely be far too tedious a foray into now forgotten minor authors and barely-opened books, but as a kind of shorthand we might note that in in his 'The Idea of a Literary Review' in the January 1926 re-launch issue of *The Criterion* Eliot did offer, not a programme, but what he termed a 'tendency', indicated by a short 'required reading' list for his pupils:

*Réflexions sur la violence*, by Charles [*sic*!] Sorel; *L'Avenir de l'intelligence*, by Charles Maurras; *Belphégor*, by Julien Benda; *Speculations*, by T.E. Hulme; *Réflexions sur l'intelligence*, by Jacques Maritain; *Democracy and Leadership*, by Irving Babbit.

Ever since the publication of that declaration and its manageable mini-syllabus, critics of Eliot have dutifully perused these approved books, either to damn Eliot's reactionary and fascistic tendencies or to defend his righteous stance as monarchist, classicist and Anglican. However, in my view, such a task is to a considerable extent mis-directed. I suggest that Eliot never had anything in the way of a political or cultural ideological programme any more (or less) intellectually rigorous, logically coherent, or philosophically cogent than the shared nostrums of an entrenched English conservative, though he admittedly expressed those prejudices and assumptions in somewhat more elevated language than the average retired army major in the local pub. To subject *The Idea of a Christian Society* to a critical 'close reading' is to induce only a state of extreme intellectual exasperation.

Eliot himself, with his usual mock humility but in my view quite rightly in this context, once remarked that he had no capacity for precisely rigorous thinking. To some extent indeed his much vaunted but epistemologically peculiar notion that (I put it slightly unfairly) one should smell a thought as vividly as a rose, is a bizarre indication of what his peculiarities in that respect were, and his careful annotations on Russell's mathematical treatises or a convoluted account of F. H. Bradley's epistemology are not convincing counter-evidence – but that is yet another story.

So, when challenged as to his declared admiration for Charles Maurras, leader of the proto-fascist L'Action francaise, Eliot was probably not merely being evasive but essentially muddled, like any average English Tory, when he resorted to vacuous clarifications: that everything of interest in fascism he had already learned from Maurras – but what, precisely? That some of his views were deplorable – but which? It is marginally more intriguing that Eliot should have cited Georges Sorel (though a misprint called him Charles), with his support for a potentially violent General Strike, in the Britain of 1926, precisely the year of Britain's only general strike.

In 1939 Eliot discontinued *The Criterion* after seventeen years of committed editorial effort, but despite all his endeavour the diagnosis he offered of the state of European culture at that date was if anything even more bleak than that indicated by, or attributed to, *The Waste Land* in the first issue. In the closing paragraphs of his *The Idea of a Christian Society*, published in October 1939, he wrote:

I believe that there must be many persons who, like myself, were deeply shaken by the events of September 1938, in a way from which one does not recover; persons to whom that month bought a profounder realisation of a general plight. It was not a disturbance of the understanding: the events themselves were not surprising. Nor, as became increasingly evident, was our distress due merely to disagreement with the policy and behaviour of the moment. The feeling which was new and unexpected was a feeling of humiliation, which seemed to demand an act of personal contrition, of humility, repentance and amendment; what had happened was something in which one was deeply implicated and responsible. It was not, I repeat, a criticism of the government, but a doubt of the validity of a civilisation. We could not match conviction with conviction, we had no ideas with which we could either meet or oppose the ideas opposed to us. Was our society, which had always been so assured of its superiority and rectitude, so confident of its unexamined premises, assembled round anything more permanent than a congeries of banks, insurance companies and industries, and had it any beliefs more essential than a belief in compound interest and the maintenance of dividends? Such thoughts as these formed the starting point, and must remain the excuse, for saying what I have had to say.

It is a strong and forthright comment. The sentence which 'many people . . like myself ' might now be tempted to single out – in the wake, not of the Munich piece of paper flourished by Chamberlain in 1938 but of the financial debacle seventy years later in 2008 and its continuing aftermath even as I write – is that perhaps unexpected question: 'Was our society... assembled round anything more permanent than a congeries of banks, insurance companies and industries, and had it any beliefs more essential than a belief in compound interest and the maintenance of dividends?'

Even before he had closed *The Criterion* Eliot had joined the group which called itself The Moot and was happy to describe itself as a Christian 'conspiracy', intending to influence covertly as well as openly the social, cultural and political thinking of its time. Its few dozen members had impressive pedigrees and credentials, with a range of occupational opportunities to lean directly upon the established levers of power in Britain, and they regularly met over several years to discuss how to analyse and remedy the plight of the country, according to their own chosen Christian criteria. The deliberations of The Moot engendered Eliot's summation of his considered response to the 1938 crisis: 'We could not match conviction with conviction, we had no ideas with which we could either meet or oppose the ideas opposed to us.'

As to Eliot own 'ideas', I will again gratefully resort to Terry Eagleton, for a succinct account of the core of Eliot's socio-political views, since Eagleton gives them rather more cogent articulation than Eliot did.

Eagleton is here summarising both *The Idea of a Christian Society* (*ICS,* 1939) and *Notes Towards the Definition of Culture* (*NDC,* 1948).[40]

> What Eliot means by a Christian society ... is one whose common and unconscious rhythms will 'incarnate' Christian value. 'For the great majority of the people – and I am not here thinking of social classes, but of intellectual strata – religion must be primarily a matter of behaviour and habit, must be integrated with its social life, with its business and pleasures . . . For behaviour is as potent to affect belief, as belief to effect behaviour' (*ICS* p. 30). The Christian society 'would be a society in which the natural end of man – virtue and well-being in community – is acknowledged for all, and the supernatural end – beatitude – for those who have eyes to see it' (p. 34). Insight into this supernatural end will be the characteristic of the conscious Christian majority, and more particularly of that section of the Church which Eliot calls the 'Community of Christians' (p. 35), a version of Coleridge's clerisy, whose role, as the spiritual elite, would be actively to nourish the values which the rest of society lived unconsciously. It is only from these men that 'one would expect a consciously Christian life on its highest social level' (p. 28); the rest of society, unable to bear too much reality, would live its Christianity through behaviour and conformity: its faith would be 'communal before being individual'. ...

---

[40] Terry Eagleton, 'Eliot and a common culture', in *Eliot in Perspective,* edited Graham Martin, London, 1970, p. 281f.

By appealing to the quality of unconsciousness in a common life, Eliot can press for a return to a Christian society in the context of a disbelief in the ability of most people to believe very much at all.

A different way of indicating Eliot's basic position is to point out that much of what these two books both assume and explicitly propose is already implicit in *The Waste Land* and in its reception.

The poem might be seen as itself both embodying and exemplifying the distinctions between levels of 'consciousness' and of 'culture' which Eliot was later to expound as a social ideal. Leaving aside the representation within the poem itself of the 'different voices' which are variously demarcated according to their cultural and educational characteristics, above all by their social class, the chosen forms of publication of the poem assume that there will be only a small minority who are capable of reading and responding to the poem with anything approaching a fully appropriate awareness of its many levels of allusion and reference –at its core, in fact, a very small band indeed, perhaps even consisting only of himself (and, maybe, Ezra Pound).

There will then be others who will respond to the poem, as several of the earlier reviewers did, by attempting to articulate its presumed overall meaning and structure, with some of this group reliant upon the props given by Eliot's Notes, while others would at least welcome the reassurance of the tradition ostentatiously displayed in those Notes.

Beyond that still smallish circle, there may be a larger ripple of readers gradually assimilating and adjusting to the undoubted challenges posed by any attempt to read the poem – and it is for these that so many later expositions, commentaries, and glosses, in addition to the authoritative but enigmatic Notes themselves, will be increasingly provided. Eventually, of course, the poem itself will figure on educational reading lists and be placed before thousands of hapless students in examination halls. By then, in the 1950s, Eliot was proposing that the number of university students should be reduced to a third of the prewar intake.

However, in propounding his social, political, and cultural views about the nature of a Christian society, and then his variation upon these ideas in *Notes Towards the Definition of Culture,* Eliot effects a dubious slide from a possibly plausible claim that a Christian society might incorporate different levels of comprehension of underlying theological claims. It may be the case that it takes an educated philosopher (or a Dante) to grasp the intricacies of argument in Thomas Aquinas's *Summa Theologia*, but that the general gist of the positions outlined and argued for in Aquinas's comprehensive work can be to some extent extracted, summarised, paraphrased, and popularised, in the sermons of a relatively (un-)educated parish priest, while his congregation may at various more or less comprehending levels assimilate the required theological gist, while in any case obediently observing the moral injunctions and the behavioural implications of that teaching in their liturgical and even everyday lives.

Nevertheless, to carry over this conception of different layers or levels of theological understanding into some notion of a culture which is 'common' yet is grasped at different levels of consciousness and participation is surely specious. Though it may be the case (and may well *not* be the case) that an aristocratic landowner has an informed connoisseur's appreciation of the painted landscapes or family portraits hung upon the walls of his country mansion, the response of his housekeeper or gardener to those same paintings may be sharply different (paintings have to be dusted for a start, and any actual topiary has to be constantly clipped), and hardly to be characterised as some form of second-degree level of the *same* understanding and appreciation. The attitudes of tenants whose rent pays for the classical statuary on the lawn may be wholly different from, rather than some lesser variation upon, an owner's cultural admiration for his own possessions. Even if or when, as Eliot himself recognised with some superior surprise, those who attend workers' educational classes are often among the most motivated of students.

There is in any case an element of circularity in the claim that theology underpins belief which itself underpins behaviour, since included in that very behaviour is an acquiescence in the authority of the theology which defines the belief. Just as there is a degree of circularity in the notion that an editor might commission criticism which supports the poetry which justifies the reputation of the editor, and so on.

Eliot remarks in *The Idea of a Christian Society*:

> When we speak of culture, I suppose that we have in mind the existence of two classes of people: the producers and the consumers of culture – the existence of men who can create new thought and new art (with middlemen who can teach the consumers to like it) and the existence of a cultivated society to enjoy and patronise it. (p. 77)

Eliot became most decidedly a 'middleman' of culture, albeit remaining also an intermittent poet and a Celebrity Writer. Since it undoubtedly remains true, by definition, that within any stratified social formation there are intermediate ranks, may I indulge in a spot of old-fashioned marxist fun: grounding Eliot's socio-cultural views upon his almost proto-typically insecure petty bourgeois in-between class position....

As we can now read for ourselves, Eliot's letters during the early years of marriage and of Vivien's severe illnesses (and the increasingly expensive medical bills) are full of acute and understandable worries about money. One could try to work out the precise financial situation of the newly married Eliots – as indeed they constantly did themselves. From September 1915 through to late 1918 Eliot undertook a variety of schoolmaster appointments and adult education evening classes, as well as considerable *ad hoc* reviewing, all poorly paid and precariously short-term arrangements. Eliot began work at Lloyds Bank in March 1917 on a fairly meagre 2 pounds and 10 shillings a week, though by 1920 he was on £500 a year, but still supplemented by more or less hack journalism (over a hundred short publications in five years). The letters concerning Pound's Bel Esprit project to subsidise Eliot's income are riddled with calculations as to precisely how much Eliot needed to secure, per year, for how many years, and how far he could realistically supplement his income from continual literary journalism. Editing *The Criterion* was at first unpaid, though the periodical did pay contributors £10 for 5,000 words. When Faber took *The Criterion* over, the firm paid Eliot a yearly salary of £350 as editor, plus £175 as a director. The $140 Quinn gave Eliot for the early manuscript notebook converted into £29, which equalled three weeks of his bank salary, while the $2,000 from *The Dial* award represented at least 40 weeks income.

And so on. As we read through the correspondence, the financial details and the demands upon his income are both remorseless.

Eliot might therefore, in a somewhat Lukacsian or Goldmannian way, be seen as occupying an unusual, but undoubtedly insecure, petty bourgeois class position, as his aspiration to the position of an independent man of letters became grindingly transformed first into that of a hack writer, a temporary adult education tutor, and a (rather superior) bank clerk, and then into a career as a conscientious middle-aged middle-man of the culture industry – though perhaps disconcertingly with himself as also one of the new iconic products of that proliferating industry, a celebrity poet.

As has often been argued in general terms, it was this vulnerably unsatisfactory intermediate economic position which in the 1930s frequently generated dangerously resentful versions of Eliot's own ideological stance, one in which he could both explicitly declare himself in sympathy with whatever was 'of interest' in Fascistic doctrine yet simultaneously proclaim his loyalty to the traditional class structures of English aristocratic society, whilst also castigating its actual core constellation of banks and insurance companies in the back-rooms of which he had so conscientiously worked in 'the City', and the streets of which had provided the explicit topography of *The Waste Land*.

That highly intellectual aristocrat Lord Bertie Russell had been Eliot's initial point of entry into the privileged 'intellectual aristocracy' of England, and perhaps the peculiarly condensed English ruling-class formation struck Eliot as much more a matter of *the* elite than the not quite corresponding American formation he was familiar with – which perhaps influenced his entangled discussion of Karl Mannheim's notion of elites. Eliot's family was long intertwined with New England's own intellectual aristocracy, but there was perhaps not as much cultural overlap with, say, active Wall Street speculators or Texan oil barons as in the Old England counterpart, where financial City and cultural Bloomsbury were but a short walking distance apart (Maynard Keynes was not the only regular go-between, though Bradford millionaires were uncommon).[41] Eliot had intimately encountered the concentration of power and privilege, of financial and cultural capital, in those two very small corners of London, and had also extended his outsider observation of the English social spectrum much farther afield, not only by regularly sampling the ramified network of country houses, but also by venturing tirelessly into the realms of the more elevated English titled Philistines (including the odd Duchess) in search of subscribers to *The Criterion*, a territory almost as alien to this emigré American as that of his working class adult students in Yorkshire.

If, therefore, one sought a further resonance with the work of Lukacs one might even suggest that Eliot's overall trajectory quite neatly matched Lukacs's criteria for the appropriate protagonist of a quasi-historical novel in whom the contradictions of an entire period converge, and that perhaps Eliot's early articulation of his uneasy class position was precisely what underpinned the continuing resonance, among a similarly positioned Anglo-American readership, of *Prufrock* and the other pre-1922 self-deprecating satires.

It may at this point be worth registering that one of the rare moments in the *Waste Land* material where we can sense an actual sympathy for its unappealing characters concerns

---

[41] See chapter 2 of NDC. Mannheim was a leading member of the Moot. Compare Noel Annan, 'The Intellectual Aristocracy', Studies in Social History, ed. J. Plumb, London 1955, and Eric Sigg, 'Eliot as a product of America', in The Cambridge Companion to T. S. Eliot, ed. A. D. Moody, 1994.

a very precisely located small businessman's daughter (Facsimile p. 51):

Mine were humble people and conservative
As neither the rich nor the working class know.
My father had a small business, somewhere in the city
A small business, an anxious business, providing only
The house in Highbury, and three weeks at Bognor.

The revised version rightly cut most of these execrable lines – but added: 'What should I resent?'

I can cheerfully leave aside whether such an approach might be worth pursuing any further, but what is of relevance to my overall argument concerning *The Waste Land* and the significance of the facsimile material for understanding it, is that Eliot's precarious financial and social situation during the years of composition and publication of *The Waste Land* – an insecurity which lasted at least until he was firmly established at Faber – meant that any public admission which recognised the decisive contribution made to the poem by Pound might well have been perceived as threatening the status not only of the poem itself but thereby also the very foundation of Eliot's new prospects in the wake of the remarkable success of the poem. It is not therefore at all surprising that Eliot suppressed these particular 'relevant historical facts'.

Of course, the very notion that such a poem might have had, in effect, two composers might have been a tricky idea to sell to *The Dial* — despite the varying precedents of, say, Beaumont & Fletcher, the *Lyrical Ballads*, Gilbert & Sullivan, or even the cooperative scriptwriting practices of the film industry. But in any case, to put it at its very lowest, there was an extremely pressing financial motivation indeed for Eliot to claim a sole authorship which brought him not only an extraordinary reputation and, even in the first instance, the equivalent of perhaps $100,000 in today's terms, but also secured the basis for his later almost untouchable dominance.

Yet what remains most important, beyond any quasi-biographical interpretation, is that the peculiar compositional passage of the 'long poem' ended in the publication of an immensely influential work which, whatever the intentions or even despite the incomplete comprehension of its contributing authors, did indeed constitute a radical formal innovation and perhaps, one might say, a peculiarly impersonal achievement.

I can conclude this admittedly somewhat jaundiced account, rather sadly. Perhaps the closest Eliot ever came in his published work to acknowledging the odd and almost accidental basis upon which his extremely successful career had been constructed was in the penultimate poem in the last edition of the *Collected Poems* published within his lifetime (my emphasis): [42]

> ... In the effort to keep day and night together.
> It seems just possible that a poem might *happen*
> To a very young man: but a poem is not poetry –
> That is a life.

*

---

[42] *Collected Poems 1909-1962,* Faber and Faber, 1974, p 229: *A Note on War Poetry,* 1942.

# *Interludes*

The next part of the book basically comprises two previously published pieces, but I want to preface them with some brief general considerations prompted by aspects of those essays. In 1984 I published a short book entitled *The Literary Labyrinth*, mainly composed of fictive reviews of imagined books I did not have time actually to write. One of those illusory texts was *Literary Conversions*, which incorporated a version of the argument around Eliot's *Four Quartets* which I had tried to develop in conversation with Leavis, as recounted earlier. *The Literary Labyrinth* also included a line-by-line rewriting of the first two of Eliot's *Four Quartets,* as a somewhat tongue-in-cheek exercise in what the Situationists called *détourenment* and also as a sort of swan-song for my concern with Eliot. 'Give up literary criticism', Wittgenstein had said to Leavis. *Literary Labyrinth* as a whole was a kind of farewell to literary criticism, since in the mid-1980s I was transferring my interests to the rapidly emerging domain of multimedia computing and what was to become the Internet.

However, I was occasionally drawn back to Eliot. An invitation from David Moody to contribute to *The Cambridge Companion to T. S. Eliot* (to be eventually published in 1994) intrigued and even amused me, since it was stipulated in the commissioning letter that contributors would not be allowed to quote from Eliot's work. Though dubious about the suggested topic, 'modernism and post-modernism', the copyright restriction seemed challenge enough, and has indirectly provoked some of the following considerations.

Then, on a trip to India in the 1990s, proselytising the Internet, I was persuaded by an old friend to give a lecture to students in the English department of the University of Calcutta, and foolishly offered the title '*Dayadhvam: looking for the key*'. I was mortified to discover several staff from the Sanskrit Department among my audience, since I was mainly intending to talk about my students' various exercises in turning *The Waste Land* into interactive multimedia computer applications. However, several years later, a written version of the lecture was coaxed from me for the wonderfully wide-ranging *DA/Datta : Teaching The Waste Land*, edited by K. Narayana Chandran, but that publication, as a special edition of the Hyderabad *CIEFL Bulletin*, was not quite the context in which to explore the further implications and possibilities arising from that piece, which I will now try to sketch.

### *i : copyright and criticism*

First, let us consider some of the issues raised by trying to write on Eliot without quoting him. I have just spent the last twenty minutes conscientiously counting words. The section – or should I call it a lecture, or perhaps an essay? – which you have just (perhaps) read is some 20,000 words long. Of those, I reckon 535 words are quoted from Eliot's prose. In addition, I have quoted thirty scattered lines from *The Waste Land* material and four lines from one other poem by Eliot. These figures are disputable: should I include the 112 words from a Faber blurb which is not definitely by Eliot? Or the 152 from the publisher's flyer for *The Criterion*? What of the phrases from Eliot quoted by others whom I quote? Should I also include the titles of poems: how many times should I count my repeated use of the words *The Waste Land* – or does that phrase perhaps count rather as a line from the poem? And do I count repetitions of the same quotations anyway?

I am nervously anxious about these matters because when I first contemplated writing about Eliot I contacted Faber's Permissions Department and was told that I would be charged £75 plus VAT for every 10 lines quoted from Eliot's verse. Thankfully, I was also very kindly directed to the 'Fair Dealing or Fair Use' page on the Faber website. There I find the following stipulations (I trust I am not violating copyright by quoting them):

If a publication is for a purely academic market and for 'the purposes of criticism or review', we allow:

The quotation of 10 lines, or multiple extracts up to 25 lines, dispersed throughout your work from an individual poem without charge, providing that this does not constitute over 25 percent of the poem. Please note: an 'individual' poem does not include book-long poems such as *The Waste Land* by T. S. Eliot or *Omeros* by Derek Walcott. These are treated like a play (see below). A long poem with several parts is treated as if the part - i.e. 'Little Gidding IV' is an individual poem.

Up to 250 words of prose, or multiple extracts up to 800 words, dispersed throughout your work. In a collection of essays, it is treated as 250 words per essay.

Up to 18 lines of a play/ book poem, or multiple extracts up to 70 lines, dispersed throughout your work.

Now, after careful counting, I think I have quoted consideraly less than 70 lines, overall, from *The Waste Land,* and I calculate – depending on whether one counts blank spaces as included or not – that my quotation from *A Note on War Poetry* constitute only 15.6% of that poem (leaving aside Eliot's three introductory prose lines). So I am safe. I hope.

The prose count is obviously trickier. If I had arranged this book simply as a 'collection of essays', which was indeed an option, I would now have to go back and excise 285 words from my reconstituted Kent lecture, treating it as a single essay, though I could then perhaps have been able to redistribute the saved words into other 'essays' in the book. But to be sure, and as a safety measure, should I now ask you not to read some of those prose quotations, or perhaps even suggest that you go back and cross out an appropriate number of words from your copy – except that, unfortunately, you may have read them already. Drat.

In fact, I have just realised that in this coming part of the book I actually quote another passage from Eliot's prose, so I have now had to excise a passage with the same number of words from the first part. I'm sorry about that. Should I instead have got in touch, yet again, with Faber to see what they would charge for, say, an additional hundred words or so of prose? They don't, as far as I can tell, specify a fixed word-rate for prose, though I was assured that overall I would probably not be charged more than £500 (plus VAT?). So, if you find that there are actually more than 800 words of Eliot's own prose dispersed throughout the book as a whole you will be relieved to know that that's probably what I have done. Though in that case you may, as a result, have by now paid a little more for this book then you would have done.

I raise these delicate matters not because I have any particular complaint against Faber and Faber (though some of my more disgruntled colleagues have indeed been particularly harsh about the level of Faber's copyright charges, in the past), but because I am interested in two wider issues.

The specified Fair Dealing And Fair Use provisions apply only, it says:

> If a publication is for a purely academic market and for 'the purposes of criticism or review'.

That phrase 'purely academic market' rather bothers me. As does that 'and'. And the further provision:

> ... to qualify as an academic publication, a book must have a total print-run of 500 or fewer in hardback, or 1,500 or fewer in paperback.

This rather implies that I can only freely quote the limited amount allowed if I am writing 'criticism' but ('and') it is intended for no more than 1500 'purely academic' readers. Is this perhaps an interesting 'evidence' I should now promptly send to the RED website, to be recorded for a sceptical future? And should I have specified in the Foreword that if you are not an accredited 'purely academic' reader you should refrain from reading this book at all?

Now, as I understand it, under the present legal provisions in England and indeed in most of Europe, Faber and Faber will be able to enforce this kind of copyright control over Eliot's work, and therefore over criticism of it, for seventy years from the date of his death in 1965. That *really* bothers me. I was born almost on the very date that *Four Quartets* was first published as a single volume in England, in October 1944. I was twenty when Eliot died. So I was decidedly of that generation for whom Eliot was a pervasive presence and influence, not just in the classroom or the lecture theatre but in my own reading of and response to literature in general. Yet it seems that I will have to survive till I am at least ninety years old before I can freely quote extensively, in England, from

Eliot's work. Is that one of the gifts reserved for age? Sorry, delete that phrase, or I might have to pay for it. Should I at least put my files in order and contact RED, before I expire, to leave with them a comprehensive record of my reading of Eliot, but only to be published on the website after 2035? After all, by the time I am 90 I may have forgotten what it was like to read Eliot.

For – as I have already indicated –my generation regarded as a crucial component of the process of intelligently and appropriately reading the work of Eliot (and any other poet) that one should attend closely to the exact words he or she had written. This was the case even, difficult as it may now be to remember, when one's reading of literature was not 'purely academic'. What counted as 'criticism', for anyone strongly influenced by Leavis, was a detailed response to 'the words on the page'. Any appropriate published criticism was then an attempt at a written version of that 'close reading', a kind of imagined dialogue with one's own reader about a shared text in front of both. It was simply unacceptable and wholly inadequate to offer only a summary or paraphrase of a poem in lieu of exact quotation. This mode of 'practical criticism' was partly derived from Eliot's own work, both as a response to the very nature of his way of writing poetry and as indebted to some aspects of Eliot's frequent practice of enforcing a critical judgement by direct quotation.

But to publish criticism on Eliot's poetry in England now means that one is highly unlikely – except at considerable expense for copyright permissions – to write the kind of detailed critical analysis which developed alongside of, and was partly prompted by, the adoption of Eliot's poems into the teaching curriculum. There was an obvious relationship between the emergence of 'difficult' modernist literary works and the pedagogical emphasis upon close attention to the text. Since, however, the whole purpose of writing critically about Eliot's poems was to encourage one's readers to read, to read again, and to read more closely, Eliot's own work, with extensively quoted passages acting as a prompt  towards reading more closely, it might be regarded as somewhat counter-productive for a publisher's copyright restrictions to prevent such critical writing upon the poets they publish.

I would here like to insert, for comparison, examples from Leavis's published critical analysis of *Four Quartets* alongside corresponding excerpts from David Moody's own essay on *Four Quartets* in the *Companion* volume from which quotation from Eliot had been largely excluded – but clearly any such exercise would itself eat into my quota of quotations.

Needless to say, the relative demise of close reading or 'practical criticism' has been shaped by many other factors than simply the impact of copyright restrictions: other procedures and preoccupations have understandably emerged. Moreover, it is not only Eliot whose work has been so restricted by publishers and copyright holders. Critics and scholars are by now miserably familiar with the various ploys for extending the regime of required paid permissions by, for example, commissioning elaborately edited 'critical editions' which claim to establish the only 'correct' text of literary works which are already in the public domain, so that any cautious academic is constrained to cite only those critical editions—and has to agree to pay handsomely to do so.

Which takes us back to the provision concerning 'a purely academic market' and its coupling with the phrase 'the purposes of criticism or review'. Since an academic publication is defined as having 'a total print-run of 500 or fewer in hardback, or 1,500 or fewer in paperback' it would seem to be assumed, or even intended, that any 'criticism' will normally be directed at, and restricted to, only a handful of academic readers.

There was indeed, as we have already seen, an element in both Eliot's and Leavis's views on the function of criticism and its relation to an alleged 'minority' culture which might have endorsed such a deliberate curtailment of numbers, but Leavis at least would certainly have demurred at the apparently preferential treatment of a 'purely academic' market. So, I would like to assume, would Eliot – though as himself publisher and middleman at Faber he presumably enforced his own firm's copyright rules.

However, it is not only or even primarily the fate of Leavisite literary criticism that concerns me. What of the poems themselves? The situation here is not only somewhat counter-productive but now almost absurd. Faber would still wish to extract a fee from me for quoting from *The Waste Land, Prufrock,* or *Gerontion,* and would certainly charge me considerably for quoting the whole of such poems in, say, an anthology or on a website. Considering the price-tag of £75 plus VAT per 10 lines, Pound's remark that *The Waste Land* is the longest poem in the English language takes on an interesting new resonance, though I doubt if he actually had in mind the task of calculating forty-five times £75 (plus VAT).

Yet I can now go on the net and within seconds download, without charge, all Eliot's early published poems in full, since they are available on-line quite legally on American websites. That is not necessarily to say that I can legally download them to my own computer, or even read them on my own screen, if I – unfortunately – happen to be in England at the time, though it is perhaps a moot point as to precisely when, during a flight back from an American trip, I am legally obliged, somewhere in mid-Atlantic, to delete a downloaded copy of *The Waste Land* from my laptop hard drive. This is an almost farcical situation, particularly since even the T. S. Eliot Society, with its distinguished patrons and supporters, notifies me on its own website where I can freely download from globally accessible US sites the whole of Eliot's *oeuvre* up to 1923. Without paying a penny – or cent – to Faber.

## *ii : digital do-it-yourself?*

We should put these issues of copyright and digital downloads into a somewhat larger context. Let me therefore return to the first appearance of *The Waste Land* in *The Criterion* and to a comparison which has already been partly gestured at: that Perry Anderson's article 'Components of the National Culture' could almost be regarded as *The Waste Land* for a New Left generation, in so far as both texts operated as 'manifestoes' for the respective journals in which they appeared.

At its launch in 1922, Eliot saw *The Criterion* as deliberately constructing a programme of influence and leverage within the cultural domain, and in later years he perhaps increasingly regarded his editorship as somehow serving a mission, however indirectly, to Christianise his readers, thereby fostering a religious 'conversion of England', to use the phrase from Faber's blurb for the 1928 selection of Pound's poems (note how carefully I have formulated that, though I sincerely hope that Faber have not in fact copyrighted 'the conversion of England').

From its re-launch in 1963, however, Perry Anderson's *New Left Review* proposed an even more challenging mission: to transform not just the cultural terrain but the entire political and economic formation, to bring about a socialist Britain. Yet the dominant strategy in *New Left*

*Review*, signalled in the 'Components' article, was in practice to promote an alternative cultural agenda, and to provide indeed a new intellectual pantheon, rather than to specify a detailed transformative economic programme and a coherent political strategy for implementing it.

One might well suppose that, given the lack of effective leverage of any form of oppositional cultural or intellectual intervention upon the English political and economic 'elite', those who actually exercised power in Britain were probably quite content to yield much of the cultural terrain to an energetic but merely intellectual criticism. So, while a novel and even impressive 'cultural studies' flourished in (mainly) academic institutions, such as the University of Kent in the 1970s, and even influenced some cultural practices beyond the 'purely academic' environment, the efficient implementation of a neo-liberal economic programme relentlessly reshaped the political terrain. *New Left Review* had no more success in bringing about a socialist Britain than *The Criterion* did in effecting a Christian Britain.

But it is not, of course, any shared ideological objective which has prompted me to couple Eliot and the new New Left in this way, but rather their situation within the changing apparatus of communication. By this I mean that the editorial programmes of both T. S. Eliot and Perry Anderson sought to emulate or implement strategies of persuasion and public intervention which were basically inherited from the 19th century: the belief that by editing a periodical and organising a publishing house they could influence the current of ideas within British culture. Indeed they could, and did.

But such a strategy further assumed that the percolation of alternative ideas generated from some relatively compact or even conspiratorial intellectual grouping (such as The

Moot) could have an effective leverage upon the sources of power and decision-making within the social formation as a whole. This was, of course, a perspective which had once been widely shared among a range of intellectual initiatives across Europe, covering the entire spectrum of political persuasion: one only has to list the many periodicals, from Karl Kraus's *Die Fackel* to the Frankfurt School's *Zeitschrift fur sozialforschung*, from *Esprit* to *Les temps modernes,* even perhaps all the way from Coleridge's *The Friend* to Leavis's *Scrutiny.*

But it was, I am suggesting, increasingly immaterial from which end of the political spectrum such projects were launched, since intellectual-cultural interventions of a traditional kind had already proved relatively ineffective and indeed almost irrelevant in a European political situation increasingly marked in the 1920s and 1930s by concentrated state violence and international armed conflict. In previous periods, it might have been plausibly claimed that the structures of power and control had required and benefited from explicit ideological justification, whether in the form of supposed religious authorisation or alleged philosophical justification, including claims of economic rationality. The positive support or critical acquiescence of the cultural and literary opinion-formers might be regarded by those seeking to seize or retain power as strategically desirable, and it had sometimes been in part the function of the media of public discussion, including academia, to sustain those justifications, and indeed to present and percolate them as the 'common sense' of the culture. There had therefore been a recognised and sometimes even accessible terrain upon which counter-interventions might be made, a so-called 'public sphere'.

Eliot's valediction upon closing *The Criterion* in 1939 clearly recognised that any such European common ground had dwindled to almost nothing. And it is perhaps ironic that just as the post-1960s New Left were rediscovering Gramsci's 1920s notion of 'hegemony' the battleground of 'common sense' was itself being increasingly marginalised in the post-war period by primarily financial means of social control, which were by their very nature largely indifferent to any explicitly oppositional intellectual interventions, and not so much reliant upon ideological justification but rather embedded within the emerging structural transformations of 'the economy' itself.

This is not to say that 'culture' in the wider sense deployed by both Eliot and Williams, as 'a whole way of life', was not a crucial component of nationalism, fascism, communism, or even the post-war Attlee programme in Britain. Clearly, too, the more specific terrain of public communications, including the 'culture industries' and, in a broad sense, the educational apparatus, remained of apparent strategic importance. Yet the potential contribution of any programme of critical intellectual intervention was arguably diminished by pervasive and fundamental transformations – to which we will return.

In this overall context, we might briefly ponder Eliot's own shifting relationship to changing forms of communication, including the printing of a mere 450 copies of *The Waste Land* on their hand-press by the Woolfs in their own house, or the circulation of *The Criterion* probably never reaching above a thousand, yet ironically supported by the financial resources of Lady Rothermere, the somewhat estranged wife of the owner of the largest-circulation popular newspapers in Britain, H. S. Harmsworth.

Eliot remained throughout his writing career ambivalent about the relationship between his poetry and his élitist views on culture and education. When the sales of the first Quartets began to number in the thousands Eliot was uneasy, remarking that if *East Coker* had sold 12,000 copies it was probably a sign that it was a bad poem.[1]

Yet in the 1950s Eliot embarked on a further phase in his career – motivated, it would seem, partly by his personal mission of Christian proselytising (and perhaps even by a certain underlying rivalry with Noel Coward?) – as he wrote commercially successful plays for the West End and Broadway theatre, which in the case of *The Cocktail Party* eventually attracted an overall audience of perhaps a million and a half, while nevertheless offering a remarkably explicit dramatic presentation of his Christian ideology. He was, of course, dead before *Cats* grossed a billion or so.

Meanwhile, Eliot's work and particularly *The Waste Land,* together with its now irremovable Notes and a large accumulation of supplementary annotation, became for decades an almost unavoidable set-text upon thousands of literature syllabuses across the English-speaking world, often trailing in its wake a nodding acquaintance with selected passages of Eliot's aloof critical pronouncements, themselves a point of entry into Eliot's reactionary and dogmatic social position.

---

[1] See Eliot's letter to Anne Ridler, 10th March 1941, quoted in Helen Gardner, *The Composition of Four Quartets*, Faber and Faber, 1978, p. 109

Yet, in being detached from its original published context in *The Criterion,* any function of *The Waste Land* as – to put it over-succinctly – either a diagnosis or an indicative resolution of an alleged cultural plight, personal or social, became subsumed under, and displaced by, an increasingly institutionalised patrolling of any possible personal impact the poem might have upon its readers. Eliot's poems had become part of that 'culture', in a far more restricted and increasingly 'purely academic' sense, for which one now had to sweat, but without that pedagogically required effort being any longer assumed to issue into anything more creatively responsive or socially transformative  than an essay in well-trained 'close critical reading' and a commendable examination grade.

Moreover, even as the general reading public for Eliot's work expanded – the Penguin edition of his *Selected Poems* after he won the Nobel Prize in 1948 had an initial print run of 50,000 – the cultural weight and political leverage of that widening readership arguably declined. A generation later, the apparent success of the New Left cultural revolution could also be measured in terms of the considerable sales of such academically influential authors as Raymond Williams and Terry Eagleton and by the undeniable ideological capture of parts of the tertiary sector of education. Yet underlying developments which rendered these apparent successes less generally transformative were also at work.

Even before the launch of *The Criterion,* the 'great' periodicals had long yielded ground to proliferating 'little magazines' with rapidly diminishing circulation figures, and even as *New Left Review* established its publishing house in the late 1960s, the post-war wave of affordable serious paperbacks, exemplified by the success of Penguin, yielded ground to the successive intrusion and eventual  welcome into every household, across all classes and educational levels, of radio, television, and the personal computer, as the primary channels of cultural dissemination, with first the BBC and then the Internet, Google and Wikipedia operating as, functionally, the contemporary successors of any pervasive 'clerisy'.

The computing revolution had effectively originated, not least through Turing's work in wartime Britain, in the very years that Eliot wrote the four successive Quartets, while the future contours of the Internet had first become apparent in 1968, with the Pentagon implementation of APARNET, even as the student revolt unfolded on the streets of Paris and Perry Anderson put the finishing touches to his 'Components' article. But cultural and even political commentators were slow to recognise the coming impact of this combined development, and to register that this was a transformation not restricted to so-called 'information processing' or simply to the received modes and means of communication. Even Vannevar Bush's proposed Memex machine in the 1940s or Ted Nelson's Xanadu project in the early 1960s did not anticipate the ramifications.

Having a computer on one's desk, or increasingly in one's pocket, was not merely like having a book, periodical, or newspaper on one's coffee table, or even a television set in one's living room. The internet-linked computer was not only a replacement for the postal service, the library, or the cinema, but also for the most basic exchange processes of the economy: money too could be uploaded and downloaded, digitally transmitted and indeed created, and radically transformed in the process.

Most crucially, for my immediate argument here, an internet-linked computer is, potentially, an immediately accessible two-way channel as the ordinary phone once was for voice exchange: we can not only download a text, image, or song, but also upload our own. More generally, not only can any individual now browse an astonishing range of global cultural production, more or less freely or cheaply available, but can also, with access to the appropriate software, make her or his own contribution, often in the form of re-mixed, sampled, or collaged versions of previously existing material, offered to a global audience as putatively creative combinations and reworkings of, in effect, quotations. Those procedures, indeed, might be seen as having been partly anticipated by the characteristic practices of the modernist generation of Eliot, Pound, and Joyce in incorporating into their work numerous echoes and exact or modified quotations from the entire range of previous literature.

There have thus been two almost contradictory and certainly contending aspects to these developments, as the overall culture industry itself has become increasingly a sector within the financialisation as well as the digitisation of consumption. Though, obviously, the publishing of any form of 'literature' has long been shaped by commercial factors, including the calculation of financial risk and profit, recent changes have transformed not only the procedures or practices of publishing but the very notion of the 'product' itself. When – to suggest a parallel – the prospect of digitally archiving the enormous back catalogue of the BBC was first mooted, nearly thirty years ago, I can remember suggesting that it was not a 'television programme' that future users of the archive might be primarily interested in accessing, but rather individual clips, or even single 'frames', slivers of time. The implications, not least for technologies of indexing and searching, would be considerable. The cultural artefact is now not only digitally disseminated in bytes but bite-size bits of any individual artefact are themselves potentially valorized. These fragments.

Any cultural artefact can be treated as an ongoing income stream, most obviously in the case of popular music, but also particularly those texts promoted within education. That thousands of successive pupils have been required to have temporary access to, for example, *The Waste Land* has meant that control over the right to copy it, in a 'selected poems', an anthology, or an authorised annotated edition, has been a reliably lucrative asset for its publisher or copyright holder, even more so when the minimal costs of digital reproduction could replace the substantial expense, and calculated investment, of hard-copy printing and warehousing. Yet insofar as the new digital processes have now enabled the appropriation and creative manipulation of all forms of cultural material, it has from a commercial perspective become even more imperative, and at the same time ever more difficult, to exercise control over dissemination, through enforcing copyright restrictions.

Obviously, however, the framework in which recent global battles over copyright have been conducted was not shaped primarily with the texts of poets in mind, but with regard to the interests of the music recording and film production industries. The peremptory extension of copyright to seventy years after the death of the producer was clearly shaped not by the posthumous interests of a single author – by definition, already dead – but by those of ongoing corporations, especially those located in Hollywood and in the various successors to Tin Pan Alley.

Almost accidentally, as it turned out, the resolution of the complementary issue of re-defining the retrospective chronological limits of 'public domain' meant that the date from which that status for all cultural artefacts was no longer to apply in America was fixed at 1923 – before which, of course, the quality of sound recordings and of black-and-white silent films meant that these were of very little interest to current media and financial concerns. But this almost arbitrary date also meant that Eliot's *The Waste Land* just scraped into the US public domain and is therefore available for copyright-free download in America.

Which also means, as it happens, that because the software I am using to self-publish this book allows me to choose my 'place of publication', I could have decided — by a mere click of my mouse —to publish this book in the USA and not in the UK, thereby absolving myself of any legal obligation to pay Faber any copyright fees at all for quoting from *The Waste Land* or from any of Eliot's poems published before 1923. Provided, of course, that you didn't buy this book in England.

That I am now able to self-publish this book at all indicates another far-reaching cultural development. Ezra Pound, it should be remembered, self-published his own first volumes of poems, and we have seen that Eliot's position at Faber effectively turned Faber and Faber into his own self-publishing house. But that almost anybody so inclined can now self-publish and globally disseminate their work has implications which we may not have yet fully grasped. I will offer some tentative suggestions in a concluding Coda. First, however, the following two short pieces on Eliot reflected or even anticipated in a fairly elementary way some of the issues I have just been outlining, while evoking in their different ways what are now to be seen as partly superseded phases and preoccupations.

\*

# Writing

The Eliot academic industry is formidable.

One volume covering 'Eliot criticism' from 1916 to 1965, published in 1972, listed 2,692 items, to which a supplementary volume in 1977 added a further 1,300.

A 1992 American National Poetry Foundation publication listed 1,423 additional books, articles, and dissertations on Eliot, for the decade from 1977 to 1986, as 'just the tip of the iceberg of Eliot criticism' during that time.

Since then, of course –?

Two small contributions follow.

Few readers would disagree that Eliot the man has been as much a puzzle as Eliot the poet. Two small books, with others, have now begun to clarify that puzzle[1] The chief contribution of biography is to present relevant personal facts, and Ms. Gordon's patiently assembled facts have pointed, very pertinently, to how readers might have erred in their puzzlement over Eliot by not recognizing what might now be considered obvious: that Eliot's work represents a series of efforts, each trying to make sense of a persistent moral dilemma. The *oeuvre* of T. S. Eliot will appear to us differently if, instead of treating the whole *Collected Poems* as due to Eliot's 'impersonal' aesthetic, we perceive his poetry as negotiating intractable personal material which persists even in the final form.

We now know, in some detail, that there was indeed another woman in the life of the man, and that much of the work of the poet can be seen as full of some emotional and moral matter which the writer would not expose to light, and from which he could not go away. Since the only way of negotiating a moral dilemma is to find an objective situation which corresponds to that specific dilemma, it may be that Eliot's problems were such that the very *données* precluded objective resolution.

---

[1] L. Gordon, *Eliot's Early Years* (Oxford: Oxford University Press, 1977) and *Eliot's New Life* (Oxford: Oxford University Press, 1988).

And the alternative to resolution, in anyone who knows what it means to endure a situation one wants to escape from, may indeed be a form of madness, perhaps less the intensity of insanity than the desperate role-playing of the apparent *poseur*. We need, to be sure, a great many more facts in Eliot's biography; we should like to know, for example, whether, when and in relation to what personal crisis, he read Milton's *The Doctrine and Discipline of Divorce*. Certainly his animus towards Milton can seem in excess of the verse as we know it.

That was a way of putting it. Not very satisfactory.

There are two elements at work in this passage. One concerns the claims of some recent scholarship on Eliot's life, which has established something like the following account of the relation between the work and the life:

Eliot was in love with Emily Hale. He married Vivienne Haigh Wood. The marriage was an appalling disaster. *The Waste Land* reflects the state of mind brought on by the marriage ... In 1934 and 1935, Emily is in England. Eliot and Emily visit Burnt Norton. From that comes *Burnt Norton* (what might have been . . .). In 1939, Eliot and her brother have Vivienne committed to an asylum. *The Family Reunion* reflects (on) the guilt of possibly killing a wife, together with the more buried theme of infanticide. Etc.

I offer this simply to suggest the kind of account now possible, even plausible. The accuracy or credibility of these emerging accounts is not at issue here. What is significant is that, in a considerable shift of emphasis, we can now read Eliot's work in quite radically personal ways, if we wish.

And this is, of course, to go directly contrary to Eliot's own critical stipulations and to the orthodoxy of a generation: that our concern should be with the poetry and not with the poet, that there is a disjuncture between the man who suffers and the man who creates. Certainly Eliot himself would have found my opening paragraph profoundly unacceptable. But the fact of the matter is that 'T. S. Eliot' is constructed and re-constructed according to the ways in which his work is received.

The second problematic element in that opening few paragraphs is the deliberate echoing of Eliot's own essay on 'Hamlet and his Problems.' But is the relation between my text and Eliot's a matter of quotation, or of pastiche, or even parody? In what sense might the use of Eliot here be seen as an attempt to authorize my own text—to borrow a kind of authority for it by transposing his account of *Hamlet?* (But how authoritative is that account anyway?) Or does the echoing of Eliot simply serve to get my own writing under way, by taking Eliot as a model for a certain kind of critical writing, a shadow voice I can adopt? (Yet how persuasive, now, is that very tone and mode of writing, and with it Eliot's own criticism?) I pose the issue in that way because central in various reactions to Eliot over the years has been the role of quotation, allusion, and different 'voices' in his writing.

We can initially outline these reactions as a way into tracing a certain trajectory from Modernism to Postmodernism in the reception and construction of Eliot.

*full of high sentence*

At its simplest, Eliot's use of quotations in both the poetry and the criticism can be taken as a sign of erudition, and therefore as a mark of elite authority. Many students react this way, either in awe or hostility.

Faced with the final lines of *The Waste Land* or even the epigraph to *Prufrock,* such readers may enjoyably succumb (the poetry *can* communicate before it is understood); or they may blankly decline to proceed; or perhaps reach defensively for a copy of Southam's *Students' Guide to the Selected Poems of T. S. Eliot.* Eliot's characteristic mode and tone in his critical essays can seem similarly gnomic or hermetic, superciliously dismissive of readers struggling to become even preliminarily acquainted with the range of English literature: 'The poetry of Donne (to whom Marvell and Bishop King are sometimes nearer than any other authors) is late Elizabethan, its feeling often very close to that of Chapman . . . ' The aspiring reader, apparently obliged to master both every local echo and the overall mapping of how every author relates to every other, can thus feel him or herself left in barbarian outer darkness.

Such responses might simply signal the passing of an era, the demise of any adequate readership. Eliot's own *The Waste Land* and its notorious notes can be cited in evidence: what else was *The Waste Land,* in its original appearance in the first issue of *The Criterion,* than a complaint that the great tradition of European culture had dwindled to a few disconnected fragments, a case of battered books, which would not cohere any more than the poem itself would. If the poem were to be received with incomprehension (requiring notes—though not for the elite subscribers to *The Criterion*) that very reaction would reinforce its own case. The comically wide-ranging notes reinforced an awareness of cultural fragmentation with their barbed and brittle playfulness. In such a situation, if one wanted to be a poet after one's twenty-fifth year, one would grimly have to sweat for it in the library—while acknowledging, of course, that Shakespeare had gained more from a perusal of Plutarch than most men would get from a lifetime spent in the British Museum.

Literature was now an austere and full-time profession, an impersonal task of storing up words and phrases, of becoming an ever-more finely tuned catalyst, a precision instrument of feeling, the minimum qualification being a feeling for the whole of European literature in one's very bones. Few readers could hope to follow into that sacred wood. The temptation might be to burn it down instead.

However, another way of accounting for Eliot's proliferation of quotations and quasi-quotations is indicated by Eliot himself, in speaking of how certain images can become personally charged with significance and remain rather mysteriously in the memory to be evoked years later in the poetry: the sight of an old white horse in a meadow, or six ruffians at a window.[2]

We can then begin to read even the quotations within the critical essays as resonant with personal emotional investment rather than   as exemplifying impersonal judicious authority, as saturated fragments of Eliot's own psyche rather than as fine placings of comparative merit.

Thus the motif of lost or even murdered children might be registered in the use of passages from *Hercules Furens* in 'Seneca in Elizabethan Translation' (an essay he sent to Emily Hale), echoed also in the epigraph to *Marina* (with its poignant 'O my daughter') The comments that Tennyson gives no evidence of having known the experience of violent passion for a woman and that the ravings of his lover on the edge of insanity in *The Princess* sound false might then be linked as much with Emily's 1935 visit as with any considered judgment on Tennyson. The singling out of Yeats's lines about having

---

[2] *The Uses of Poetry & Uses of Criticism*, (1932), 1964, p. 148.

reached forty-nine with only a book, not a child, to show for it might resonate onto Eliot's use in his poetry of Hieronymo's madness (at the murder of his children) or the fate of Ugolino in the tower (condemned to eat his own children). The choice of *Ion* as silent structure for *The Confidential Clerk* would go alongside Vivienne's addition to *The Waste Land* manuscript: 'what you get married for if you don't want children?' The repeated citing of the 'sufficiently unfamiliar' passage on 'the poor benefit of a bewildering minute' might be set alongside that 'awful daring of a moment's surrender' perhaps recorded most honestly in the original draft of the published lines 'Your heart would have responded.' Read along these converging lines, even Eliot's critical impersonality in his essays can dissolve into as personal and emotionally porous a medium as the poetry.

A third and even more demystifying way of reading the quotations would be in terms of a simple serendipity, not just the occasional conjuncture of Spinoza and the smell of cooking, but the storing up of words and phrases as the regular bye-product of the endless miscellaneous reviewing which Eliot undertook to make ends meet in the early years of the marriage.[3] What seems like formidable erudition often derives from happening to be reading several different kinds of book at once, producing the accidental cross-connections and fortuitous juxtapositions familiar to any working writer.

A simple example would be to trace how Eliot's close reading of Aristotle for his work at Oxford provided an epigraph for a section in 'Tradition and the Individual

_____

[3] A useful list is in C. Behr, *T. S. Eliot: A Chronology of his Life and Works* (London: Macmillan 1983), pp. 95-120.

Talent' while the same rather peculiar passage of the *De Anima* (Book I. 4) fed into the composition of 'Gerontion', a poem partly shaped by Eliot's reaction to his father's death which had itself occurred in the same year that he undertook to review *The Problem of Hamlet*.

Given also the anonymity of much cultural reviewing work in those years, a tone of authoritative omni-competence was easily available as cover for a young man's ignorance, inviting tonal camouflage for hair-raising audacities of arbitrary judgment. Eliot's 'impersonal' critical style may then be compared to Addison's construction of an urbanely 'a-political' prose *persona*: a neat resolution of an individual career dilemma, generalizable and imitable as the mode of a generation or the style of a disciple or discipline.

Eliot's status as American exile in England suggests a further element in his use of quotations, a matter of nervous anxiety rather than of aloof omniscience. His recently available letters show how linguistically precarious he could feel. We can sense him articulating his American English with an alien care. In 1914, he describes his boarding house filled with European exiles speaking several tongues; he transcribes what he calls 'brilliants' —fragments of overheard British speech and odd sayings. His correspondence adopts a variety of styles and voices, reflecting an unusually dispersed set of simultaneous social locations. His poems in French already reflect this: 'En Amerique, professeur', *etc*. Rather than being in awe of Eliot's multi-voiced ventriloquism as an index of ironic impersonal control, one can just as easily see an anxiety of identity at work, deeper than Prufrock's though in continuity with it.

As with later writers in exile (especially in Paris), there is a tendency in Eliot to erect a whole theory of language from this de-naturalizing experince of how words can fail to work for one. Being unable to say just what one means, or facing a roomful of people telling one that that was not what they meant at all, were real social experiences for Eliot during those early years in England.

His letter of June 17,1919 to Eleanor Hinckley[4] is a hilariously painful account of the social complications of meaning and of report possible in the politely vindictive world of literary London. In *The Waste Land* language itself is seen as having fallen, even from the first intelligible sound that broke the animal silence: that primitive imitation or quotation of the thunder's 'Da' is already a deeply ambiguous and enigmatic syllable. Language is to fall or fail again, in the seventeenth century, as a mysterious dissociation of sensibility allegedly 'set in', like a nervous breakdown in the culture.

But to be unable to say exactly what one feels or fail to find a formula for a precise emotion may be a matter of personal social awkwardness rather than evidence for a cultural diagnosis. To resort to other men's words, for a word within a word when one is unable to speak a word, may be the linguistic equivalent of reaching for a mask, a socially acceptable *persona*. Numerous other American visitors have, after all, registered an unexpected muffling and peculiarly annoying opacity in the language they had thought they had shared with their English hosts. And now that even that Anglo-American tongue has transmuted into the flat international 'English' of cross-cultural conversations in airport lounges, satellite-linked

---

[4] *Letters,* 1, 1988, pp. 304f.

television studios, and multi-national conferences, even the native speaker can feel irredeemably alienated from the increasingly unusable riches, resonances, and resources of the English language. Eliot's own carefully constructed speaking-voice can then seem like both a delicate negotiation of a personal linguistic uncertainty and a paradoxical anticipation of the thin air of current English. A discourse constructed from quotation and allusion may be only a shade away from a discourse consisting entirely of sound-bites.

However, a more profound level of anxiety is also at work, in the problematic relation between contextual structure and local quotation. Necessarily, a quotation involves taking a phrase or formula from one context into another. But what legitimates the new context itself, the structure into which the displaced allusion fits? Eliot had a tendency to take even the skeletal framework of a new work from another source: what he called the mythic method in Joyce, and which he uses himself, in the deployment of Jessie Weston and the Grail legend in *The Waste Land,* or the appropriation of Greek tragic plots and/or West End theatre forms in the plays. However, once the accommodating structure is itself registered as only another quotation a dizzying instability threatens.

The underlying problem is apparent in Eliot's repeated discussions of the complex relation between an artist's appropriation of dominant cultural thought-frameworks and a reader's acceptance of such frameworks, putting in question the very possibility of poetic response and belief. The essays on Shakespeare, Dante, and Blake rehearse these issues of philosophical credibility, conceptual coherence, and poetic suspension of disbelief; while the essays on Bradley and Leibniz reveal that for Eliot himself no metaphysical system, as such, could claim more than a provisional credibility or coherence. In the essay on

Bradley he characteristically puts the emphasis on Bradley's *style*. His radical epistemological skepticism is unusually explicit in an early letter to Norbert Wiener.[5] From *Prufrock* to *The Hollow Men* a similar skepticism is at work concerning any underlying psychic structure, since, as 'Tradition and the Individual Talent' acknowledges, the point of view Eliot was struggling to attack was indeed related to the metaphysical theory of the substantial unity of the soul.

Arguably, Eliot's only successful resolution of these interrelated problems was to construct an idiosyncratic form of spiritual autobiography sustained by the device of intra-textual self-quotation. In *Four Quartets* he may have begun by taking over the form of a Beethoven quartet, but the subsequent quartets, in both structure and endlessly layered local echo, primarily relate back to and interweave with the previous quartets in the overall poem, and beyond that to Eliot's own *oeuvre*, his own previous words echoing thus in our minds as we read.

*Four Quartets* thereby becomes brilliantly self-sustaining. Only an occasional, and surely deliberate, flat-footed assertiveness perhaps acknowledges a continued tension between epistemological skepticism and dogmatic authority: the hints and guesses may somehow be Incarnation but they nevertheless remain only hints and guesses. That elaborately appealing poetic solution could not be surpassed or even repeated. Indeed, in the post-conversion prose the omnicompetent tone of the earlier criticism returns, as a kind of arrogance mitigated only by pseudo-humility: ostensibly tentative notes lead only to *the* definitive delimiting of 'culture' and alternative

---

[5] January 6, 1915, *Letters,* I, 1988, p. 79.

notions can be only summarily dismissed. If Eliot did indeed move beyond the modalities of Modernism in his own lifetime, it is salutary to register where he moved to.

## *after modernism*

I am not suggesting that Eliot was or was not a 'Postmodernist', but rather that Eliot's work initiates a logic which can illuminate current notions of postmodernism, and that his ways of negotiating his particular cultural situation pre-echo some features of what is currently meant by postmodernism. The term is notoriously tricky, but the specifically architectural, and arguably still most influential, use of the term emphasizes precisely the deployment of quotation, the relation and dissociation between structure and facade in the design of buildings: while the under-girding skeleton may be the product of the latest technology, the cladding or appearance is constituted by a variety of essentially optional historical masks.[6]

Of obvious relevance to Eliot would be the example of exhibition architecture: the temporary buildings erected for various world's fairs and great exhibitions, offering artificially concentrated doses of the world's cultural styles. The classic American example was the Chicago Columbian Exposition of 1893. Stuart Ewen quotes a description of a central feature of that fair:[7]

---

[6] See C. Jencks, *What is Post-Modernism?* (London: Academy Editions, 1986).
[7] John F. Kasson, *Amusing the Million*, quoted in S. Ewen, *All Consuming Images* (New York: Basic Books, 1988), p. 37.

The Midway in effect formed a colossal sideshow, with restaurants, shops, exhibits, and theatres extending down a huge corridor, six hundred feet wide and a mile long . . Here the Beaux-Arts neo-classicism of the Court of Honour gave way to Barnumesque eclecticism, refined order to exuberant chaos. Fairgoers threaded their way on foot, or in hired chairs among a hurly-burly of exotic attractions: mosques and pagodas, Viennese Streets and Turkish bazaars. South Sea Island huts, Irish and German castles, and Indian tepees.

In 1904 St. Louis, Eliot's boyhood hometown, was the site of the Louisiana Purchase World's Fair, with its construction of an entire artificial 'Philippine' city. The sixteen-year old Eliot certainly attended the St. Louis Fair, but since his father was the President of a brick manufacturing company it was in any case unlikely that the young Eliot escaped awareness of the mechanics of balloon-frame architecture. St. Louis was once singled out, by Giedion, as providing impressive nineteenth-century examples of severely functionalist architecture, a proto-Modernism abandoned before its time.[8]

One might then see in the widespread American adoption of surface architectural imitation and facades as quotations a loss of confidence in American civic culture's having a style of its own. Pound's ransacking of Provençal, Chinese, and Renaissance Italian materials, can then seem not so distant from Mellon's stone by stone transportation of a medieval French abbey facade to his Pittsburgh

---

[8] S. Giedion, *Space, Time and Architecture* (Cambridge, MA: Harvard University Press, 5th edn., 1971), p. 393f; cf. pp. 200f.

museum, or the artificial creation of the New York Cloisters or, finally, Disneyworld itself.

Eliot's recursive recycling of past literatures to create a modern literature can be seen as a similar strategy arising from similar problems. His construction of a pan-European poetic structure, incorporating vividly compressed fragments of Wagner, Verlaine, Augustine, and Ovid, can seem remarkably akin to the poly-cultural and literally superficial displays of the Midway.

These suggested similarities are not only, in true postmodernist fashion, surface affinities but also structural. For the deeper superficialities of postmodernism are already at work in Eliot's construction of history as essentially a matter of literary taste. If a dissociation of sensibility can be so culturally devastating yet so evidently a matter of critical construction, then not only the blithely anachronistic collages of Hollywood or Great Exhibition representations of past and future are factitious and arbitrary, but the very narrative of history itself is merely a matter of organizing fragments of quotation, a textual reshuffling of an endlessly expanding but unreliable archive with no verifiable validity.

If so, then even the worst examples of Heritage history, as a pattern of essentially timeless moments, styles and motifs, are merely indicative of a deeper abyss: that History may be neither servitude nor freedom, but unavoidably Disney. It simply depends on who creates and controls the taste by which that past is not only enjoyed but actually constructed. For when the cultural past is only another country to be exploited for commercial tourism, then constructing either canon or criterion becomes critically impossible. Eliot's main cultural presence might then become only as the librettist of *Cats*.

Perhaps we should now await the virtual reality version of *The Waste Land,* offering personalized interviews with the Sybil and a chance interactively to rewrite the ending.

## *when was Modernism?*

It is time to re-examine the inherited notions of Modernism, and to consider how it was constructed and how Eliot became a key to its canon. As Raymond Williams has emphasized, what now constitutes 'Modernism' is a highly selective construct.[9] The basis for that selection was, in part, another temporal contingency: the coincidence of 'Modernism' with the emergence and development of 'English' as a respectable academic subject. What such 'difficult' writing as that of Eliot, Joyce, and Pound, potentially offered was justification for claiming the status of a 'discipline' for 'English' in the first place. The function of erudite quotations in this context was twofold: to validate the notion that genuine learning was required, and to reinforce a claim for necessary training in close and practised attention.

However, the merits of Modernism were not, of course, immediately endorsed by the academic community. Roughly, three phases can be out-lined in the assimilation and construction of 'Modernism' in English criticism.

In the first period, from say 1922 to 1945, the 'new bearings' suggested by Eliot's critical preferences and poetic practice were established as canonical, shaping the curriculum into a remapping of the highpoints of literary history, so that Eliot and his generation were seen as the

---

[9] Raymond Williams, 'When was Modernism?', *New Left Review* 175 (May/June 1989): 49.

appropriate culmination. But by the time this effort was successful the Modernist moment was already history.

After 1945, another generation of critics emerges, in the increasingly professionalized and institutionalized field of 'EngLit.' Especially in the United States, a generation of well-trained elucidators produced an impressive body of scholarly commentary, with ever-more specialized studies of every aspect of the Modernists. Eliot's own erudition was thereby emphatically highlighted, while the poetry risked disappearing into the accumulating apparatus of the knowledge industry. Student 'Guides' such as Southam's were then doubly constitutive of the canon: effectively delimiting it to those texts chosen for exegetical commentary and implying a virtue in the sheer density of allusion.

Arguably, the problem facing the third generation of critics, from, say, 1968 onwards, was both that the elucidatory work upon Modernism had been largely completed (they had been the students for whom those guides were already written) and that the redefining of the canon had been almost too successful: no group of writers later than 'the Modernists' could claim anything like their established prestige, measurable by the groaning library shelf-load. For the aspiring professional critic not content to be the acknowledged expert on the semi-colon in the later Henry James, the strategic problem was how to tackle the same terrain as before but with a different critical emphasis: how to say something new about the monstrous bibliographical construct that was now 'T. S. Eliot' or 'Joyce'.

One initially successful strategy was to find new theoretical ways of re-validating the already established valuations. The various re-theorizings of literature and /or of criticism, or the several forms of deconstructive re-

reading, tended in that respect to be professionally productive. An alternative, but more high-risk strategy was simply to expand the canon to the point where canonical considerations were entirely surpassed and 'literature' dissolved back into textuality and rhetoric, whether that of Black /Woman /Working-Class writing, Government texts, or advertising copy. The co-presence of both strategies necessitated a complex reformulation of value (as whatever yields pedagogic surplus?) and simultaneously induced a strained sense of professional overload: too much requiring to be read and too diverse a range of competences to be called upon.

In this fairly recent phase, Eliot's status was deeply ambivalent. As both unquestionably eminent and now reasonably teachable (compared with Joyce or Pound) Eliot's work figured increasingly as exemplarily canonical, yet for the same reason was imputed with a double discredit: as *ur*-draughtsman of the critical orthodoxy to be deconstructed, and as archetypal white male elitist conservative literary icon. Surprisingly little work attempted to reclaim Eliot as, say, proto-structuralist (layering myths upon each other) or precursor of linguistic constructions of illusory subjectivities (Prufrock on Lacan's couch). Instead, even in this era of authorial death and dissolution, Eliot's complicated, and exploitative, relations to women were increasingly subjected to biographical and psychoanalytic scrutiny; the 'personal' reading even of Eliot's previously erudite quotations became plausible precisely as a contribution to the necessary ideological dethronement.

One way of placing 'Postmodernism' is then to see it as the next (post-1980s?) generation's nominal resolution of a shared professional impasse (the term itself has all the marks of such a career move). 'Postmodernism' in this context refers to the fourth phase in the critical re-working of 'Eng.Lit.' (now a whole repertoire of cultural studies) in which the awesome job-description of required expertises was made tolerable by a counter-move: all previous phases of the discipline were now to be taken as providing only provisional overall structures, fabricated framings and mappings, themselves now available as material for reflexive analysis but all under equal epistemological erasure.

In this phase, Eliot is a somewhat neglected figure, but aspects of his own career might be plausibly offered as allegorical or exemplary. As in Eliot's own development, 'postmodernist' criticism has combined a kind of intellectual serendipity with a rhetorical mode that could plausibly mimic omni-competence: the remorseless over-production of critical publication, combined with the speed of theoretical redundancies, confronted younger practitioners with a variant on Eliot's own early dilemmas.

And as with the resolution offered by *Four Quartets,* some postmodernist (critical) writing tended towards self-sustaining structures, held up only by acts of inter-textuality, a form of critical suspension of skepticism, in which alternative positions are treated not as statements open to refutation but as storehouses for competing quotations, or simply as memories of once-held positions now available for autobiographical revision. The end term, as in Eliot's poetry, would presumably be a criticism composed entirely of reflexive self-quotation.

### *after postmodernism*

As an academic *topos* 'Postmodernism' was, of course, plausibly sustained only by wider cultural developments. It may be, however, that the most frequently celebrated features of Postmodernism even more rapidly waned into a new past: the period of Postmodernism (1979-89?) was soon over. In the wake of world events after the early 1990s, it now seemed merely quaint to proclaim the end of meta-narratives, the repudiation of overall histories and of overarching frameworks for interpretation, the demise of grand explanatory theories. As new world narratives popularly proliferated, from Kennedy's *The Rise and Fall of Great Powers* to Fukuyama's *The End of History,* it became increasingly plain that some central postmodernist motifs operated to undermine only certain carefully selected or targetted kinds of grand narrative, those stemming from the generally 'liberal' or 'progressive' camps of the previous decades. The appeal to 'Postmodernism' provided a way of discrediting, or avoiding engagement with, those attempts at global coherence which both repudiated and offered to explain capitalist domination. 'Postmodernist' was frequently simply code for 'post-Marxist'.

However, the collapse of the Soviet forms of Communist organization in Eastern Europe eventually removed the need for that stratagem. The more triumphalist apologists for the 'West' were therefore only too ready to reintroduce grand narratives, with predictable epic heroes (Spirit of Free Enterprise, Genuine Democracy), and global perspectives: a New World Order was (once again) proclaimed and it was rapidly possible to see what was likely to come after Postmodernism, at least at the level of political rhetoric. The somewhat unconvincing 'Victorian values' of the 1980s were revamped in 1990s America as the timeless shibboleths of Family, Nation, and Religion, while in an allegedly unified Europe these values revealed their nightmare forms: in wars fought in the name of ethno-nationalisms and ethnic cleansing, in bitter religious contestations, in enraged racist conflicts. Some commentators had already seen Postmodernism as cultural precursor to a 'soft path' fascism,[10] while others interpreted the newly rampant fundamentalisms, whether Christian, Islamic, or Israeli, as paranoid reactions to the corrosive uncertainties celebrated in postmodernist positions.

Whereas the 'Postmodernist' phase had at best an ambivalent debt to Eliot and no clear pigeon-hole for his work, in this now-emerging post-Cold War period Eliot was clearly ripe for several possible new appropriations. His own move towards a reactionary and religious conservatism will perhaps makes him congenial and useful to some of the new currents of right-wing thought. Both the various parochial nationalists and those who claim a new pan-Europeanism can legitimately cite his perspectives in support: either group can now quote *'Bin gar keine Russin, stamm' aus Litauen, echt deutsch'* with suitably different emphases. The renewed strength of religious ideologies leaves Eliot well placed for a certain resurrection: the *Idea of a Christian Society* might go down well in some circles, and any number of regressively conservative tendencies may seek support and comfort in Eliot's deliberately restrictive definition of culture. As increasingly the benefits of 'democracy' are also questioned, in favour of an incremental authoritarianism, the more anti-democratic aspects of Eliot might again find a new lease of life.

---

[10] Dean MacCannell, 'The desire to be postmodern', in his *Empty Meeting Grounds: The Tourist Papers*, (London: Routledge 1992), pp. 183-229.

It is, fortunately, possible to put this in more neutral terms. The issues treated in *Notes Towards the Definition of Culture,* of cultural community and identity, of the relations between region and nation, sect and cult, are clearly on the new European agenda. In considering these issues Jacques Derrida even brought the neglected Valery back into the debate.[11] Perhaps Eliot is now due for similar resuscitation.

Eliot's version of Modernism emerged in response to the specific cultural dilemmas of his generation of Americans faced with post-World War European culture as a questionable and uncertain option rather than as a dominant given. After the long end of the Cold War, we may all be in an analogous position for a while, as exiles —of uncertain cultural identity—from an as yet undefined future 'Europe'. Eliot's soberly pitched and profoundly problematic voice may still be one of those we must attend to, if we are not to develop merely a continent-sized Euro-Disney. We may even find ourselves, squatting in the ruins of postmodernism, re-reading *The Waste Land* afresh and reluctantly rejoicing that once more we have to construct something upon which to rejoice.

A particular strand within Modernism may be due for productive revaluation. From Imagism to, say, Eliot's essay on Dante, there is a concern with the possibility of a new kind of thinking in images, even a logic of images, more multi-dimensional and popularly accessible than that of words. If political democracy in the television and internet age necessitates a capacity for shared political

---

[11] J. Derrida, *L'autre cap* (Paris: Les Editions de Minuit, 1991) - translated by Pascale-Anne Brault and Michael B. Naas as *The Other Heading: Reflections on Today's Europe* (Bloomington: Indiana University Press, 1992).

discourse not dependent upon educational or linguistic differentiations, then these issues remain active.

Eliot's attempt to devise, or revive, a form of passionate thinking may also be worth pondering: a world of ecological awareness may well be one in which we truly do need to have our modes of feeling directly altered by our reading and thought, in which to feel our thought as immediately as the odour of a rose may be a requisite capacity.

We can return here to the opening issues. A quotation operates in a double-faceted mode: by quoting we seek authority from another, yet often it is the very act of quoting which  endows that source with its putative authority. (Student essay-writers thus face the dilemma of negotiating between mere appeal and appropriate support.) The authority of a quotation, however, is always only provisional, dependent finally upon the force of our own case or context.  We perhaps need to re-learn that all authority is indeed so delegated, however indirectly, from ourselves, and not from some pre-given superiority.  It may be time to pursue further one basic insight of Modernism, that even genius is a job, no more mysterious than turning the leg of a table. Insofar as the refined impersonality of Eliot's authority presided over, and shaped the agenda for, a whole era in literary criticism, the long-delayed demystification of both the man and the poetry, in the mainly sympathetic light of new biographical readings, may be the last and best contribution he can now make to a suitably disenchanted but open future.

*

I'm afraid that I was not aware, when writing the
following piece, of this nicely ironic snippet from the
Eliot industry.

> *Dayadhvam*: I have heard the key
> Turn in the door once and turn once only
> We think of the key, each in his prison
> Thinking of the key, each confirms a prison..

Eliot's Note reads:

Cf. *Inferno*, XXXIII, 46:

> 'ed io sentii chiavar l'uscio di sotto
> all 'orribile torre.

The Temple edition of Dante which Eliot used has a note:

> When Guido of Montefeltro took command of the
> Pisan forces in .. 1289, the keys of the prison were
> thrown into the river and the captives were left to
> starve.

The 2015 edition, I, p. 702, has a note:

> Geoffrey Carter suggests that TSE was misled by this
> [Temple edition] note and supposed that the Italian
> verb 'chiavare' was related to 'chiave', key, whereas
> Ugolino actually hears the door being *nailed* up.
> (*N&Q* Oct 1977).

The Carter article from *Notes & Queries* is not listed in
the 2015 edition Bibliography.

# *Dayadhvam*: looking for the key

*Dayadhvam.* Let us first 'sympathise ' (Eliot's translation):

> I have heard the key
> Turn in the door once and turn once only
> We think of the key, each in his prison
> Thinking of the key, each confirms a prison
> *(The Waste Land,* ll. 411-414)

Think, for a moment, of the anxious student of Eliot, looking for the key to *The Waste Land,* and about to be trapped thereby in a kind of prison, a series of double-binds constructed by the poem.

By this passage, for example. Eliot's note directs us to both Dante's *Inferno* XXXIII, 46, and F. H. Bradley's *Appearance and Reality.* The Dante reference is to Ugolino, trapped in a tower with his sons and grandsons, left either to starve or to eat his own offspring (echoes of old Father Chronos devouring his young...?). Bradley's image is of a radical solipsism, a monadic mode: 'my experience falls within my own circle, a circle closed on the outside . . . the whole world for each is peculiar and private to that soul.' Images of isolation, entrapment, starvation—yet here associated with the injunction *'Dayadhvam:* sympathise' with another—hardly an option for a monad, and a peculiarly unhelpful but perhaps compelling injunction for someone in Ugolino's situation. Are we to take *Dayadhvam* as the answer or solution to Bradley's closed circle? Or is the reader to sympathise with the prisoner, as suffering a like entrapment within the Bradleyan self? Or are we to recognise such imprisonment as merely mind-forged? The relation between enigmatic injunction and its associated lines poses a dilemma.

We are already, of course, within the context of an overall allusion, to the *Brihadaranyaka Upanishad,* V, 2 (Eliot's own reference is incorrectly to V, 1). But there the three-fold injunction of the thunderous *Da* was nicely adjusted to the three categories of auditor. Each interpreted the syllable in terms most appropriate to themselves: gods, to restrain themselves, despite their power; men, to give (honour, gifts, sacrifice, themselves?), despite a natural selfishness; demons, to be compassionate, despite their demonic character. Each, one might claim, by their differing interpretation registers and acknowledges an obligation against their own respective natures. Yet Eliot, in shifting the order and removing the differentiated interlocutors, attaches each interpretation to an apparently inappropriate context, suggesting a peculiar kind of observance which almost constitutes a violation of each injunction.

The basis for this claim, and perhaps the key to the whole passage, and with it the whole poem, lies in those partly cancelled lines from Eliot's draft of *The Waste Land:*

> The sea was calm, and your heart responded
> Gaily, when invited, beating responsive
> To controlling hands. I left without you
> Clasping empty hands. I sit upon the shore
> Fishing, with a desolate sunset behind me
> > *(Facsimile,* p. 78)

These lines, almost the final lines of the whole poem, underwent several revisions and second thoughts and finally a crucial emendation and excision. The published version makes the response and the invitation only hypothetical ('your heart *would* have responded') and removes the implication of consequence: 'I sat upon the shore' now merely dangles, unconnected to that invitation offered and accepted in a boat upon the calm water....

Our immediate temptation is to read between the lines of both the suppressed and the published versions and to recognise this encounter as in fact the culminating failure of the whole poem: the protagonist fails to respond adequately and appropriately to a genuinely responsive sexual encounter. In the published version the invitation remains hypothetical, though the response would have been forthcoming. In the suppressed version, the invitation and response were actual, but followed by only bleak withdrawal and denial. If the land is indeed blighted by a loss of procreativity then here the protagonist, in either version, is exercising too much self-restraint *(Damyata),* perpetuating either infertility or lovelessness. The refusal here is a refusal to 'give' the greatest, and oddest, gift of all, life itself: he remains trapped in his own isolation and loneliness, and in effect devours his own potential offspring by refusing to have any. The evasive revisions of these lines could then be seen, correspondingly, as signalling a kind of failure on Eliot's part, an authorial revision cloaking a deeply personal refusal or incapacity. 'What you get married for if you don't want children..' added Vivienne to the draft manuscript *(Draft,* p. 20). In a perhaps tacit endorsement, Eliot incorporated the remark into the pub scene.

We are, by now, already deep into difficulties, echoes, allusions. On this reading, the crucial memory at work in the poem is one of accepted but refused desire: a sexual invitation accepted but then withdrawn. The gift of life, that 'awful daring of a moment's surrender', with blood shaking the heart, which is the very moment of conception, though it itself never figures in our obituaries or is recorded on gravestones, that moment was not given but retracted through prudence, or prudery. And if *Damyata* is self-restraint, then here in the calm boat to observe it was perhaps to violate the other two injunctions, to sympathise and to give.

Yet we can also, of course, read these lines quite differently. In Eliot's version of the stricken waste land it is not sexual incapacity or even lack of fertility ('She's had five already') that is the issue, but the wrong kind of sexuality: this waste land is, after all, replete with rape, seduction, indifferent promiscuity, betrayal. How we respond to and judge the impact of this final sexual encounter involves, necessarily, our own criteria for appropriate sexual behaviour in such circumstances. Since the relation between the injunction and the incident is unresolved by the text itself, a critical reading at this point is also a moral decision.

We can therefore sympathise with any student faced with this passage, invited to explore its several layers, confronted not with exegetical starvation but with a plenitude of possibilities. Too many echoes crowd in. We have in play by now not just the published text, but Eliot's notes and the references they pursue; we also have the draft, and Vivienne's and Pound's various glosses, annotations and interventions; we have the whole corpus of Eliot's other work and, increasingly over the past few years, biographical information on Eliot's own life and loves and lost loves. The dense interweaving of these layers and levels may seem difficulty enough, but if we do indeed allow them to shape our responses to the poem we may only be entering into another and more complex layer of difficulty, a further trap awaiting, another key turning upon us.

Try putting these lines into a further context, that of Eliot's other poems before *The Waste Land*. If we navigate briefly through some of the intertextual echoes an unmistakable theme emerges. 'I have heard the key/ Turn' but I have also heard 'the wind under the door', though the 'wind crosses the brown land unheard', where 'the river's tent is broken', another 'broken image' from the heap that includes that 'broken Coriolanus' revived for a moment and those 'broken fingernails of dirty hands' remembered from Margate Sands but recalling also those 'exploring hands encountering no defence' or those 'controlling hands', 'expert with sail and oar'. The dirty fingernails also echo the 'nails' of a dog disturbing a bed, and those 'last fingers of leaf', clutching and sinking, like clasping empty hands. On one occasion, though, her arms were full and her hair wet, but I could not speak. On another, in *La Figlia Che Piange,* the sunlight wove into her hair and she clasped her flowers to her, and turned. So, on that occasion, 'I would have had him leave'and 'he would have left/as the soul leaves the body torn and bruised/ As the mind deserts the body it has used.' A naked body on the low damp ground, used, torn, abused? I left without you—. After a lovely woman stoops to folly, she smoothes her hair with automatic hand (or stretches it out tight? or lets it down, so?); on another occasion, it was a child's hand, automatic, and I could see nothing (behind that child's eye; looking into nothing). Do you see nothing? (I remember the hyacinth garden, and pearls, and eyes.) Only the moon, smoothing the hair of the grass, her hand twisting a paper rose, like a lovely lady twisting lilacs in her fingers. Do you have the key? The last twist of the knife—. Again and again in Eliot's verse the inter-echoes accumulate, as we mount the stairs, or turn away, imagining the response to an overwhelming question . . .

These tissues of echoes, and hundreds more, cluster round our reading of *The Waste Land,* penetrate deep into our reading of any single line. Read one way, they lead to a thoroughly biographical question (but do not ask what is it —) concerning Eliot's relations with his first wife, and with his once-beloved Emily, his opportunities and lost turnings, his lack of children, his thoughts of murder, his ache for a lost daughter, etc.

But as soon as we follow the threads in this direction a new trap begins to close, another double-bind awaits the earnest seeker.

Eliot himself insisted that the critic's concern should be the poem not the poet. He refused any biography, despite recent efforts, and the Bradley passage already cited indicates why biography would have been a peculiarly impossible genre for Eliot. But do we accept his critical injunction, practise the necessary 'self-restraint', sympathise with Eliot's personal pain, allow his plea for protective impersonality? If so, do we thereby allow the core of this poem (and perhaps the whole *oeuvre*) to elude us, the key located in that excised yet endlessly re-worked encounter? Is Eliot's insistence only a lure to distract us, a smokescreen for what he once claimed was indeed 'only a relief of a personal and wholly insignificant grouse against life.' But what if, on the other hand, we agree to accept Eliot's self-denying critical injunction and attempt to read the poem 'as a poem'?

In 1929, Eliot, discussing Dante, permitted himself a long, worried footnote, the following brief extracts from which give some indication of the paradoxes into which his own position had by then led him:

> The theory of poetic belief and understanding here employed is similar to that maintained by Mr I. A. Richards . . . I agree for the reason that if you hold any contradictory theory you deny, I believe, the existence of 'literature' as well as of 'literary criticism'. We may raise the question whether 'literature' exists; but for certain purposes . . . we must assume that the reader can obtain the full 'literary' or (if you will) 'aesthetic' enjoyment without sharing the beliefs of the author. *If* there is 'literature', *if* there is 'poetry', then it must be

possible to have full literary or poetic appreciation without sharing the beliefs of the poet. . .

I have also asserted that we can distinguish between Dante's beliefs as a man and his beliefs as a poet. But we are forced to believe that there is a particular relation between the two, and that the poet 'means what he says'. . . And the statement of Dante [*la sua voluntate e nostra pace*] seems to me *literally true*. And I confess that it has more beauty for me now, when my own experience has deepened its meaning, than it did when I first read it. So I can only conclude that I cannot, in practice, wholly separate my poetic appreciation from my personal beliefs.

*(Selected Essays,* pp. 269-271)

The double bind here is palpable. If we accept this version of Eliot's injunction then we should be able to read *The Waste Land* 'as a poem' without sharing the beliefs of the poet, of Eliot himself. But if we can indeed read it without sharing Eliot's particular belief in the impersonality of poetic art, then we no longer need to read it 'as a poem' in Eliot's sense, and we may therefore just as well read it as a deeply personal and autobiographical 'piece of rhythmical grumbling'. But then why not just read the biographies instead?

Two issues intertwine here, both of which can become central to any 'teaching' of *The Waste Land.* One is the basis for Eliot's own views on the relation between poem and poet. The other is whether *The Waste Land* can indeed be read 'as a poem' at all. Take one aspect of the poem already alluded to: the notes provided by Eliot himself. Such a provision seems to acknowledge that this poem requires something more than the text of the poem itself, a set of references, of keys. Yet on its first publication the poem had no notes. In the first issue of *The Criterion,* edited by Eliot, the poem—almost in lieu of an editorial—in effect acted as a kind of manifesto, indicating the journal's cultural critique and programme.

For those first readers of the new journal, the very 'incomprehensibility', the structural oddity, the fragmentariness, of the poem could be taken as indicative of the cultural malaise the poem was seen as diagnosing under the figure of the Grail myth: that European culture was now only a heap of broken images, a case of battered books, so decayed and sterile that poetry could no longer be written, that cultural creativity was no longer possible. The poet's own incapacity would then be as symptomatic as that of the Fisher King: the apparent inability of the poem to succeed in becoming 'a poem'stemming from a radical failure of creativity and of cultural potency in post-war Europe. Yet to take the poem in this way was already to enter another double-bind: for if we can after all successfully read *The Waste Land* as a poem concerned with these issues, then its diagnosis is thereby shown to be either incorrect (this culture can still, after all, produce *The Waste Land*) or at least as already in the process of cure, the capacity for diagnosis of the cultural malaise itself being the first step in overcoming that malaise.

The obvious way out of the dilemma posed by this problematic status of *The Waste Land* is, of course, to postulate that the poem is indeed incomprehensible but only to some readers (the vast majority) but not to others: a deep cultural sterility may have affected most of Europe but a small elite, including the poet and the subscribers to *The Criterion,* have, nonetheless, no need of notes or additional elucidation. In his 1919 essay on Ben Jonson Eliot had estimated that Jonson's qualities 'ought to attract about three thousand people in London and elsewhere'.

The remark is of a piece with Eliot's later explicit analysis of cultural levels and elites in *Notes Towards the Definition of Culture* and in *The Idea of a Christian Society*. From that line of thinking would emerge the conservative stance which would recommend in the mid-1950s that the post-war student population be reduced to half the pre-war figure. For *The Waste Land* to be studied by thousands of (in Eliot's eyes) ill-educated adolescents would provide him with paradoxically powerful ammunition for his diagnosis of our cultural ills.

But this diagnosis goes rather awkwardly with another analysis. If there has indeed been a drying up of creativity, what are the underlying causes? Eliot's answer is to be located in that alleged 'dissociation of sensibility' which somehow 'set in' in the mid-17th century. In the essays of 1920-21, closely associated with the writing of *The Waste Land,* on 'The Metaphysical Poets' and on 'Andrew Marvell', Eliot offered a slippery and tendentious case.

Essentially, he pre-defines certain qualities as characteristic of poetry 'as poetry', including what he is to call 'impersonality', and then claims to find those qualities in Dante, Shakespeare, and the metaphysicals but not in Milton, Pope, Tennyson, Browning. Only in the present and, implicitly, in his own work is there a possible revival of those long-lost qualities, by drawing upon a French tradition which, somehow, was never affected by that dissociation, a tradition in which Racine and Baudelaire are still basically akin and Laforgue and Corbiere are closer to the school of Donne than any post-17th century English poet could claim to be. On this analysis, Milton and Dryden are both the watershed and the main culprits, though the 1921 essay on Dryden tends to leave Milton as the sole real target.

This proffered explanation for the underlying roots of the cultural malaise which Eliot offers to diagnose, or to demonstrate, in *The Waste Land* makes it clear that a little local matter like the pan-European conflict of the First World War is not really germane, but that, in effect, we have to return to a moment prior to quite another war in order to release our creative energies once again. That war is the English civil war which a later essay on Milton acknowledges as not yet completed. But Eliot's treatment of Milton reveals an underlying instability in his critical principles.

Dante, we note, can be acknowledged as a great poet even if, and indeed precisely when, we do not share his beliefs; it is, for Eliot, almost a condition of true poetry that it does not require our assent to its non-poetic claims. Milton, however, whose political views Eliot declares to be 'antipathetic', can only be read for his sound and not for his sense. In this move, we can clearly see that the alleged 'dissociation' is not, after all, so much an intrinsic feature of Milton's poetry as a tactic recommended for a reader.

One can propose a rather different diagnosis. Here the significant contrast would not be between the moment of Donne and the later moment of Milton and Dryden, but between the function of poetry in Milton's work and its function in Dryden's. In *Paradise Lost* (the *Waste Land* of its day?) Milton is himself arguing a passionate case, offering a profound diagnosis of what he sees as a cultural but primarily as a spiritual catastrophe, itself a matter of political decay and betrayal. Milton's poem is quite directly political in its import, an attempt to understand the nature of a political defeat: the paradise that is lost is that of God's own commonwealth, established by the regicides of 1649 for whom Milton was spokesman, but then defeated in the 1660 Restoration. What desperately, and almost despairingly, needed to be understood by Milton was how

God's own cause could have been so defeated within a history itself under the control of that very God. Milton's final analysis of the roots of such defeat, the paradox of history itself, drives him to grasp the nature of betrayal in paradise itself, the very structure of sin: the love of Adam for Eve taking human precedence over the love due to the divinity, a commitment at the very core of human creativity and procreativty, yet necessarily also a risk-filled declaration of independence from divine rights and duties..

For Milton *Paradise Lost* was not a 'literary' work but an attempt to justify the ways of God. He sold the poem for £5. For Dryden, the cultural matrix is quite different. He is not a passionate orator for a divine cause, nor an engaged analyst of personal and political disaster, but the supreme professional writer, a paid poet, versifying more or less to order, for a suitable return, revelling in the new commercial opportunities of the Restoration ethos as translator, theatrical adapter, provider of witty prologues and epilogues, supreme coffee-house celebrity, occasional polemicist and satirist, best-selling author.

What is at stake in this (slightly unfair) contrast between Milton and Dryden is a reformulation of the very notion of 'literature'. What had been, or at least could include, the passionate rhetorical proclamation or defence of a cause being argued for, becomes, in the politically fragile and paranoid milieu of the Restoration, the anaemic dissociation of literature from either political principle (if not from political *party-pris*) or passionate belief in any theology or ideology. From Dryden to Addison and Steele is a very short step. And in the process it is precisely Milton whose stubbornly engaged work provides the occasion for redefining what 'literature' now is: it is, of course, that which is most sublimely above the mere fray of politics and petty causes. The poem is most to be valued 'as a poem' and precisely not as any attempt to justify the bitterly puzzling ways of God, let alone those of men, and certainly not of those men who (let us now quickly forget) had executed a king. The poem can now be safely read, not for its ideological content but for its beauty, majesty, sublimity, style, its sound, not its sense.

The production of 'Literature'is now to be regarded as a professional field, almost a specialist occupation, within a delimited domain, that of increasingly 'polite culture' (fed by easy translations and memorably phrased opinions), a matter for professional writers (Grub Street awaits) and for a new breed of consumers, leisured readers for whom 'literary writing' is an entertaining spectator sport and is expected to provide the specific pleasures of the imagination. To service this new consumer product sector, an ancillary profession will soon emerge, that of the critic, preferably that species of perfect critic whose task is to attend to the poem strictly as a work of art, leaving aside any mere agreement or disagreement (where unfortunately present) with the actual content of a poet's work. Eventually, for the well-trained critic, any merely personal emotion will, of course, be left at the door of the study. It is such critics who will retrospectively apply an aesthetic notion of literature to Dante, Shakespeare, Donne. And Eliot.

This cultural history underpins not only *The Waste Land* but the context into which Eliot's work was almost immediately to enter in the 1920s: the establishment, and proliferation, of university literature departments in which the study of literature was to become an increasingly specialist and professional matter. Any reader of poetry, of literature, was now caught in a very odd kind of prison indeed, upon which a curious key had firmly turned.

That these pleasures provided by the professional writer had become the object of a curiously intense scrutiny, itself increasingly professional, raises inevitably the question, even as I read, of how I can read the poem 'as a poem' while also studying it as a prescribed pedagogic exercise. This history, and these intertwined issues, seem to me to pose acute dilemmas for any student of literature, and perhaps above all for any postgraduate researcher, hovering on the brink of contributing to and perhaps joining that highly professional field.

*

Let us pause and clarify what is now at stake. There are, I have suggested, three ways of responding to a work of 'literature". One is to regard it precisely as a work of art, to attempt to read it and respond to it 'as a poem'. The second is a close cousin of that mode, but is separated from it by a crucial divide: it is to read the poem as a critic would, as someone engaged professionally within a specific field of intellectual and mainly academic production. The third, the oldest but now the least acceptable to that professional field, and even to the common reader of 'poetry', is to respond to the poem not 'as a poem' but as an utterance, a position, a case, an argument, an ideological assertion, a specific practice.

To read *Paradise Lost* as an attempt to justify a god's ways to men and to judge and argue with the poem accordingly is a manifestly different activity from judging it according to either some canon of critical taste, or the criteria of the latest attempt to theorise the very notion of literature. If either of the first two positions is adopted, the logic of Eliot's essay on *Hamlet* is almost inescapable: that the sole appropriate contribution of 'criticism' is to provide 'relevant historical facts which the reader is not assumed to know.' But, in the very same essay, Eliot also maintains that our attention should be on the poem not on the author, despite the perhaps inescapable point that historical facts about the author might well be regarded as among those most relevant to the poem. But in either case, providing relevant historical facts does not itself constitute a reading of the poem as a poem. The appropriate response to a mode of reading that actually treated *Paradise Lost* as an argument about *why* paradise has been lost would presumably be a writing of one's own, another theologico-political analysis, not a stylistic comparison; and indeed the appropriate response to *The Waste Land* might well be another poem—provided, of course, that *The Waste Land*'s diagnosis of our cultural malaise did not preclude such responsive creativity in the first place.

Given this overall framework of an approach to *The Waste Land,* we can now see how it might directly affect the teaching of the poem. I want to outline some actual experiences of trying to 'teach' *The Waste Land,* but one further element of context needs first to be clarified.

Eliot's notion of the role of the critic has a long history behind it, going back through Matthew Arnold's notion of 'aliens' within every class and Coleridge's scheme for a cultural 'clerisy', to Hooker's views on the role of the clergy in a national church. A consistent theme in this tradition is the attempt to locate some agency or mechanism within society for purveying the best that has been thought and said throughout the whole of society, of delivering to the wider population what has originated in some centre of excellence. The older model for this envisaged a clergyman in every parish, and Coleridge's clerisy were still essentially territorial, an educated leavening in each locality. Arnold's aliens had no specific sociological or geographical location but were associated with a newly important communication medium, the periodical press: ideally, the journal and with it the writings of the critic could reach every educated household, and even beyond. The obvious inheritor of this putative leavening function was, of course, the national broadcasting institutions, and part of the familiar *animus* against television among earlier generations of critics lay partly in their sense of displacement. More recently, however, television has begun to converge with the personal computer as the mechanism for making available in every home the global resources of cultural production. One would rather like to imagine Coleridge designing his Clerisy World Wide Web home page!

It is in the context of that convergence of communications technologies that much of my own teaching occurred during the 1980s and early 1990s and this included a number of separate student exercises around *The Waste Land.*

I can outline these, briefly, in order to return to some of the issues already broached above. In describing these projects I have offered examples chosen more for convenience of description than because they were necessarily fully implemented (copyright constraints effectively precluded full realisation) and I have somewhat conflated various stages of work done with several different students, dating back to the late 1980s. [Since that period, some apects of these exercises have become more generally familiar, but the issues involved are still worth rehearsing.]

*Exercise I:* A Hypertext Guide to *The Waste Land*

The initial idea was fairly simple and very much in line both with Eliot's own notion of the function of the critic and with traditional approaches to teaching the poem. We set out to use computer-based hyper-text possibilities to allow students easier access to some of the material that might be regarded as relevant to a study of *The Waste*

*Land*. The first project was realised on an Amiga 2000 computer, using a basic hypermedia program, *Hyperbook,* which allowed the inclusion of pictures, text and sound, with hot-spot links between pages and the conversion of any portion of a page into a button or hot spot which would, when clicked upon, activate some further element of the overall composition. Later exercises along similar lines used the *HyperCard* program on a Macintosh and the *Guide* program in Unix.

The first stage involved typing the text of *The Waste Land* onto several Hyperbook pages and then constructing interactive hot-spot buttons over those elements of the text to which an explanatory note or other content was to be attached. On first entering the Hyperbook only the primary text of *The Waste Land* as published would appear. The user could then click on a word or a line and the attached note would appear in a pop-up text box, a small window appearing on top of the main text like a standard help file in many Windows programs. The first layer of these notes was provided by Eliot's own notes and by B. C. Southam's *Guide to the Selected Poems of T. S. Eliot.* To take a simple example, at the following lines

> With a wicked pack of cards. Here, said she,
> Is your card, the drowned Phoenician Sailor,
> (Those are pearls that were his eyes. Look!)
> Here is Belladonna, the Lady of the Rocks...
> (ll. 46-49)

the reader might click on line 46 and bring up Eliot's note on the Tarot pack; clicking on the word 'Belladonna' would make a small text-box with a translation appear; a further click would then bring up Southam's various glosses on the several meanings associated with the word. Clicking on line 48 would open a box giving the reference to *The Tempest* I.ii, and clicking on that reference would move the reader to another page with the appropriate passage from *The Tempest,* with a button to enable return to the primary text at line 48.

Even at this first level of implementation several design issues were soon in play. We distinguished by colour coding within pop-up text boxes between Eliot's own notes and Southam's, but we also experimented with different ways of alerting the reader to the presence of a hot spot button, by colour-coding the text itself (words in red indicating an attached note), or by underlining, or by only highlighting hot spot information when the mouse cursor passed over an active word. Each mode had its drawbacks. We also experimented with different ways of presenting the additional layers of information, by having text boxes superimposed on the primary text or in the margins, or by jumping instead to a complete page of annotations keyed to specific groupings of line references. An overall option button allowed the reader to choose between text with and without visible line numbers, and another offered options as to the size and type of font (designing a decent equivalent for the familiar Faber & Faber font proved surprisingly difficult on the computer screen).

Including Eliot's Notes and Southam's explanations was, however, only an initial level of possible hypertext. We also tried several ways of allowing the reader access to the draft of *The Waste Land,* both as a document in its own right and as a locally accessible 'level' within the primary text. So, at the lines:

Sighs, short and infrequent, were exhaled,
And each man fixed his eyes before his feet.
Flowed up the hill and down King William Street,
To where Saint Mary Woolnoth kept the hours
With a dead sound on the final stroke of nine
(ll. 64-68)

it was possible not only to call up glosses on King William Street and Saint Mary Woolnoth, or the Dante reference in line 64, but also the several options considered in Eliot's draft, each rejected version momentarily replacing the text as published, for example:

> Sighs, short and infrequent, were expired
> And each one kept his eyes before his feet....

Pound's various comments could also be brought into view alongside, over or instead of the original draft version.

Already, this level of additional information from the draft proved difficult to present without untidily cluttering the screen, but decisions as to what to include raised interesting critical issues. For example, there were two obvious ancillary texts to attach to the 'Death by Water' section: the earlier poem '*Dans le Restaurant*' and the much fuller draft version with the long account of a shipwreck. Including Eliot's discarded 82 lines with Pound's comments, was the first level of addition, requiring several extra hyper-pages. But we then tried also including a version of the section as it might have been, had Eliot actually accepted Pound's more detailed cuts and suggested changes, rather than deleting the entire passage. The result was at least worth considering, as in the drastic reduction of lines 13-29 *(Draft,* pp. 63-64) to:

> With a light fair breeze
> We beat around the cape
> From the Dry Salvages
> A porpoise snored on the swell astern.
> Opened, a water-cask smelt of oil
> The garboard strake began to leak
> The canned beans were stench
> Two men came down with gleet;
> "Eat!" they said, *etc.*

We also attempted to incorporate, for example, the allusions sketched above to various earlier poems by Eliot and to passages from the essays written in the years immediately around *The Waste Land* in 1920-22.

It would have been theoretically possible to pursue this exercise almost *ad infinitum,* juggling layers of glosses, annotations, quotations, critical comments, allowing the reader to 'zoom in' to almost any level, asymptotically incorporating every text by Eliot and perhaps eventually the whole of literature! However, what was already palpably clear even from the partial exercise was that the 'primary text', thought of as the poem itself, quickly became swamped, obliterated from view by the various layers of information being superimposed upon! it.

What the exercise demonstrated in a highly visible and dramatic way was how easily 'scholarship' can come between the reader and the poem. A conscientious user of our hypertext guide might have seven or so supplementary text windows open simultaneously and overlapping each other. Here was a new variation of an old problem, familiar to any reader of, say, a critical edition of Pope's *Dunciad* or those old Arden Shakespeare editions where a single line of text on a page might have suspended from it several paragraphs of footnotes. In academic practice, many of us end up having a 'clean' copy of a major text for re-reading, a heavily annotated personal copy, and a critical edition with printed apparatus.

The hypertext guide was beginning to work as a conflation of all three, but it was increasingly difficult to practise the required self-restraint to have only the unmarked primary text visible on screen.

The effect of this first hypertext exercise had been to turn the primary text of *The Waste Land* into itself only another level of information, a layer or window which one might, or might not, have 'open' alongside others.

A second, and more productive, lesson was that trying to decide in advance what 'the reader is not assumed to know' was far less fruitful than providing students with the facility to add their own choice of additional texts and hyperlinks to the overall hyperbook.

A third lesson, difficult to grasp quite so clearly without the severe practical demands of trying to realise it in specific hypertext links, was the sheer density of possible intertextual echoings: it could seem at times that every line of Eliot might well be linked to every other line, across the entire range of his *oeuvre.*

These conclusions from the first exercise could, of course, have been ruefully anticipated by anyone already familiar with the history of literary scholarship.

*Exercise II:* A multi-media Opera

However, we were also hopeful that an approach quite different from providing 'relevant facts' might also be possible: that of treating the 'primary text' of *The Waste Land* not as one more level of information in a critical guide-book, but more as a kind of libretto for a multi-media score, an 'opera' version or performance of *The Waste Land.*

The provision of layers of textual information had already raised the issue of whether to include audio as well. We had two recordings of the poem available, that read by Eliot himself and a tape of a BBC radio broadcast version from the 1970s, which had 'dramatised' the poem by having several male and female voices perform the lines, acknowledging and enacting both Eliot's draft title, 'He do the police in different voices' and the note on Tiresias which claims that the various characters melt into one another and that 'the two sexes meet in Tiresias'.

The BBC's claim for this aspect of their multi-voiced version seemed less important in practice than the simple impact of hearing the opening lines divided into several overlapping voices, overheard as if in the Munich Hofgarten, amid a mild clatter of coffee cups and background conversational murmur, as recreated by the BBC special effects department or the radiophonic workshop. Equally memorable was the effect of hearing the Wagner fragments actually sung, or the surprisingly moving use of Wagner's 'Lament of the Rhine Maidens' as the record which the typist puts upon the gramophone, allowing that strange lament to sound throughout the following lines, from 'This music crept by me . . .' and crescendoing very appropriately at the otherwise indecipherable 'Weialala leia' of line 277.

What this way of dramatising the poem, almost as a radio play, suggested and prompted was some attempt to compose a computer-based multimedia version, not so much a faithful rendering of Eliot's poem as a reworking in a new medium. Several possibilities were explored in a second exercise, focussing not just on the use of visual or audio elements but on the difficult issue of overall structure. For this exercise we mainly used the *Macromedia Director* program on a PC. The program allows the inclusion of text, graphics, sound, digital video and a sophisticated range of transitions and hyperlinkages between elements. It also allows non-linear jumps throughout, while using an essentially linear scoreline for overall design and composition.

There is a clear invitation to visualisation in several scene-settings within the poem (the depiction of the room or the pub scene in 'A Game of Chess') and extensive use of visual imagery (white towers, inexplicable splendour of Ionian white and gold). We spent some time simply finding or trying to create in paint programs images appropriate to these various settings, or images of crowds flowing across London Bridge, the Tarot cards, the sweet Thames running softly, the torchlight red on sweaty faces (merging at some level of montage with the sweating river). We found ourselves raiding everything from classical paintings to newsreel footage. But more intractable was the issue of how to give an overall organisation to these elements of visuals, text and audio. Here we seemed at times close to the problems Eliot had had in organising his own material and like him we reached for existing patterns or analogies.

Computers are already strongly associated with one model of non-linear but quasi-narrative structure, that of the video game, the interactive adventure. Since *The Waste Land* itself deployed the mythic structure of the Grail adventure, with its questor and obstacles, perilous journeys and magical agencies, it seemed feasible to construct a kind of Waste Land game, with Christian mythology providing the underlying structure but with various other possible approaches and roles for players to follow.

This exercise proved more interesting simply to map out than to try to implement in detail (for example we concluded that in this video game 'success', arriving at 'Shantih', could only be achieved by the player giving away all competitive points gained!). We also considered merging aspects of both the informational hypertext exercise and the 'opera' exercise by making Eliot's own text into the playing field of the 'game'—with the Key to the meaning of the poem as the sought-after grail or goal.

But it was then less clear what the final reward might be for a successful player: what, in this game, could be the equivalent of the rain arriving or the thunder speaking?

This second exercise was an intriguing challenge in its own terms, and it raised genuine critical issues. One argument that immediately arose, of course, was whether it was at all appropriate to re-think, to re-imagine, *The Waste Land,* or any poem, in these terms, as a computer game, or even as a Third Programme radio drama.

A range of issues could be explored here, going back at least to Dryden's adaptations of Shakespeare for his very different kind of theatre, or Eliot's own appropriation of West End boulevard theatre conventions as a shell for his reworking of Euripides' *Ion* or as a vehicle for his Christian proselytising. Within the context of teaching *The Waste Land* the 'opera' exercise was a highly productive way to raise issues not just about the overall form of the poem but also about such various issues as, for example, Eliot's attempted use of 'demotic' speech in the pub scene, his deployment of musical references, his admiration for Marie Lloyd. It also led us to consider such other re-workings as Martin Rowson's graphic novel version of *The Waste Land* as a hard-boiled detective story (1990).

*after the exercises*

The essential further question raised by both exercises taken together was precisely that which can be regarded as central to the poem itself: whether any form of creativity is still possible, and in what medium. Insofar as Eliot was asking that question for his own generation, two responses might now be appropriate. One would be to acknowledge this as indeed the issue posed by Eliot in the poem, and to treat his cultural diagnosis with the same kind of respect, scrutiny, and critical contention as that invited by Milton's argument in *Paradise Lost.* This involves, in my view, declining to restrict one's reaction to the poem 'as a poem'. If these exercises raised that issue for the era of the computer then they might well constitute an apt response to Eliot's original intentions. These may well, now, be the right questions to ask in a new form of critical practice.

But does simply asking the question release the waters? Eliot perhaps found a way of offering a diagnosis that was also in part a cure. What emerged from the second exercise took us into territory at some distance from any explicit concern with the poem, or even with 'literature'. Since it was clear, when we first began, that the software available to enable ordinary mortals to compose interactive multimedia presentations was fairly limited (and mainly designed with brief business presentations in mind), one student (Howard Williams) responded to the difficulties of composing his multimedia *Waste Land* 'opera' by settling down to write his own multimedia authoring program software instead, designed to be as user-friendly as possible, partly with an eye on the desirability of any reader being able to add their own contributions to the original hypertext guide. (In this, he effectively anticipated the later development of HTML.)

Writing computer software may seem a radically different kind of creativity from writing literary criticism, but it has at least some affinities with the task of composing a poem, an exercise of imagination and intelligence of a fairly high order. Another student (Eldad Druks) eventually used that first student's programming code to construct not a personal version of *The Waste Land* but an interactive multimedia '*De Chirico Labyrinth*', based upon digitized images of de Chirico's architectural paintings and mysterious cityscapes. That project subsequently grew into a proposed, and partly implemented, *De Chirico City* in 3D animations, with the prospect eventually of a virtual reality city constructed from de Chirico's architectural imaginings, which the viewer (player?) can enter and explore...

*

The point of briefly outlining these several further projects and directions which developed from the initial *Waste Land* exercises is to highlight, in conclusion, a crucial aspect of any 'teaching' of this poem. In undertaking to teach it, we are teaching not a poem but students (and they are teaching us). But one question to be considered in any teaching context is precisely the appropriateness of that teaching to its wider cultural context, including whether teaching the poem, or even teaching literature, is any longer appropriate to those students.

Teaching *The Waste Land* should, for reasons I have tried to outline, inevitably raise those interrelated issues of whether 'literature', the 'poem as poem', even exists, whether scholarship, information, knowledge about this poem or any poem, is now endangering what we used to value in 'literature', whether such a notion is itself an ideological nostalgia, an after-effect of a historically specific and now-departed cultural moment.

But, more positively and productively perhaps, what teaching *The Waste Land* also raises today, as in 1921, is whether the demands and opportunities of a new and still emerging cultural moment and medium now invite us, once again, towards a renewal of creativity in a different mode, to developing quite new forms of creativity in what might otherwise be regarded only as a digital waste land.

If we are to be true to that marvellous insight, that culture—even language itself—begins from an act of ambiguous imitation, from that polysemic mis-appropriation of a single resonant syllable (*Da*), we must also recognise that true creativity goes beyond such acts of imitation and mere stammering mimicry. We, and all our students, must find our own voices and our own media in which to speak. That, finally, is today's lesson from *The Waste Land.*

\*

# Re-Reading

*...mixing memory and desire...*

A niggling problem with my reconstructed lecture on *The Waste Land* was that I paid almost no attention to *why* Eliot seemed to have had such difficulty in arriving at an appropriate form for the poem. Moreover, I only suggested a rather vague schema for what Eliot might have originally intended as the overall shape of his 'long poem'. By concentrating upon Eliot's attempts to shape the various materials into a final form, I rather neglected the actual content, not only of the published *The Waste Land* but also of the collection of materials which went into its making.

In addition, insofar as my argument emphasised Eliot's concern to occlude, or at least not to make public, the role played by Ezra Pound, I paid insufficient attention to the more obvious element which he undoubtedly wished to preserve from prying readers: his tortuous relationship with Vivien.

My account was primarily shaped by the new evidence which the facsimile edition provided in 1971 for Pound's interventions, but it was difficult at that time to offer much beyond second-hand reportage concerning what many speculated had been the appalling state of Eliot's marriage. Quite how that marriage might be related to *The Waste Land* was therefore unclear, though the publication of the first volume of the letters in 1988 did at last give a detailed and painful insight into the relations between Eliot and Vivien and their various tensions, illnesses, and financial difficulties.

Then the long-delayed publication in 1996 of *The Inventions of the March Hare*, which made available the poems in the notebook sent to John Quinn in 1922, prompted a tentative reconsideration of the composition of *The Waste Land*.

A lecture, of course, especially one by a junior lecturer, had to offer at least the appearance of a confident and structured argument, which partly accounts for the unsatisfactoriness of my previous account of *The Waste Land*. But having left the somewhat paranoid field of professional literary criticism in the mid-1980s, I subsequently read the newly published material concerning Eliot in a more suitably relaxed manner. The form of the following notes therefore reflects a fairly hesitant process of simply trying, as more Eliot material was released, to explore more fully the issues of composition, form, and content which continued to puzzle me in reading *The Waste Land*. As working notes, there is an element of tedious plodding, and they are clearly intended to be read alongside the material discussed, since quotation is kept to a minimum. Page references are normally to the 2015 edition.

*i : ... inventions of a March hare...?*

In 1996 the edition of the *March Hare* poems usefully included a tentative chronology of the order of composition of all Eliot's poems leading up to 1920. The 2015 edition of the poems has more recently offered some different datings, which supplement or correct the dates given in 1996.

What is interesting, when we consider the overall chronology, is that a small cluster of the poems included in the material which Eliot sent to John Quinn as somehow related to the composition of *The Waste Land,* seems to be dated to 1915, in particular the following perhaps less poems – using the dates of composition in, and page references to, volume 1 of the 2015 edition:

*Do I know how I feel? Do I know what I think?* – January/April 1915. [p. 269 ]

*The death of Saint Narcissus* – April/May 1915. [p. 270 ]

*So through the evening, through the violet hour* – July 1915? [p. 272 ]

*After the turning of the inspired days* – July 1915? [p. 271]

*I am the Resurrection and the life* – July 1915? [p. 272 ]

The last three poems may, however, date from earlier, perhaps 1914 (Gallup) or even 1913 (Rainey).

I can label this group of poems 'Cluster B'. Located chronologically alongside them are two other unpublished poems [*To Helen*] and *Introspection* which were apparently not included by Eliot in the material for *The Waste Land.*

Added to Cluster B in *The Waste Land* material are three poems which can only rather tentatively be dated, which I will call Cluster C:

*The Death of the Duchess* – 1919?, possibly 1916? [p. 281]

*Dirge* – 1919?, possibly 1921. [p. 285 ]

*Elegy* – 1919?, possibly 1921. [p. 284]

The latter two poems might simply be included instead among the several new drafts which date from 1921 and which we think of as the main material intended for *The Waste Land*, while *The Death of the Duchess* may possibly date from 1916, shortly after the Cluster B poems. The *Duchess* poem was not printed in the *March Hare* edition but was already available in the 1971 facsimile.

Another group of poems is noticeable in the overall chronology, which were apparently not part of the material for *The Waste Land,* but are probably dated immediately prior to Cluster B. They invite the label Cluster A, in which I would include:

*The little passion: from "an agony in the garret"* – 1915?, possibly 1911? [p. 263]

*The Burnt Dancer* – June 1914. [p. 262]

*Oh little voices of the throats of men* – July 1914. [p. 264]

*The Love Song of St. Sebastian* – July 1914. [p. 265]

*Paysage Triste* – 1914/1915? [p. 267]

*Suppressed Complex* – 1914? by 2 Feb. 1915. [p. 268]

*Afternoon* – 1914? by 25 Feb. 1915. [p. 267]

*In The Department Store* – 1914/1915? [p. 268]

Cluster A is most obviously inter-connected as a group of poems concerned with, or rather disturbingly expressing, a state of considerable sexual frustration and tension which sometimes takes the form of almost sado-masochistic fantasies (or memories?). Some brief quotations, though the whole group should be read in full:

> I know he used to walk the streets...
> ... knowing well to what they lead...
> (*The Little Passion*)

> Within the circle of my brain
> The twisted dance continues....
> Caught on those horns that toss and toss
> Losing the end of his desire...
> (*The Burnt Dancer*)

> I would flog myself until I bled...
> I would come with a towel in my hand
> And bend your head beneath [between] my knees .
> And I should love you the more because I had mangled
> you ...
> (*The Love Song Of Saint Sebastian*)

One can suggest a fairly obvious relation between this group of poems and Eliot's personal situation during the few months he spent in Europe between leaving Harvard in June 1914 and arriving in Oxford in September 1914. I am even tempted to map his trajectory across Europe by noticing in some poems specific echoes of Paris and Germany. But Eliot's intended stay in Marburg to study German philosophy was abruptly terminated by the start of war hostilities in August 1914 and he found himself unexpectedly diverted to Oxford. That the sexually charged mood of these poems continued in Oxford is clear from his remarkably confiding letter to Conrad Aitken on 31st of December 1914 (*L1*, p. 80f). After thanking Aitken for ensuring the delivery of a bouquet of roses to Emily Hale, Eliot recounts that he has been 'going through one of those nervous sexual attacks' which he suffers from 'when alone in a city', and that 'this is the worst since Paris': 'One walks about the street with one's desires, and one's refinement rises up like a wall whenever opportunity approaches'. In an earlier letter to Aitken, 25th July 1914, from Marburg (*L1*, p. 48) Eliot mentions a possible sequence of poems with the working title 'Descent from the Cross', which echoes a line from *The Little Passion* where walking the streets leads to '... one inevitable cross / Whereon our souls are pinned, and bleed.'

Within Cluster A there is some material which eventually appeared in *The Waste Land*, as indeed did the dirty broken fingernails in the 1911 *Interlude: in a bar* (*March Hare*, p. 51), but none of this cluster of poems, though sent to Quinn in 1922, was apparently indicated by Eliot as associated with *The Waste Land*. The Cluster B poems from 1915 were, however, somehow to be connected with the making of *The Waste Land* and to be regarded as such by John Quinn. They might perhaps be thought of as among whatever sheaf of old drafts or folder of unfinished poems, in manuscript or typescript, or simply in memory, which Eliot took with him to Margate or to Lausanne for possible inclusion in, or adaptation for, his intended long poem.

The main poem from Cluster C, *The Death of the Duchess*, was definitely part of Eliot's working materials for the 'long poem' and the typescript was vigorously annotated by Ezra Pound. Dating the *Duchess* is problematic (see the discussion in *2015*, I, p. 1181f.) but it is possible that it was composed alongside, or shortly after, *Gerontion* – a poem which as late as January 1922 Eliot was still proposing to include as a kind of prelude to *The Waste Land*. However, there are also some arguments for dating *Duchess* to 1916, shortly after the Cluster B poems. 1919 was the year in which Eliot first clearly envisaged his new 'long poem', and *The Death of the Duchess* was perhaps the third longest poem he had yet written: 56 lines and almost certainly unfinished. Some of the early poems which now appear as longer are composites of short poems, whereas the division of *Duchess* into two numbered sections, as printed in the 2015 edition, was a revision, a handwritten after-thought, as is clear from the *Waste Land* facsimile.

On the back of *The Death of the Duchess* typescript is scribbled what may even be a schema for a possible long poem, though Valerie Eliot interpreted it as a summary (albeit inaccurate) of *The Duchess of Malfi,* a performance of which Eliot had seen in 1919. The rough jotting might be a preliminary stab at designating parts of a 'long poem', though it bears no obvious relation to *The Waste Land* as we now have it. There are simply five words on separate lines: encounter, (a blank line), imprisonment, flight, meeting, afterwards. Was this possibly a broad outline narrative for a long poem of which *Death of the Duchess* was a kind of beginning? (See *Facsimile*, p. 107.)

The *Duchess* certainly contributed to the final composition of Part II of *The Waste Land,* and may originally have been intended as an intact segment of the envisaged 'long poem'. It was one of the components which Pound considerably reduced without entirely rejecting and which Eliot, perhaps mistaking Pound's annotations (see my earlier argument), completely excised. Three separate passages from *Duchess* survived into the final *The Waste Land,* including a variation upon the lines accompanying 'my nerves are bad tonight' which Vivien annotated as "wonderful". Some lines from *Duchess* are almost familiar:

> Under the brush her hair
> Spread out in little fiery points of will
> Glowed into words, then was suddenly still.

> ...the closed carriage at four ... play a game of chess..

Other less familiar lines are worth noting:

But it is terrible to be alone with another person....

If it is terrible alone, it is sordid with one more.

We can definitely connect *The Death of the Duchess* to a poem from Cluster B which the *March Hare* edition did not attempt to date, though the 2015 edition notes Rainey's dating to January-April 1915. The first line of the poem was *Do I know how I feel? Do I know what I think?* and the unfinished *Duchess* may, as a re-working of *Do I know how I feel?*, date to around 1916, though it could also fit with Eliot's situation in 1919.

In January 1919 his father had died (without ever meeting Vivien) and Eliot was concerned even more than before to make sure that he had a volume of poems published as justification for his drastic decision to stay in England and to abandon a possible career as an academic philosopher. In a letter to Quinn dated 6th January Eliot emphasises the importance of getting his book published because he is planning to visit his family in America in the summer or autumn, and the book will be almost all he will have to support  the his claim that he found England more favourable to the production of literature, despite his family's strong opposition. In March he was offered the post of assistant editor of the *Athanaeum* and in April a letter from Harvard tried to to persuade him to come back as a  philosophy don. By May his main literary ally Ezra Pound had left London permanently for France, but also in May 1919 the Woolfs' Hogarth Press did finally publish his slim volume of only seven new poems simply entitled *Poems,* and in February 1920 John Rodker's limited edition of *Ara Vos Prec* added *Gerontion* and included the poems from the *Prufrock* volume of 1917.

In all, 1919 was a year for memory and for self re-assessment by the 30-year-old Eliot. It had begun with a letter to his mother on 12th January reacting to his father's death on 7th January, and remarking 'I have been over all my childhood' (*L1*, p. 316). It ended with the firm resolution to write a long poem. A letter of 18th December (*L1*, p. 424) to his mother specifies that his New Year's Resolution is 'to write a long poem I have had on my mind for a long time and to prepare a small prose book from my lecture on poetry'.

In October 1919 Eliot published the essay on *Hamlet* in which he emphasises what he sees as Shakespeare's inability to find an 'objective correlative' for the 'intractable' material which he was struggling to bring under control in the play. The term 'objective correlative' has notoriously generated much debate, but it is perhaps partly clarified if one thinks of the problem which had so desperately preoccupied Eliot himself in the years since the sudden marriage in 1915: the nature of his relationship to Vivien. Eliot was, it seems, enduring his own confrontation with the 'intractable' in his struggle over the next two years to find an appropriate correlative for the material, including several previously unpublished poems, which he was already struggling to shape into what became *The Waste Land*.

One aspect of the 'intractable' problem could be formulated precisely in terms of the title of the (July 1915?) poem *Do I know how I feel? Do I know what I think?* – phrases which reappear in the opening lines of *The Death of the Duchess* :

> The inhabitants of Hampstead have silk hats
> On Sunday afternoon go out to tea...

They know what they are to feel and what to think,
They know it with the morning printer's ink...

They know what to think and what to feel
The inhabitants of  Hampstead are bound forever on
the wheel.

Vivien's family at that time lived in the fashionable middle-
class Hampstead area and the newly-married couple
occasionally not only visited but stayed in the Hampstead
house. With those Hampstead Sunday afternoons in mind,
one can register the contrast between the febrile sexual
preoccupations of the poems in Cluster A, dated to the
months immediately preceding the sudden wedding, and
the situation conjured up in the perhaps enigmatic poem
*After the turning of the inspired days* which has been very
variously dated (see *2015*, 1, p. 1158) but the handwriting
of which matches a letter to his father of  23rd  July 1915.
The short poem ends:

After the ending of this inspiration
And the torches and the faces and the shouting
The world seemed futile – like a Sunday outing.

The eventual adaptation of these lines for inclusion in Part
V of *The Waste Land,* with the explicit overtones of the
agony in Gethsemane garden and a coming crucifixion,
retrospectively reinforces an unavoidable sense of ironic
play in the final phrase: Christ may have experienced a
transcendent Easter 'Sunday outing' in exiting his own
tomb, but that is not the primary sense of Eliot's sardonic
use of the phrase. Perhaps Vivien's 'inspiration' had already
ended and Baudelairean boredom or Hampstead *ennui* had
– in a painful dissociation of sensibility – 'set in'.

The tortuous complexity of what Eliot thought and felt about Vivien in the apparently dreadful years after the sudden decision to get married is reasonably clear from the letters which have now been published, but it is far less clear quite what – and why – he had originally thought and felt about her in 1915, however briefly. It was perhaps very rapidly unclear even to Eliot himself. There is a pointed or perhaps poignant aside in a review in *The Monist* for April 1918: Eliot remarks that 'strong passions do not need explanation' but then speaks of a man 'who is not very much in love' and who 'excuses the follies which he has committed for the purposes of appearing passionate'. A few months later Eliot was to write in *Gerontion*: 'I have lost my passion: why should I need to keep it / Since what is kept must be adulterated?'

What one can certainly say is that Eliot first met Vivien in late April 1915 and that they were married on 26th June 1915. The day of the wedding was itself extra-ordinary: they were due to arrive at Ezra Pound's for a routine afternoon tea but failed to appear, and it only transpired later that instead they had gone to get married at the Hampstead Registry Office, with only two witnesses and no other friends present. Neither set of parents was informed in advance. The unexpected and sudden decision in effect reshaped both their entire futures.

Insofar as Eliot's future was soon to be seen as drastically blighted by that decision, the month of April, in which he first met Vivien, may well have been for Eliot the cruellest month of his life. We are now so familiar with the opening lines of *The Waste Land*, as finally published, that it is worth emphasising what an extraordinary and highly charged statement it is.

April is the cruellest month, breeding
Lilacs out of the dead land, mixing
Memory and desire,....

My emerging suggestion is, therefore, that when in 1921 Eliot reviewed his existing drafts and various unfinished or unsatisfactory poems to see if he could assemble them into the intended 'long poem', a significant part of the material he focused upon dated from the period immediately after that unexpected set of decisions in April to June 1915, both to get married and to abandon, in effect, his likely career as a Harvard philosophy academic. Another cluster of material perhaps dates from 1919, when, after the death of his father, he tried, again, to come to terms with the consequences of that decision, perhaps by (re-)drafting the fairly long but unfinished Hampstead / *Duchess* poem which was then laid aside, though at about the same time he did complete *Gerontion* which he was later to consider as possibly a part of *The Waste Land*.

Certainly, in late 1921 Eliot did not simply assemble all his previously unpublished poems but made a selection mainly focused around the period immediately following the marriage. Insofar as he was still trying in late 1921 to make sense of that moment of catastrophic decisions, it was the various short poems he had written at that time – those sometimes unfinished complexes of thought and feeling – which would have recalled most vividly and encapsulated most precisely the intractable problems for which he was trying to find a shape.

So, after reading *Inventions of the March Hare*, the hypothesis seemed irresistible that *The Waste Land* might be read, even sequentially, as a kind of autobiography. Indeed, once we know the details of the biography, it is tempting to try to map the various sections of the poem onto specific episodes in Eliot's life, from the crucial encounter with Vivien onwards, to trace in the poem his complexly entangled trajectory of thought and feeling from 1915 to 1921 as originally caught in the poems drafted during those years. When Mary Hutchinson first heard Eliot recite *The Waste Land* she is supposed to have immediately remarked that it was 'Tom's autobiography'. However, to read *The Waste Land* as a simple and direct auto-biographical account would clearly be implausible and inadequate, not least since the opaque form, the palpable intractability, of the draft components of the poem suggests that several other factors were also in play.

Nevertheless, it seemed worth jotting down the following rough notes. Obviously, what is being tracked here is not a narrative of incidents such as might be recounted by a biographer, but a clutch of poems which encapsulated or came out of a sequence of experiences. Those poems or fragments were not necessarily 'about' specific incidents but nevertheless originated in and were prompted by, and probably written or drafted contemporaneously with, particular moments. So the following somewhat tongue-in-cheek outline should be read as partly complementing my previous sketch of a possible arrangement in terms of the titles of the material which went into the making of poem.

*Part I:*
The original opening episode of a drunken night out in Boston and a visit to a dubious house of pleasure can be seen as standing in for those various poems in Cluster A which Eliot was undoubtedly wise not to publish, so this finally excised section had perhaps offered only a guarded glimpse into his (partly fantasised?) situation before he left Harvard and during his journey across Europe, which included Munich as the setting for the overheard exiles' conversation in the Hofgarden, recalling his aborted visit to Germany in the gathering storm clouds of 1914.

That 'April is the cruellest month' can be read as a bitterly ironic reference to the spring month in which Eliot first encountered Vivien, the start of his new life, while the Hyacinth girl can operate as a version of that encounter, whatever form it actually took.

Eliot hesitated in the overall draft as to whether the question 'what are the roots' etc. should come before or after the Hyacinth garden, but the phrases and imagery in this passage come in any case from the (July 1915?) poem *The Death of Saint Narcissus*, which, one might – optimistically – see as articulating a satirical repudiation of Eliot's own endemic narcissism in the wake of the life-changing wedding, or – less sympathetically – as a self-mocking recognition of how impossible it was for him to overcome a narcissism fatal to any genuine falling in love with another.

Madam Sosostris may have been the wisest woman in Europe, as well as a comic caricature of some inhabitants of his new British environment, but Eliot in reckoning up the nature of his destiny or accidental fate could ruefully reflect that no fortune-teller had told him that as soon as he arrived in Marburg a world war would break out, still less that when he diverted to Oxford his future would suddenly be irreparably skewed by the most significant decision of his life. That sequence of events was hardly on anyone's cards.

Indeed, something wholly unpredictable had happened: he had ended up as a bank clerk in the decidedly unreal financial City of London, the newly familiar streets of which were – to put it mildly – largely inhabited by Dante-esque figures bleakly suspended between life and death.

On the other hand, being diverted to England at precisely that rather unreal time had produced the equally unexpected bonus that he also encountered the strange figure of Ezra Pound (the Stetson is irresistibly Pound's) who promptly introduced him to the dog-eat-dog world of London literary life, giving him an opportunity to unearth his unpublished poems and unexpectedly to become the kind of Baudelairean literary figure he had often wanted to be: the *hypocrite lecteur* of his newly inaugurated literary career.

*Part II.*

On my reading of the contribution of *The Death of the Duchess*, the whole section evokes that disturbing new social world in which Eliot then found himself, partly composed of Hampstead Sunday outings and of very conventional people knowing very firmly what they think and feel, whereas he and his alarmingly unpredictable wife Vivien spent a great deal of time not at all understanding either how they felt and thought or how the other felt and thought, with breakdown and chaos daily threatening or, perhaps even worse, a sterile marriage with a stranger, reduced to playing chess every nervously silent evening. A truncated 'Duchess', of course, gives 'chess'.

Quite who the contrastingly aristocratic and ambivalently formidable Cleopatra may have been in this new social nightmare depends on whose social gossip one believes (Ottoline, Nancy, Virginia?) while at the other end of the social and sophistication spectrum from over-cultured Bloomsbury we can hear the Eliots' Cockney housekeeper's anecdotes from a territory as quintessentially English, and as utterly alien to Eliot as either the City banks or his evening adult education students.

*Part III:*

Silly and pathetic Fresca, if fully retained or reinstated, would have taken the poem even more jaundicedly into the world of literary London and its aspiring female literati, including Vivien herself. When Pound truncated Fresca, Eliot substituted a further reference both to the London Thames and to the world he had now find himself trapped within, of callow City directors indulging in the opposite of Spenserian wedding celebrations.

It's plausible to register a certain guilty echo of his father's overseas death in 1919 (the king my father's death) and perhaps some rather more dubious memories (Mrs Porter's Boston brothel reappears?), juxtaposed with present temptations (Mr Eugenides), while the perky but sad typist girl is (salaciously fantasised as) sordidly typical of those vulnerable lower-grade female employees now intruding into the male enclave of Eliot's London banking world, a modern working girl, neither bored Duchess nor irrepressible Cockney, and not and asprint poetess but a daily sight hardly to be ignored by a still sexually frustrated Eliot.

The clattering fish-market workers from the local Thames wharves who lounge at noon, Eliot's pedestrian routes along familiar Queen Victoria Street and Lower Thames Street, his lonely lunchtime church visits, and the daily sight of the river's drifting barges, together encapsulate the contemporary London in which Eliot is now doomed to make a kind of half-living, while the almost-mythical memory of Elizabeth and Leicester (another thwarted desire, a mistaken option, or unrealisable relationship?) conjures up the capital's contrasting costume-drama past.

The three Thames naughty daughters take us from the outer reaches (those Sunday outings?) of Richmond and Kew to the holiday excursion sands of Margate and thus to the actual location where the increasingly stressed Eliot wrote these parts of his still accumulating long poem.

*Part IV:*
If I doggedly attempt to follow through this kind of quasi-autobiographical sequencing it is perhaps barely persuasive to regard the original draft of Part IV, with its Gloucester seamen and the Dry Salvages, as directly evoking both the alternative American life which Eliot perhaps at some point ruefully reconsidered, but we might at least recall the genuine fear of 'death by water' (from wartime submarines)

which Eliot confronted on his transatlantic voyage back to his American family immediately after the marriage.

That the sequence ends with Phlebas – from the French poem *Dans le restaurant* – brings into indirect play two other 1917 poems in French which ambivalently marked a crucial moment in his life: a poem about a hollow honeymoon (*Lune de Miel)* and one quite explicitly about his own successive and competing roles with a title rather startlingly evoking adultery (*Melange Adultere de Tout*).

In July 1917 Eliot published those two French poems together and then chose them as the concluding items in the Hogarth Press volume of 1919. Notoriously, so it is said, Bertrand Russell had seduced Vivien even before the couple's quasi-honeymoon, while Eliot was away in America. In the *Prufrock* volume published in June 1917 the priapic *Mr Apollinax* (undeniably the Russell who had first met Eliot in Harvard) was perhaps significantly juxtaposed with the *Hysteria* which might in 1915 at least have warned Eliot off Vivien.

In *Ara vos prec* he omitted *Hysteria* but then reinstated it in the American edition. The *Prufrock* volume, his first book of poems, was almost insultingly dedicated not to his wife but to the dead Jean Verdenel, who had been killed in May 1915 – half-way between Eliot meeting Vivien in the cruellest month of April and the rushed wedding in June.

*Part V* begins with a re-working of that bitterly ironic poem possibly composed immediately after settling into marriage agony and which had originally ended in the insufferable Sunday outing. But the most obvious *sitz im leben* (to use the apposite phrase of biblical scholars) of most of this rapidly composed Part V is precisely the disturbing and exhausting experience of continuing breakdown which had led Eliot to that hole among the mountains (a perhaps unfair description of Lausanne and its environment?), complete with (re-worked) hallucinatory visions and nightmares from earlier poems, bats with baby faces and a woman drawing her long black hair out tight.

The three passages under the Sanskrit rubric of DA could fairly easily be mapped onto actual past moments of misguided surrender, of intolerable imprisonment, and perhaps of a regrettably lost opportunity and alternative.

If the awful daring of a moment's surrender had now led to a key turning inexorably in a prison door, there had perhaps just once been a different moment in a boat when a heart did respond gaily, when invited – but only in the draft, and even in that version she was cruelly left behind, clasping empty hands.

The published poem ends in a grimly resigned state, perhaps still close to an anxious form of madness, but now reconciled to at least trying to set in order a future to be spent in the probably futile shuffling around of dissociated literary fragments –now the chosen territory of his new but arid and impotent life...

### ii : ..a new life?

I was not being entirely serious, nor merely facetious, in thus crudely summarising a set of biographical or auto-biographical episodes as matching and shaping the sequential structure of the poems which eventually made up *The Waste Land*, but once the emerging biographical information was placed alongside a reading of *The Inventions of the March Hare* and its chronology of the poems, the connections seemed plausible enough.

However, as I somewhat idly elaborated this hypothesis, it eventually struck me that the literary model I half-consciously had in mind – even if Eliot did not – was the *Vita Nuova* of Dante. Which prompted some further tentative exploration.

Just as the (published) *Waste Land* begins with a mingling of memory and desire, so the *Vita Nuova* opens with a reference to the book of memory, a memory of what began as desire, and the clear statement that Dante has composed the *Vita Nuova* by assembling and ordering a number of poems which were written separately and at various past moments in the trajectory of his relationship with Beatrice. Dante arranged those short poems of various forms in a kind of chronological sequence which is commented upon in the interposed prose passages. The opening of the *Vita Nuova* can be translated as:

> In that part of the book of my memory previous to which is little that I can now bear to read, there is a heading, saying *Incipit Vita Nuova*: here begins my new life. Under that rubric I find written many things, and among them the texts which I intend to assemble into this book; if not all of them as such, at least their significance.

Dante's composite work sequences its components in such a way as, ostensibly, to illuminate the successive phases of his relations with Beatrice, from childhood infatuation and adolescent desire, through a process involving various alternative possible love objects, leading eventually to his recognition of the ultimate love object: the divine itself.

For later readers of Dante this process of composition and the formal structure of the finished work inevitably raised the much-disputed question of the actual relationship between autobiographical fact, the personal life of the poet, and the literary value and significance of the *Vita Nuova* as a finished poem: the issue, to use Eliot's term, of poetic 'impersonality'. In some respects therefore, the *Vita Nuova* was a literary precedent which could have fed into Eliot's continuing engagement with the issue of what his own long poem might be like and how it might relate to his personal life, his own 'new life' which had begun in April 1915.

It is worth recalling that the book which Eliot had hoped to publish in 1919 was to be composed of both prose and verse, and in April 1921, in an article for *The Chapbook*, Eliot even considered the possibility of combining prose and verse in a single composition. The two obvious exemplars of this form were the *Vita Nuova* and *The Consolation of Philosophy* by Boethius. It is perhaps ironic that in the first months of the marriage Eliot did indeed seek the consolations of philosophy by completing his thesis on knowledge and experience in Bradley, and asking Vivien to type it for him. It is also rather curious that when John Quinn was discussing the final submission of *The Waste Land* he once asked Eliot to send it to him when it was complete, 'both prose and verse'.

Obviously, Eliot did not provide linking prose passages in *The Waste Land* but we can, after all, ask how we would now understand the *Vita Nuova* if we attempted to read its sequence of sonnets, ballads, and canzoni, without ever having known the explicatory biographical glosses provided by Dante's prose commentary. Eliot once spoke of the alleged obscurity in modern poetry as being mainly derived from the writer simply leaving out the links which the reader had expected. He did, of course, provide the partly misleading prose Notes to *The Waste Land*, which include five specific references to Dante, to the *Inferno* and the *Purgatorio*. The Notes include no mention of the *Vita Nuova* but Dante's work itself suggests echoes.

For example, a single passage from *Canzone II* is variously resonant:

Then saw I many broken hinted sights,
In the uncertain state I stepped into
Me seemed to be I know not in what place,
Where ladies through the streets, like mournful lights,
Ran with loose hair, and eyes that frighten'd you
By their own terror, and a pale amaze...

And birds dropp'd in mid-flight out of the sky;
And earth shook suddenly;
And I was aware of one, hoarse and tired out,
Who ask'd of me: "hast thou not heard it said? ...
Thy lady, she that was so fair, is dead."

I quote the translated version given in Ezra Pound's *The Spirit of Romance,* from which, of course, Eliot was to take the dedicatory phrase *il miglior fabbro.*

With Eliot's essays as well as *The Waste Land* in mind, it would be worth exploring further echoes from Pound's chapter on Dante in his 1910 book: his dismissal as 'arrant nonsense' the notion that the *Vita Nuova* is merely 'embroidered with conceits'; his insistence that the *Commedia* is written in the traditional four senses – the literal, the allegorical, the ethical, and the anagogical, – and in the third and fourth senses the whole poem is to be read as 'an expression of the laws of eternal justice ... "il contrapasso", as Bertran calls it', or – says Pound – 'the law of Karma if we are to use an Oriental term' (compare: the collocation of .. eastern and western asceticism...). Pound briefly compares the *Commedia* to *Hamlet,* picks out from *Inferno* Canto V concerning Francesca the phrase 'that seemed so light upon the wind' (... What is the wind doing?...). From the Charon Canto Pound cites the simile 'as the leaves of autumn fall one after one until the bough sees all its pageantry upon the earth' (..the river's tent is broken, the last fingers of leaf ...) and from Canto XIV concerning Capanaeus the line 'what I was living that am I dead' (.. We who were living are now dying / With a little patience..).

Allowing for all this, however, a comparison between the *Vita Nuova* and *The Waste Land* would immediately highlight the difference that – as Eliot and Pound recognise – the *Vita* is written in the familiar mediaeval mode of four senses, which can be read as supervening upon one another, so that a contemporary reader of Dante might well begin with the 'literal' or 'historical' sense (precisely that which is made more explicit in the prose passages) but would then advance through the other three levels of meaning towards the more profound and hidden or mysterious sense, with the significance of Beatrice figuring differently at each level of the interpretation.

By contrast, *The Waste Land* does not at all lend itself to any immediate 'literal' interpretation, and indeed Eliot can be said to have so constructed the poem that without a fairly detailed knowledge of his suppressed biography, which was simply not available to his first readers (or to several generations of later readers), any 'literal' level or sense of the poem was the *least* accessible to interpretation. In Dante's poetics, the relationship between the life or personality of the poet and the meaning of the poem is subsidiary or even irrelevant in a literary mode in which the literal meaning was only one of four possible significations. In the case of *The Waste Land,* however, any other possible levels of supervening interpretation were also effectively veiled from most readers. However, those who had read Eliot's various essays might have found themselves intrigued by possibly suggestive connections. One instance would be the crucial Hyacinth girl episode, to which I can now return in more detail. Eliot's Notes, of course, partly misdirect our attention towards fertility cults and the death of Osiris, but an awareness of Dante may be more illuminating.

In his essay on Dante published in April 1920, and chosen as the final essay in *The Sacred Wood*, published in November 1920, Eliot reproaches Walter Savage Landor for his alleged mis-comprehension of the episode of Paolo and Francesca in *Inferno* Canto V. Landor had written:

> In the midst of her punishment, Francesca, when she comes to the tenderest part of her story, tells it with complacency and delight.

Eliot acidly corrects him. Francesca does indeed have a memory of the past delight of her desire, but – pronounces Eliot – not to have remembered the delight of the love between her and Paolo would have meant ceasing to be human, and such amnesia would therefore also have provided a 'relief from damnation'. It is crucially part of damnation to experience desires which one can no longer gratify and, indeed, it is constitutive of being damned that one still will not and perhaps now cannot repudiate those very desires which shaped one's past life. In a sense which totally escapes Landor, not only were the desires voluntary but the damnation itself is voluntary. Eliot emphasises that it is indispensable to Dante's hell that the sinners are not only in hell as a result of their choices but that they remain there *by choice*. Those in the *Inferno* perpetuate their own distinctive punishment by each still cleaving to their individual sinful passions in life, whereas the sinners mercifully assigned to Purgatory continually choose not the perpetuation but the painful purgation of their sinful desires.

In the draft of Part II of *The Waste Land* Eliot had originally included 'I remember the Hyacinth garden' as an (unspoken?) comment by the male speaker in response to the questions whether he knew nothing or remembered nothing – but the revised version excised the line. The oddly-phrased question 'What thinking?' itself echoes

Dante's 'Che pense?' at V: 111. Eliot also removed the answer to the question as to what the wind is doing – but in the draft the wind was carrying away the little light dead people, and a reader might well have remembered the wind which swirls around Paolo and Francesca. Particularly so if *The Waste Land* had still retained the long passage in Part III concerning Fresca – a name which is, of course, short for Francesca. Her shortened name also echoes the 'fresh' (*Frisch*) wind of the Wagner phrase 'Frisch whet der Wind' which introduces the Hyacinth episode, so that the connections between the Hyacinth girl and Fresca (Vivien?) were thereby woven even more completely into the textual fabric than the published version indicates....

*iii : varieties of metaphysical poetry.*

I will perhaps return to this facet of *The Waste Land* later, but at this point let me bring into the developing hypothesis another belated publication. In 1993 Eliot's Cambridge Clark lectures from 1926 were finally published, under the title *The Varieties of Metaphysical Poetry*. There are numerous local moments in the lectures which throw a retrospective light upon *The Waste Land*. Many of Eliot's touchstones, those brief passages which he frequently quoted here and elsewhere, can be read as intensely evocative of aspects of his own relationship with Vivien.

For example, one might add to the skein of associations already sketched around the Hyacinth episode, that in the first of the 1926 lectures the Paolo and Francesca lines were cited by Eliot shortly after he had referred briefly to Sappho's 'great ode' – presumably the *Ode to Anactoria* which includes such elements, variously echoing passages of *The Waste Land*, as (adapting Symonds' translation) :

If I see you for only a moment, my voice fails me, my
tongue is silenced ...
my eyes see nothing, and the noise of roaring waves
sounds in my ear...
sweat runs down in rivers, a tremor seizes all my
limbs...
caught by pains of menacing death, I faint, lost in a
love trance

However, what was most intriguing about the 1926 lectures
was that they seemed to offer a significant, yet not fully
acknowledged, revision of Eliot's earlier arguments
concerning the English 17th-century metaphysical poets,
and indeed the very meaning for him of the term
'metaphysical'.

Eliot's earlier review-essay entitled *The Metaphysical
Poets* had appeared in the *TLS* on October 20th 1921 and
was the last article published by Eliot before he arrived in
Margate to struggle with his long poem. The argument of
that essay is familiar and was for a time remarkably
influential: that in the work of Chapman and even more in
that of John Donne what we find is a form of sensibility
which can fuse thought and feeling, can coadunate
different experiences into an emotional-intellectual
complex, and that, as in Donne's poems, the fundamental
creative activity of any poet is to bring together such
apparently disparate experiences as the smell of cooking
and reading Spinoza, falling in love and the sound of the
typewriter. One might incidentally recall Eliot's domestic
situation in 1915-16, which included Vivien valiantly
typing his Ph.D. thesis shortly after they were married – a
not unfamiliar task for a new academic wife – while Eliot
produced philosophical reviews and articles on such not
inappropriate topics as Leibniz's theory of monads. The
predatory Russell also took considerable advantage at that
time of Vivien's ability to type from dictation.

But, argued Eliot in 1921, something happened between the time of Donne and the time of Tennyson and Browning: in 17th century England a dissociation of sensibility had set in, which was aggravated by Milton and Dryden. The implication of the 1921 essay was that this disintegration had occurred after the work of Donne and insofar as the task of the contemporary poet was to recover from that disabling dissociation, one might see in Eliot's 1919 poem *Gerontion* an attempt at an impressive emulation of John Donne's complex, dense and dramatic mode. Quite briefly in the 1921 essay, two other moments were also brought into the argument. The work of Donne and some of his contemporaries was rather perfunctorily proposed as akin to that of Dante and his circle in 13th century Italy and also comparable to certain successors of Baudelaire in 19th-century France, particularly Laforgue and Corbière.

Yet in the 1926 lectures the emphasis had shifted somewhat. The argument about Dante is much more elaborated, particularly in terms of the relationship between poetry and philosophy. Here Eliot is partly expanding a case which had been sketched in the 1920 essay on Dante: that the mediaeval poet was able to draw upon an ordered schema of moral judgement which informs and penetrates his entire presentation of the relations between individual episodes in the *Commedia*. The coherent and articulated philosophy, primarily that of Aristotle as commented upon and endorsed by Aquinas, is not some mere external scaffolding, an artificial framework, but inter-fuses Dante's entire way of thinking and feeling. In *The Sacred Wood* the Dante essay was immediately preceded by an essay on William Blake which, by contrast, emphasised Blake's lack of a comparable philosophical framework and his un-satisfactory attempts to construct an idiosyncratic system of his own.

But the 1926 argument proposed that, unlike Dante and rather more like Blake, Donne himself had lacked a coherent philosophy, and though the positive assessment of his poetry still emphasises Donne's capacity for a fusion of thought and feeling, Eliot's position is now that the disabling disintegration had *already* 'set in' and was discernible even in Donne's best work. Though individual poems might have something of the quality Eliot was applauding, Donne could only draw upon an impressive but fundamentally miscellaneous and eclectic range of reading, which resulted in what Eliot calls 'scraps' or 'fragments' of a variety of incompatible philosophies.

Clearly the 1926 argument is, as much as that in 1921, intended, however implicitly, to be applicable to Eliot's own situation. But Eliot in his Harvard years and up to the mid-1920s had patently been in a position far more comparable with that of Donne than with that of Dante. His description of Donne's ransacking of available philosophies matches Eliot's own eclecticism in his early work in philosophy: some of his Harvard courses were only for a slight term or two, but he had a moderate acquaintance with a range of disparate philosophies from the Pre-Socratics to the present, including Aristotle whom he also studied more closely at Oxford, Descartes and Leibniz, Hegel and Fichte, Royce and Bradley, Husserl and Meinong, Russell and Whitehead, the main American pragmatists and transcendentalists, Bergson and the French Neo-Thomist school, with intermittent forays into Buddhist and Sanskrit texts.

But it was clearly impossible to take all these together as constituting a single systematic metaphysical philosophy, or as providing Eliot with any unified structure, a cogent intellectual framework, by which the concerns of the poet might be shaped and given order. In particular, Eliot lacked what he saw as underpinning Dante's work: an authoritative schema of moral judgements, a moral hierarchy, such that exacting discriminations can be made in the *Inferno* and in the *Purgatorio* between kinds, categories, or levels of sinfulness.

Here, the even more delayed publication of Eliot's early philosophical papers becomes interestingly relevant. The recent online availability of the *Complete Prose* means that for the first time it is feasible to read a great deal of Eliot's miscellaneous occasional writing, published reviews and unpublished papers, even without access to major research libraries.

*iv : the desolations of philosophy :*
*thought, feeling, and the object.*

There were two entwined aspects of Eliot's problematic situation after the wedding in 1915: the nature of his feeling, past and present, for Vivien, and the extent to which he had unexpectedly entered into and was still inextricably committed to an unwelcome moral situation and decision. That decision had involved, among other consequences, a choice for an uncertain career in literature over an assured academic position in philosophy, but he continued to be preoccupied with both areas of thought and feeling.

Immediately prior to the meeting with Vivien, Eliot had been producing weekly essays for his Oxford philosophy tutor and though they would be worth examining in some detail I will simply point to some aspects of the issues considered in them. What largely preoccupied him in those tutorial papers, and in the thesis he was now planning on F. H. Bradley, was the curious nature of an 'object'. At one stage the title of his proposed thesis seems to have been explicitly concerned with Meinong's notion of object as well as with Bradley. These short tutorial papers have such titles as 'Objects: Content, Objectivity, and Existence' and 'Objects: Real, Unreal, Ideal, and Imaginary', while another series included 'Thought and Reality in Aristotle's Metaphysics' and 'Form and Matter.' In a 1918 review, Eliot was to offer the characteristically lordly remark that the 'Theory of Objects' is a topic 'manipulated by such writers as Driesch, Messer, Meinong, Husserl, Orestano and Ehrenfels.'

The most obvious sense in which Eliot in 1914-15 was philosophically concerned with the issue of 'objects' was to clarify the epistemological relation between the object of experience and the object of knowledge, but this also involved the issue of how far one can operate satisfactorily with the very distinction between subject and object, and what indeed constitutes the subject. One approach was to regard the subject as a 'point of view' or as the focus of 'immediate experience' – for which Bradley sometimes simply, or confusingly, used the term 'feeling'. (See for example Eliot's Michaelmas term paper 'Finite Centres and Points of View'.)

But at least two further 'objects' posed more than philosophical problems for Eliot during that period. One was the possible object of belief, which was later to loom ever larger in his thinking and feeling, and the other – a far more immediate preoccupation – was any possible object of desire, of lust, perhaps of love..

His letter to Conrad Aitken of 31st December 1914 is an eloquent articulation of his sexual frustration throughout the trip to Europe and his even worse situation in Oxford, his continuing misery at not finding an appropriate object even of lust, still less of desire, a love object. The poem *Paysage Triste*, in what I have called Cluster A, evokes a Clough-like situation in which even when he might have fleetingly found someone to 'answer' his 'appreciative' stare, the 'experienced' girl who 'mounted in the omnibus', he was only too cautiously aware that such a woman – an 'almost denizen of Leicester Square' – could never accompany him, say, to the opera or a soirée. In meeting Vivien Haigh-Wood, however, he might seem to have unexpectedly found that 'object' correlative with his desire and one far more appropriate to his social situation. We don't know what specific form the 'encounter' took, though one account apparently tells of their going punting together, and one may be unfairly tempted to recall the phrase 'supine on the floor of a narrow canoe'. In any case, it would then seem that his choice of love-object (and, reciprocally, that of the equally doomed Vivien) was quickly and shatteringly invalidated, though again we do not – and cannot – know the extent of this change of 'feeling' or how immediate it was.

At this point we can turn directly to a philosophical paper Eliot wrote while at Oxford, which he delivered on 12th March 1915 to a meeting of the Moral Sciences Club in Cambridge. The paper is now available as *The Relativity of the Moral Judgment*. It is twenty pages long and my paraphrastic summary does not do it philosophical justice, but what is salient for my present purposes are elements of both the internal argument and the external context.

The argument revolves precisely around the relationship between feeling and thought in moral judgements. Basically, for Eliot's position, a moral judgement *is* a 'feeling' and though a philosophical system of moral judgements might necessarily be arrived at only by a primarily ratiocinative process, at the core of any actual moral response is the 'feeling' which makes and indeed is the moral judgement, though any particular 'feeling' can also, normally, be given some degree of intellectual formulation. When we judge that someone is 'a bad man', says Eliot, this may be simply an expression of the fact that we dislike him, but even if it isn't merely such a feeling of dislike, the moral judgement is nevertheless itself a 'feeling'.

Here Eliot is partly drawing upon that distinctively expanded sense of the term 'feeling' in Bradley's philosophy, so that what is involved in 'feeling' is the whole person at a certain moment, the totality of the subject's immediate experience which essentially constitutes the subject at that moment.

One obvious problem arising for this position is how, if at all, one might construct a systematic organisation of moral judgements if at the core of each particular judgement is a specific feeling. Since every moral judgment 'pretends to be consistent' with other moral judgements which we regard as correct, we reject any single judgement which conflicts with our existing personal system of 'true' moral judgements, because we recognise that implicit in any genuinely new feeling-judgement is an entire alternative system of judgements into which the wholly new feeling is capable of dangerously expanding.

Eliot's paper therefore considers the almost paradoxical possibility of an *in*correct or *un*true moral judgement, which on this account must have taken the form of a 'wrong feeling', even though the 'wrongness' of the feeling would not and could not have been accessible at the moment the judgement was made, precisely because the judgement was itself that feeling. The very next moment, says Eliot, may show that I was wrong but at that moment and for that consciousness, 'the value was there, and remains inexplicable'.

One passage in the paper pre-echoes related formulations in *Tradition and the Individual Talent*. Eliot argues that, as Hegel recognised, 'a change of mind is not merely a change of mind, but is also to some degree a judgment upon the past', so that 'every stage in our progress is a self-consciousness of the preceding.' The same passage also anticipates a remark in the Dante essay: that 'in the moral and emotional and intellectual development of a human being, the past is never discharged or disbanded.' Dante's inhabitants of hell are eternally fixed in their own identity.

What was perhaps bitterly ironic in rapid retrospect was that Eliot had delivered this paper on relativism in moral judgement in Bertrand Russell's rooms in March 1915, a month before he met Vivien, and a few months later it seems to have been the same Russell who severely sabotaged the marriage with Vivien. Russell had readily offered to share with the newly-married couple his own London flat, where Vivien remained while Eliot was away most week-nights on his various demanding and distant teaching commitments in Yorkshire and elsewhere. Russell had not only given Eliot an entrée into professional reviewing and a social introduction to Bloomsbury literary circles, but had even provided him with a loan of £3000 worth of debendtures. In January 1916 Russell even took Vivien off for a shared holiday in Torquay, without Eliot. This relationship *à trois* was to continue until at least 1918.

Was it, in these circumstances, open to Eliot fully to recognise the role which Russell played in the first years of the marriage, and what would it have meant for him to have to come to the conclusion that his friend and patron Russell was or was not a 'bad man' – or indeed whether he Eliot was or was not himself a bad man, perhaps in his not even admitting the situation to himself. In what sense, and at what risk to his whole life-situation, could Eliot come to any coherent moral judgements concerning the respective situations of himself and Vivien? Do I know what I feel? And how is this related to what I think? Perhaps also: who is the third who walks always beside you?

Eliot's philosophical paper on the relativism of moral judgements might very quickly have seemed both intensely relevant and utterly useless.

We can now return to Dante. There is a distinct echo of these concerns with moral judgement and the possibility of a moral system in Eliot's 1920 essay on Dante. He argues that it is a mistake to think that in Dante's work there is a 'philosophical' element and a 'poetic' element which can be isolated from each other. Rather, there is available to Dante a coherent and authoritative philosophy, which is essential to the structure of Dante's poem and that structure is itself essential to the poetic beauty of the poem. This does not make the *Commedia* a philosophical poem in the sense that the *De Rerum Natura* of Lucretius expounds a specific philosophical system. Rather, Dante's poem is 'penetrated' by a philosophical position, which does not simply provide a schematic scaffolding but rather informs and permeates the essential organisation of the poem. That organisation is an ordered presentation of emotions which is at the same time a system of judgements. The specific emotion presented by any single episode is thereby made dependent upon, and reciprocally contributes to, the whole schema. The 'structure of emotions' of the entire work, insists Eliot, ranges from the most sensible to the most intellectual and the most spiritual, and each single episode in this panorama and narrative necessarily – given the very location of the action of the poem – invites our own moral judgement, whilst also enacting a divine judgement, not only upon each individual inhabitant. And that judgement occurs in the actual process of our reading, as in the minute particularities of Dante's writing, precisely as an intense fusion of what we think and what we feel. On this account, Dante might seem to have offered Eliot as poet a possible alternative to any dissociative choice between philosophy and literature.

We can now consider further how far the emerging structure of the 'long poem' might have been shaped by Eliot's continuing engagement with Dante. One fragment preserved in the *March Hare* materials is suggestive. On miscellaneous leaf 13 of the *March Hare* notebook (*March Hare*, p.83, *2015*, I, p. 275) Eliot wrote out in pencil and underlined three lines from Dante's *Inferno* Canto III, leaving a considerable blank space between each line but with a quatrain following the third line:

> *Justitia mosse il mio alto fattore*
>     BLANK
> *Mi fece la divina potestate*
>     BLANK
> *La somma sapienza e il primo amore*

The quatrain begins:

> O Lord have patience
> Pardon these derelictions –

The three lines from Dante form the second tercet of the inscription over the gate into hell which reads 'abandon hope all who enter here':

> Justice moved my high maker
> What made me was the divine power
> The supreme wisdom and the primal love –

The final phrase could equally be translated 'first love'. Eliot leaves sufficient space for two more inserted quatrains but did not complete this partial structure for a poem. The 2015 edition rightly points out that the word 'dereliction' may echo the title of John Donne's poem: *Desertion, or Dereliction* and may have the more specific sense of forsaking or abandoning, as well as more generally a neglect of duty. Eliot's fragment is impossible to date. Whether the unfinished schema might have been contemporary with or an alternative to the possible outline on the back of the *Duchess* draft is therefore uncertain. But I am tempted to date both as having some reference to a situation in which Eliot was either contemplating the end of his marriage or reflecting upon a lost alternative to it.

Another poem, *Exequy* (*2015*, p. 286), concludes with an entire capitalised line from Dante (from the same Arnaut Daniel *Purgatorio* Canto XXVI which provided the title of the *Ara vos prec* volume), and was certainly part of *The Waste Land* material, though Pound could finally find no place for it. The poem imagines a time when 'persistent lovers will repair / to my suburban tomb' and ends with one pilgrim hearing a breathless chuckle from underground with the refrain 'Sovegna vos  a temps de mon dolor' – remember the time of my misery. If the finalised *Waste Land* now opens with memory and desire it might at one stage have concluded with remembrance of a time of misery.

However, unlike Dante, Eliot in composing his 'long poem' did not have available to him a philosophical system upon which he might shape the overall structure of his poem. The attempt in *Gerontion* to write like John Donne may itself have brought home to him the extent to which even Donne's mode, alone, was an unsatisfactory solution. But the draft outline of a possible poem based upon or intertwining with three lines from Dante perhaps indicated another possibility: that of actually using Dante's own work as, in part at least, a framework or scaffold, not a philosophical system but a 'structure of emotions' made up in part of the specific emotional-intellectual texture of previous literary moments.

Indeed, how far might the full range of literature itself be deployed to provide the function which philosophy had once made possible for Dante?

After all, it is not only Donne's sensibility which suffuses the poem *Gerontion* but, as the 2015 edition and many previous commentaries have highlighted, the poem is deeply saturated with half-buried literary echoes. This is not of course a wholly new feature of Eliot's writing: many of his poems from *Prufrock* onwards had been tissues of more or less explicit semi-quotations, but a poem probably written immediately prior to *Gerontion* suggests an interesting new explicitness.

Eliot in various letters in 1919 emphasised that his poem *Burbank with a Baedeker: Bleistein with a Cigar* was among his most serious recent attempts. The immediately noticeable feature of the poem is the seven-line epigraph which simply juxtaposes six extremely fragmentary quotations. Previous poems had provided succinct epigraphs with more less decipherable applicability to their content. The elliptical character of the *Burbank* epigraph poses a different kind of puzzle to the reader until – with whatever degree of assistance – one recognises that all these fragments evoke Venice, with different significances for the several authors thus abruptly recalled, though the core quotation from *Othello* encapsulates lust, jealousy, alleged adultery, and wife-murder. This catena of disjunct quotations is later most obviously echoed in the concluding collocation of fragmentary quotations in the final passage of *The Waste Land*.

When Eliot was compiling *Ara vos prec* in late 1919 he selected *Gerontion* and *Burbank* as the opening poems of the collection and the two have continued in that juxtaposed order throughout the various editions of the *Collected Poems*. At about the same time, Eliot was writing in *Tradition and the Individual Talent* that the aspiring writer must have the whole of European literature from Homer onwards in his bones, and that the genuinely new – not unlike an act of retrospective moral judgement or an Hegelian moment of historical self-consciousness – can and must radically modify the existing order. He also remarked in the *Relativism* paper that philosophical idealism – 'the philosophy of the historically minded' – attempts to take 'the delicate and evasive truths of historical and literary criticism, truths which are the intuitive apprehension of a trained mind and a trained taste' and inappropriately imposes upon those 'truths' a preconceived and mistaken dialectical ordering. For Eliot, perhaps those delicate and evasive truths to be discovered in literature and literary criticism might form the nodes for an ordering of value judgements structurally different from that of a philosophical system.

As a lecturer in the adult education sector Eliot both enjoyed a freedom to offer, and confronted the challenging scope of, a remarkable range of courses in literature and history, and it may be partly thanks to the pedagogical demands of that experience that Eliot could at least suppose, or allusively propose, some coherent pattern to be discerned in the entirety of European culture. Unlike Ezra Pound, whose own long poem 'with history' developed an increasingly intrusive dependence upon cited archival documentary fragments, Eliot constructed his critical essays (and his long poem?) not upon biographical or historical documentation but almost solely upon quoting selected passages which now seem intensely saturated with personal significance for him, and upon the basis of which he also assembled a more explicit (and specious) overall historical argument, as in the quasi-academic 1926 lectures. But the demanding scope of his engagement with literature 'from Homer onwards' did make palpable to him the possibility of recognising substantial differences in emotional-intellectual sensibilities and, therefore, in the very nature of feeling, thought, and belief, across distinct and varying periods and cultures.

But while his overall critical case concerning a sudden 17th century dissociation of sensibility may seem less than convincing, the intertextual saturation of *Burbank* and *Gerontion* in 1919 anticipated the most salient aspect of *The Waste Land*: that Eliot's poems comprise a dense tissue of literary references. In a fairly obvious sense, then, what the reader is presented with in *The Waste Land* is not at all, on the immediately legible surface at least, a sequence of moments in the biographical trajectory of Mr. T. S. Eliot but rather a range of characters, situations, and episodes which form, in variously over-determined ways, a network of literary interconnections between them and beyond them. Moreover, what is pervasively at work is a shaping of the various components of the poem not just by more or less specifiable references or footnotable allusions to so many literary and musical works, but most effectively by an incorporation into the very texture of Eliot's own poem of the characteristic different modalities and sensibilities of previous literary texts and moments. It was not, for example, merely a 'parody' or 'pastiche' of Pope which Eliot was so precisely attempting, but, among other effects, a mode which significantly associated Fresca with the 'typist'.

The 'intractable' material for which Eliot never found an appropriate form was the nature of his 'wrong' moral feeling or judgement in relation to the sudden decision to marry Vivien and the after-effects of that moment for the still ongoing and daily decision not only to continue in that relation but also to live out its consequences. Dante might have said that Eliot knew with a kind of inexorable horror that he was voluntarily in hell and was voluntarily remaining so.

However, it would be far too simple to see the poem as conceived only as an exploration of that private or individual situation – as merely Eliot's version of the autobiographical component of the *Vita Nuova*. As with Dante's vision of hell in the *Commedia*, we might see it more as an attempt at an articulation of a range of related situations. The intractable question which shapes *The Waste Land* is not only how its various sections are connected in terms of literary form, but how the different voices, characters, and situations which it assembles are related at some level of moral judgement – but moral judgement in Eliot's own sense, of specific and particular combinations of feeling and thought.

It would also be too simple to say that Eliot's several characters are in a version of hell, or perhaps each in a personal and individual hell (each trapped in its own monadic self, the key turning upon each separated self), and that they are and remain there voluntarily, even if we recognise that it is plausible that between them the various protagonists do indeed cover a range of 'wrong' moral decisions and situations. The intractable problem which Eliot confronted – in accordance with his own argument which emerged explicitly only later, in the 1926 lectures – is that there was for him, and for his readers, no authoritative or given moral framework in which to locate and order this variety of situations.

Dante could, for Eliot, essentially categorise the various inhabitants of his *Inferno* according to a coherent moral (which for Dante meant a philosophical-theological) framework which was more than a mere external scaffolding but was implicated in the very responses of thought and feeling which Dante is concerned both to explore and to insist upon as we encounter each inhabitant.

Eliot's problem was therefore even more intractable than, though it had some relation to, that which he had discerned in *Hamlet*: how a literary work could indeed enact a judgement in his sense of the term.

Here a fundamental feature of the poem comes again more clearly into view. If there was no given or acceptable philosophical-moral framework, system, scaffolding or ordering, what else might partially substitute for that lack? Eliot's Notes make an uncertain and unconvincing appeal to the anthropological approach of Fraser and Weston, but the emphasis is misleading. Insofar as the Grail legend does indeed enter into any of our actual responses to the poem, it is not through consulting the explicit account or explanation of it to be found in anthropological treatises, but in the vividly remembered or dimly evoked literary material itself of the Grail stories.

And it is this which is most fundamentally characteristic of Eliot's approach in *The Waste Land*: that each episode or character within the poem insinuates into our response echoes and allusions to a range of previous literary moments, experiences, presentations, encapsulations, such that a single line or phrase can bring into play the concentrated sensibility of an entire work, or even of an entire *oeuvre*. This is not simply a matter of alluding to the content of previous literary works but of deploying their actual form, quoting or imitating their meter, rhythm, feeling, incorporating fragments, plucking them out of the past but bringing with them and in them 'the delicate and evasive truths' they incarnate.

A musical memory from Wagner or a single line from Baudelaire, a phrase from Verlaine or an echo from Chaucer, may combine to at least provide gestures towards a complex moral assemblage constructed not from one coherent or many competing philosophical systems but from previous literary articulations, written instances of both unique and deeply historical structures of feeling. In considering the actions of the typist home at tea-time our reactions are shaped simultaneously by the presence of Greek myths, Ovid's poetry, and the verse patterns of 19th-century French ironists. In imagining the encounter in the Hyacinth garden and its aftermath both the terrible poignancy of Paolo and Francesca and the horror at the heart of Conrad's darkness together shape our complex layering of responses. Eliot claims in the 1921 Marvell essay that in a single line of Catullus is an entire civilisation. Elsewhere, he says that the single line from Baudelaire which he quotes in *The Waste Land* sums up for him the entirety of Baudelaire's *oeuvre*. When he inscribes the enigmatic syllables 'weialala leia' he is inviting his reader to hear the whole of Wagner and in the intensely repeated single word 'burning' to enact the core sensibility of Saint Augustine.

When Eliot said of Dante and Aquinas that one has to feel like them in order to think like them, he is partly claiming that in reading Dante appropriately one can enter into the 'immediate experience' (in Bradley's sense) of each presented situation, that the reader can grasp in an emotional-intellectual unity the specific fate of each inhabitant of the *Inferno* or the *Purgatorio*, but also that Dante's poem taken as a whole offers a kind of immediate experience of the entire civilisation of 13th century Italy. It is the poetry which gives us access to that sensibility. In this he was not that distant from Pound of the early Provencal and Chinese translations.

In *The Waste Land* Eliot might be seen as presenting a new contemporary sensibility, radically different from the Provencal canonisation of the love object as secured by her being already married, a kind of adulterous fidelity, or from Dante's idealising or sublimating of the love object as an anticipation of the divine. The modern sensibility for Eliot is one in which all forms of sexual relation are shaped by de-sublimation, by the distortions of desire. One might be induced to see in the poem a repertoire of betrayals or inadequacies, of impotence and false choices, mainly evincing a variety of forms of unsatisfactory sexual relations.

But Eliot seems also to have been attempting to perceive in the entire repertoire of literary – or more generally cultural – works of the past the possibility of an ordered structuring of the crucial defining complexes of both thought and feeling, which would somehow serve as comparative moral judgements. If for the Eliot of the *Relativism* paper the feeling (in the extended sense of total experience) *is* a judgement, then juxtaposing this array of situations in his long poem was an attempt to assemble a judgement – and the fundamental judgement would seem to be that these people are in, or indeed constitute, a voluntary hell.

At the core of this judgement is precisely Eliot's intractable material: what *The Waste Land* traces but also conceals is that the steps which had led Eliot to his condition in 1921 were not due to some pre-destined and foretold fate or merely to the unexpected geopolitical situation in 1914 which accidentally impinged upon his personal plans, but rather, like Paolo and Francesca, he had chosen his situation and was still choosing to perpetuate his punishment: the feeling was the judgement.

On my reading of the process of composition, if Eliot had retained more of the original apparently miscellaneous but indirectly very personal materials he might have made it much clearer (perhaps even to himself) what he was attempting to achieve by this patterning of personal experiences upon historical-literary forms and genres, as shaping the individual episodes and situations in the poem. But by prematurely and drastically cutting so much of that material Eliot left himself, and the reader, with only a much more enigmatically disconnected set of fragments.

On the other hand - have we come all this way for a chimera...? Arguably, all this, even if a plausible account of what Eliot might have been working towards, would have been a forlorn attempt anyway, since his own sense of the 'mind of Europe' as being simultaneously present in a writer's 'very bones' was surely another form of Hegelian idealist construction. In the *Relativism* paper he remarks that the most successful, and perhaps the only, attempt ever made to 'organise history (including of course the history of value) into an intelligible process' was the philosophy of Hegel. He adds: 'its failure is even more instructive than its success'.

For Literature, however idealised, cannot substitute for a philosophically coherent moral system, though by intensely combining thought and feeling individual literary works may try to reproduce in a responsive reader the actual dilemmas of specific complex moral judgements. What was profoundly at work in Eliot and his generation of modernists was perhaps an attempt to construct a 'chapter of the moral history' (to use Joyce's phrase) of Europe but without the philosophical and theological underpinning which had sustained previous cultural formations. And they failed.

Eliot in the later 1920s partly reverted to a traditional Anglican scaffolding, however problematic his relationship to Christian theological doctrine may have been. Joyce never wholly abandoned the Catholic mentality he had so ambivalently but deeply inherited. Pound, possibly the most tragic of the trio, eventually acknowledged his failure to make it cohere, politically, aesthetically, personally.

It was surely the ultimate irony of the doctrine of poetic impersonality that the Bollingen Prize should be awarded to the incarcerated Pound, nevertheless judged either criminal or insane or both.

One extension of this argument would be to trace a fairly obvious line from Matthew Arnold's touchstones of poetic value through Eliot's noticeably repetitive selection of personally resonant moments within the European literary corpus, and on to Leavis's attempt to inculcate a capacity for a form of discrimination simultaneously aesthetic and moral which could be registered in the very texture of a passage of writing, but which could only be arrived at by the potentially interminable exercise of close comparison between texts. But I have touched upon these issues earlier, so let me instead return now to further aspects of memory and desire.

*vi : I gotta use words… my words echo in my mind…*

In 1930, in various letters, Eliot wrote that *Ash Wednesday* put into words a certain 'stage of the journey', that all his previous poems represented 'previous stages' of his journey, and that *Ash Wednesday* was only a 'first attempt' at an application of the 'philosophy of the *Vita Nuova*' to modern life (see *2015*, I, p. 730) . But it may be that the various 'stages' discernible in *The Waste Land* were also, taken together, an earlier stage of Eliot's long *Vita Nuova* before he had fully assimilated what he later saw as its 'philosophy'. But what was that philosophy for Eliot?

The final brief section of the pivotal 1919 essay *Tradition and the Individual Talent* has its own epigraph, a phrase from Aristotle, though without attributing it, from *De anima*, 1.4. 408b: 'Mind is, no doubt, something more divine and impassible' (as rather enigmatically translated by J. A. Smith, a Professor of Philosophy at Oxford with whom Eliot had studied Aristotelian logic). When Eliot then writes that he proposes to halt at the frontier of metaphysics it might seem that he is merely acceding to a disciplinary boundary, beyond which lies 'philosophy'. However, if we now bring together some strands in this (still highly tentative) argument, we can perhaps recognise that here Eliot is touching upon another aspect of the formidably intractable material he was trying to engage with, not only the object of desire but the subject itself..

It would not be worth investigating in full detail what 'metaphysics' meant to Eliot, but quite often in the 1926 lectures it denoted something much closer to 'mysticism' than the term would normally be taken to mean. Whereas for Aristotle the investigation of the nature of the concept *being* led him towards a systematic investigation of other related concepts, for the generation of European philosophers after the First World War there was a tendency to regard 'being' as somehow itself the object of enquiry. Within that approach figures such as Jacques Maritain, whose work Eliot was reading, with considerable reservations, while preparing the Clark lectures (*L2*, pp. 795ff.), seemed inclined to regard mere wonderment at the very notion of being as the culmination of metaphysical enquiry. In the 1926 lectures so deliberately entitled *The Varieties of Metaphysical Poetry* Eliot at times struggles somewhat unconvincingly to clarify what he sees as the relations between philosophy, metaphysics, and mysticism but in explicitly differentiating 'philosophical' poets from 'metaphysical' poets he shows an inclination to slide towards assimilating metaphysical thinking into mystical awareness.

It is, arguably, the Neoplatonist strand even in Thomism which he sees as structuring the ascent of Dante not only through the circles of hell and purgatory but also through the states of being which constitute the hierarchy of paradise. Defining each individual state in the *Divina Commedia* is precisely the relationship between the objects of desire and the memory of that desire: those whose life has finally been suffused with a growing desire for the ultimate divine object can continue their ascent to the limit of their personal capacity, while those still caught in the trammels of unrepudiated earthly desire are allocated a place in the decending circles of hell appropriate to the precise degree of degradation of their object of desire. What constitutes memory and desire ranges from the rending re-enactment of (frustrated) bodily passion to an almost non-corporeal spiritual contemplation.

On some (earthly) accounts, what constitutes the subject, the agent of moral decision-making, is not a focus of immediate experience or the momentary articulation of a point of view, a 'feeling', but rather that form of continuity provided by memory. It is only through memory that one could retrospectively challenge or endorse a decision which continues to shape one's life. But the notion that memory could constitute a coherent identity may not have been wholly satisfactory to Eliot, despite the early influence of Bergson. Perhaps, for Eliot from 1915 to 1922, memory was only too dangerously entangled with desire, but more a retrospective desire, for the lost object, perhaps Emily Hale, than any present or prospective desire for Vivien, now also but in a different way a lost object. Desire and thought entangled, thinking may have aroused desire, recaptured as remembered immediate feeling, but the object of desire was not present except in memory, whereas the object of past moments of desire, Vivien, is indeed daily present but no longer as the object of desire. There is, to adapt a phrase, no objective correlative to the desire he actually feels, and the desire he increasingly wishes to feel is an intellectual desire, the object of which is not human love but, ultimately, divine love.

In his Oxford tutorial paper on form and matter in Aristotle, Eliot singles out the problem of individualisation: is it through or in form or matter that the particular is differentiated (one contentious issue between Aquinas and Scotus). This perennial problem of form and matter is fundamental to the subject-object relation in Aristotle and is often later posed simplistically in terms of body and soul or mind and body. Eliot is quite right to pour scorn upon Descartes' incoherent version in Lecture II of *Varieties*, though perhaps unfair to associate the 6th Meditation with I. A. Richards's remark that 'love is a spontaneous emotion bearing no relation to the object of affection.' One crucial problem for Eliot was how a substantial change (not necessarily in the technical sense) could be effected – as in his life-changing decisions of April to June 1915. In what sense could a decision – a 'wrong feeling'– be inappropriate to the person who actually made it? In what sense might a choice of object change the very identity of the subject? If I do not know what I feel or what I think, what is this 'I' which thinks or feels anyway?

Consider the very first line by Eliot in the *Collected Poems*: let us go then, you and I.... Who is the I? I don't mean simply in the poem. One could say – fairly generally – that for most people 'memory and desire' are indeed constitutive of the I that they think of themselves as being. And however much people may appeal to some notion of a 'mind' in ordinary experience memory and desire are inextricably corporeal: it is the body which desires and remembers though one can equally say that memory and desire, and indeed the body itself, are intertwined in and as both thinking and feeling to constitute our personal existence. This familiar conundrum can be traced in Eliot's work from the early *First Dialogue of the Body and Soul* through to his comments about John Donne's presentation of 'the fusion and identification of souls in sexual love' (*Varieties*, Lecture 1). It also underlies Eliot's comment that only those who have personality and emotions know what it means to want to escape from these things.

Here the overall approach of the 2015 edition of Eliot's poems is unexpectedly illuminating and also disturbing. What is extraordinary about the commentary included in this weighty edition is that the editors seem able to find, often with a high degree of persuasiveness or plausibility, that almost every line or phrase which Eliot ever wrote was resonant with other phrases and passages which he had read and for the most part remembered with a sometimes startling accuracy – even when he did not consciously remember that he had remembered a particular passage. There are well-known instances in, for example, *Gerontion*.

The dense apparatus of the edition might be seen as inappropriately burdening the words of Eliot with a plethora of mere parallels, but Eliot seems to have had an extraordinary memory at least for literary texts, though in many instances he slightly misremembered words and phrases, even in passages which he had clearly taken to heart as his equivalent of Matthew Arnold's touchstones. A study of these parapraxes might be revealing. The 1926 lectures are particularly replete with quoted passages often familiar from Eliot's other writings. The footnotes to the lectures as edited in 1993 also show just how extensive his reading – indeed, his close reading – of literary texts tended to be. We can add the contributions to his saturated textual memory of his constant 'occasional' writing, which reviewed or otherwise dealt with an extraordinary range of disparate publications, and no doubt both as the editor of *The Criterion* and as a publisher he also read and commented on a great many more miscellaneous manuscripts.

Yet the very omnipresence of memory-traces of an abundance of miscellaneous texts in his own writing suggests that this capacity or habit may have been problematic for Eliot himself. On one occasion, he claimed that he had provided the Notes to *The Waste Land* in order to defend himself against the charge of plagiarism which had been directed at some of his early poems similarly saturated with echoes of other writers. But if his work was indeed so permeated with echoes and allusions, how was his own identity to be constructed? Not just his poetic but his 'personal' identity? When Eliot writes of the thousand sordid images of which your soul was constituted or of a life composed so much, so much of odds and ends, it can be directly associated with the notion that he must borrow every changing shape to find expression and that unless he finds his own words in the words of others he remains doubtful, not knowing what to feel or if he understands. As he also recognised, despite the intentionality of most deliberate references and allusions, quite often the textual memories operate as mere fragments, like dream shards, removed from their original setting without intentionally invoking those contexts at all but simply pinned and wriggling as fragments he has shored. Against what?

The issue raised by this kind of omnivorous memory is whether there is indeed an ego or identity distinct from this cluster of memories derived second-hand from other people's writings. Eliot's whole activity at times seems to have been constantly and voluntarily revolving around a concatenation of miscellaneous texts, as reviewer, as editor, as publisher. On one occasion he said that he needed a more or less constant injection of three or four new books. The result was a mind-ful of quotation – these fragments – including the touchstone quotations to which he returned again and again.

Whereas for most of us there may be some kind of vaguely articulated duality between what we experience or conceive of as body and soul, or mind and body, what seems to happen in Eliot's case is that a curious third element becomes crucial: his memory of other people's fusions of thought and feeling, his intellectual-emotional saturation with previous texts in the form of vicarious 'feelings' or what he sometimes called 'art emotions'. This takes him beyond the familiar practice of critical quotation. His way of reading seems to have involved an intense engagement with an emotional structure, or structure of emotion, which he is easily prompted to recall (it is a crucial part of what makes him an impressive critic). But at the same time it seems that he was often either incapable of responding in a similar engaged way to actual people around him, including most especially Vivien herself, or perhaps that in a mode of self-defence he deliberately suppressed such ordinary human capacities. The nickname Possum is only the most legible sign of the iceberg which he once partly disclosed, for example, in the extraordinary letter to John Middleton Murray of (mid-April?) 1925 (*L2*, p.627), in which he speaks of having deliberately made himself into a dead machine in order not to feel and even at the risk of 'killing' both Vivien and himself.

How far Eliot took it for granted that others did or even could read literary texts in a similarily intense and vicarious way is unclear. Certainly he sometimes seems to assume in the critical writing that his reader will not only recognise a fragmentary quotation but also be able to summon up the entire context of the work cited, and even to make more less instant judgements as between one whole body of work and another. The remark about having the whole of the literature of Europe in one's bones seems at times to define a pre-requisite for Eliot's readers as well as for putative poetic practitioners.

It is this complex and almost contradictory relationship between words, phrases, lines, passages, which seemed to have an intense personal resonance for Eliot, or which he could adopt as providing a voice for his personae, and his use of quotations which can sometimes operate as isolated fragments and sometimes as concentrated encapsulations of previous literary sensibilities, which seems to me to most characterise Eliot, as poet, as critic, and perhaps as person. It is not simply that we now know 'Eliot' only through those words on the page, but almost as if it was Eliot's own repeated impetus to construct a persona made so entirely of others' words which at the same time speak in the most personal manner possible and yet refuse or decline anything in the way of expressing or revealing a personality. One might again put this in terms of the notion of 'impersonality' which had puzzled me as a teenager, or perhaps even formulate it with reference to Eliot's intermittent engagement with Buddhist notions of the not-self, but its most palpable demonstration is that so very much of the 2015 edition consists of quotations, not least from the grand old *OED* itself.

Traditionally, issues of identity have been explored and debated within the fields of philosophy and psychology and ultimately as a matter of metaphysics. But what Eliot seems to insist upon in the Clark lectures is his own somewhat idiosyncratic use of the term 'metaphysical' as more less akin to 'mysticism' and I want to bring these tentative notes towards a conclusion by suggesting that what Eliot eventually produced as his own version of a contemporary 'metaphysical' poem was in effect a spiritual autobiography, that *Four Quartets* offers us a presentation of that curious complex of thought and feeling which for Eliot constituted his very identity but which was at the same time directed towards a non-identity, a hollowing out of the personality which T. S. Eliot had once been, in the hope of arriving at an evacuated and impersonal loss of identity in some form of mystical immediate experience. The focus of the whole poem is not, in the end, Incarnation but glimpses of a timeless contemplation, culminating in a quasi-Dantesque finale.

The way in which *Four Quartets* is constructed – as I had once argued with Leavis – is essentially through the intertwining of textual memories within the poem itself, echoes of words upon words. It is the accumulating memories of previous and coming textual moments, as we read and re-read the quartets, which constitutes the very fusion of feeling and thinking which is the immediate experience of the poem. But, unlike most of Eliot's previous poems, this work is not primarily constructed from the existing corpus of past literary works, phrases, and lines, but from and as those given to us within Eliot's poem itself. And again, I would tentatively suggest, the poem was constructed through the complex relationship between remembered significant moments of his own life and the composited poems or segments which for him evoked those particular moments and which are woven into and thereby constitute the structure of the overall poem.

However, let me now return one more time to *Gerontion*. One of the few moments in the 2015 edition where the editors seem to miss an obvious literary allusion concerns the lines:

> I have lost my sight, smell, hearing, taste and touch:
> How should I use them for your closer contact?

The commentary cites *As You Like It* and John Henry Newman, but anyone familiar, as Newman certainly was, with Aquinas will immediately recognise an allusion to his Corpus Christi hymn: 'sight, taste, and touch in thee are all deceivèd.' But whereas Gerontion seems to regard the senses as irredeemably inadequate or inappropriate as a way of making contact with the 'you', who may or may not be divine, for Aquinas the senses may indeed partly deceive us on occasion but can only do so absolutely in the unique context of transubstantiation: the immediate experience of tasting the consecrated bread and wine is exactly what the senses expect and what one gets from the experience of eating bread and wine, but it is only in this one instance that for Aquinas the God-given senses are not intrinsically reliable provided we do not abuse them. The Eucharist uniquely constitutes – to adapt Eliot's earlier terminology – a 'wrong feeling', a judgement which is false if we believe that what we are experiencing is bread and wine.

Eliot's *Gerontion* has significantly twisted the sense of Aquinas's verse. For Aquinas it is the consecrated bread and wine upon the altar which through transubstantiation supernaturally deceives us, by retaining the misleading but actual and familiar experience of our various senses, whereas Gerontion sees his human senses as intrinsically inadequate and naturally deceptive. It will be characteristic of the later Eliot almost to deny the possibility of approaching the divine through the human senses, and to try to invoke in his poetry quasi-mystical moments of transcending and even repudiating the senses and the natural world itself. By the time of *Four Quartets* Eliot has moved far from the position of Saint Thomas which (with whatever qualifying reservations) had indeed informed and sustained Dante's work[1]

---

[1] Let me here acknowledge a long-standing debt to my one-time neighbour, Kenelm Foster, O.P., whose *The Two Dantes* (1977), chapter 4, offers a succinct account of the relation of Dante to Aquinas. See also Patrick Boyde, *Perception and passion in Dante's Comedy*, 1993.

One might argue – on some other occasion – that Eliot's account of the relationship between philosophy and literature in the 13th century was in any case unconvincing, but I am here simply trying to suggest that the enigmatic composition of *The Waste Land* is partly illuminated by Eliot's overall argument in the Clark lectures, whatever the validity or otherwise of that argument, and that the process of thinking which went into those lectures – partly perhaps stimulated by the very composition of *The Waste Land* a few years before – takes us back precisely to the period in which his long poem was being gestated, in conjunction especially with the 1920 Dante essay and the 1921 *Metaphysical Poets* essay. Though *The Waste Land* can indeed be situated in the political and cultural context of 1922 and Eliot's programme for *The Criterion*, as I have previously argued, it can equally be located at the intersection of intensely charged dilemmas not only of Eliot's thought and feeling focused upon April 1915 but also of his critical and philosophical thinking and feeling about what it means to know what it is to feel and think.

However, for Eliot after *The Waste Land* the desire increasingly explicit in his work is to endeavour to release himself from the senses, from sensuousness, even from the body itself, and perhaps even to to transform thinking into believing and feeling into pure contemplation. And at this point I find myself returning to those arguments long ago with F. R. Leavis as to where *Four Quartets* went 'wrong'.

*vii : my end is my beginning*

When Leavis, back in the 1960s, insistently asked where *Four Quartets* 'went wrong', I had taken him to mean – as I am still reasonably sure he did at that time – that there was some flaw in the composition of the poem such that at a certain moment in reading through it one became dis-satisfied and had to judge that the poem had at that point begun to fail. What was however difficult for me to grasp – and this was, of course, in line with Leavis's whole approach to such questions – were the grounds for making such a judgement: what was it about this or that passage which constituted, in his adverse response, a local inadequacy, and how and where precisely could one put one's finger on it, quite literally? I knew enough at the time not to dare ask Leavis for his 'criteria', some explicit and articulable norm against which a poem might or should be measured.

I had also by then imbibed two other guiding approaches to the practice of criticism, apparently rather similar but actually rather divergent in their implications. One, which derived in part from Eliot himself, was the notion that a major poet creates the taste by which he is enjoyed (it was always 'he' in those days). The other, which I understood or misunderstood from reading Adorno, was that each major modern work of art now had to construct its own unique form, an invention specific to that work, a compositional totality created according to its own unique and, in a sense, internal rules. Clearly, several issues were intertwined here, including the relationship of the work of art to 'tradition', and the apparent circularity of both positions: what if the 'taste' in question was itself shallow, and how could one possibly know – as writer or composer, as working practitioner – at what moment the current work in progress was in any sense finished, complete, done?

Yet when, in 1975, no longer in touch with him, I read Leavis's extraordinary account of *Four Quartets* in *The Living Principle: 'English' as a discipline of thought* it seemed that now it was the whole poem that was 'wrong', which did not preclude that some passages in it were wonderfully right. What Leavis now emphasised in his extraordinarily attentive yet characteristically convoluted close analysis, was what he saw as the fundamentally self-contradictory character of the poem: that Eliot's marvellously creative capacities had constructed a denial or repudiation of that very creativity. It is impossible to summarise Leavis's hundred or so pages, but if his analysis is at all compelling, one is brought to recognise how Eliot had successfully, within the poem itself, created the intellectual, moral, and spiritual position from which the poem insisted that it be judged, yet also at the same time one had to regard that position as itself inimical to that very judgement of success, since any actively co-creative reader, in positively responding to the poem, has to reject Eliot's own stance as undermining the very possibility of that denial of creativity which the poem endorses. Leavis puts this case in an unfolding and incremental critique of considerable length, slowly and patiently probing the poem's self-contradictory character. One partial formulation:

> Eliot's kind of 'humility', consistently believed in, amounts to nihilism. But he is not, of course, consistent: what a part of one believes isn't necessarily believed by the whole. ... the inconsistency that stares us in the face is his seeking to establish the inevitability of his pondered negation by the exercise of intensely skilled human creativity – his own as a poet. (p. 215)

This is almost, on one reading of *The Waste Land*, a reversal or variation upon the double-bind I have earlier suggested as originally constructed by the 1922 poem, when it appeared in the pages of *The Criterion*: that the very achievement of the poem refuted any claim that such poetic achievement was impossible in the contemporary fragmented and sterile cultural situation.

From another perspective, the issue is, again, whether one can read a poem 'as a poem' while not sharing, or even actively dissenting from, the poet's own beliefs which inform that very poem.

Here, Adorno's dictum (as I understood it) came into play, particularly after I first read perhaps the finest critical essay published on *Four Quartets* since Leavis's own. In 1992, Tony Rudolf's Menard Press published *Quatre Quatuors*, a translation of Eliot's poem into French by Claude Vigée. The volume included the original French version of 'Listening to the Voice in Four Quartets' by Gabriel Josipovici, which through whatever publishing grace or accidental blessing, apparently escaped the usual copyright restrictions on quoting the poem, even in its English version.[2] The essay takes the form of a commentary, beginning with the opening lines of *Burnt Norton* and ending with the closing lines of *Little Gidding*. In that respect, it evinces a reader embarking upon and completing that process of a continuously attentive reading which my own earlier position saw as always to be defeated.

Necessarily, within the compass of only twenty pages or so, Josipovici offers a highly selective commentary. He singles out for quotation several passages upon which I shortly want to focus since they can serve to suggest a direct contrast with Leavis. First however, to use an old formula, let us compare and contrast Leavis and Moody.

Leavis continues the paragraph just quoted as follows:

———————————————

[2] I quote from the English version included in Jospipovici's *The Singer on the Shore*, Carcanet, 2006.

And there is perhaps a kind of felicity in his lapsing once more, as he insists on his anti-creative 'humility' (or avowed impotence), into a stylistic infelicity – an embarrassingly infelicitous 'use of words' that reminds one of Pound:

> And so each venture
> Is a new beginning, a raid on the inarticulate
> With shabby equipment always deteriorating
> In the general mess of imprecision of feeling,
> Undisciplined squads of emotion.

There can't, I think, be any defence of this. It is an error of taste that, in such a place, seems to have a significance that makes it worse than that. The informal self-communing manner, which Eliot shows in *Four Quartets* that he can use with success, was meant here to have an effect of unstudied spontaneity that would give convincing rightness to an intimately personal avowal. The actual wrongness is of a kind one is familiar with in his work when he affects colloquial licence. One feels that he couldn't have fallen into it here if the conditions making a profound and difficult sincerity possible for him had obtained with any sureness. (p. 215)

Leavis had just commented on Eliot's lines which immediately precede those quoted (the opening of part V of *East Coker*):

> … it is an odd infelicity in a poet, and such a poet as Eliot, to speak of the developed 'practitioner' as having learnt 'to get the better of words'. *Four Quartets*, for the responsive reader, testifies that 'using words' is a misleading way of describing its author's relation to the English language. It is actually his incomparable living ally, and more, for its life is active within him; as a

sentience that can think and feel and judge man to be abject in his impotence, he is in essential ways constituted of the language he speaks, uses and lives. It is *in* the English language that he conceives, feels, refines, and achieves subtleties of definition (definition that is inseparable from communication, or, at any rate, from making communicable). In the English language he is drawing on the creativity of numberless generations of mankind and profiting collaboratively. (p.214)

Compare this with Moody on the same passage:

Getting the better of words is of the essence of *Four Quartets*. Its major design is to so use words as to make them mean what is beyond words; or, to put the same idea another way, to so transform the understanding of the world which is in its words that it will be perceived as the divine Word in action. (The two themes, that of conquering time, and that of getting the better of words, are drawn together, since words are the medium by which the mind may attain the consciousness which transcends time.) The theme of words that must strive and fail to reveal the Word is stated explicitly in BN V, briefly restated in EC IIb, partially developed in EC Va - then apparently left aside to be finally developed only in Little Gidding.
*(The Cambridge Companion to T. S. Eliot*, p. 147)

Moody's recourse to summary reference in a catena of abbreviations rather than providing specific quotation (an option largely precluded by copyright restrictions) highlights, of course, the practical difficulty of making a fair comparison. But that Leavis is fundamentally at odds with Moody is clear from his comments on what Moody sees as 'stated explicitly in BN V':

Perhaps the questionableness of what Eliot does with 'pattern' comes out most significantly when he associates it with 'words' and associates 'words' with 'music':

> Words, after speech, reach
> Into the silence. Only by the form, the pattern,
> Can words or music reach
> The stillness ...

It is astonishing that a 'practitioner' whose genius manifests itself in his practice as a rare intelligence about the language in which he works should, obviously without self-suspicion, exhibit so grave an unintelligence here. What, when it is said of words ('after speech'), we may ask, does 'reach into the silence' mean? What is it meant to convey? Actually, of course, seeing the word 'pattern' ahead, we know at once what kind of effect Eliot intends the sentence to contribute to. (p. 227)

And in another passage:

> We are considering the part played in Eliot's creative thought by 'pattern' and 'dance', ideas or themes that, as we apprehend them, are involved in a complexity of varying and cumulative evocation. It seems, then, the obvious thing to turn with our questions a couple of pages on from the passage in movement II of *Burnt Norton* to the opening of V:

> Words move, music moves…
> *[Leavis quotes seven lines;*
> *but I have almost reached my 25 line quota*
> *for this Quartet.]*

The distinctive kind of creativeness with which Eliot's genius focuses consciously on language is illustrated in the last two lines in the way the 'still' (placed with a characteristic perfection of art at the line's end) of 'still moves perpetually' stands enclosed between the repeated 'still' of the first and the concluding 'stillness' ....*[but]* The question that engages us is again: What is the relation between 'the still point' and the 'dance' (or 'pattern')? It seems me plain by now that Eliot has no intellectually statable answer in his mind for us to elicit from the 'music'. We have perhaps been led to take 'pattern' with a mistaken kind of seriousness....(p. 174)

The reality his concern for which explains the emphasis laid on 'pattern' and 'dance' in his 'music' is, in contradistinction to the physicist's, spiritual.... Not only is 'spiritual' an equivocal word; it may cover irreconcilable intentions. Let me say at once that it does in Eliot – or at least that it points to a paradox that, when one considers it in the complexities of his poem, one has to to judge to be an essential contradiction. The ultimate really real that Eliot seeks in *Four Quartets* is eternal reality, and *that* he can do little, directly, to characterise. (p. 175)

Yet now compare Gabriel Josipovici with both Moody and Leavis on this same passage, the opening of *Burnt Norton* part V:

Now, the lyric being over, we return to the longer meditative line as the voice, having faced both ecstasy and apathy, prepares for one final assault on meaning. This time it will question its own performance as well as the other issues which have been touched on and then left in the air in the course of the poem:

Words move, music moves...
*[Josipovici quotes 13 lines]*

This is the Symbolist aesthetic, made manifest by the poem ('Words, after speech, reach / Into the silence...') as well as elegantly summarised. The last three lines deftly relate it to the earlier thoughts on time, so that we are not far here from Yeats's meditation on the 'great-rooted blossomer' and from his rhetorical question: 'How can we know the dancer from the dance?'

But, as we know, the way human beings are constituted makes this only an ideal, never a liveable reality. For, in reality

Words strain,
Crack and sometimes break, under the burden,
Under the tension, slip, slide, perish,
Decay with imprecision, will not stay in place,
Will not stay still. Shrieking voices
Scolding, mocking, or merely chattering,
Always assail them.

I find these lines are among the most moving and *encouraging* in the entire poem. By admitting what he does, the speaker reaches across to me in a way that he has not quite done so far. For this is something we all know, how our need to speak, to articulate our fears and desires, is always frustrated by the fact that words seem to have a life of their own, how they refuse to perform as we want them to, how they slip and slide away from us and how other voices, voices we did not know existed and didn't want to hear, voices which shriek or merely chatter, constantly interrupt, disrupt and mockingly destroy even our most heart-felt efforts.

Already in *The Waste Land* Eliot had been able to
articulate in memorable poetry the failure of poetry and
memory:

> On Margate Sands
> I can connect
> Nothing with nothing.
> The broken fingernails of dirty hands

We have all felt this but literature has, by and large,
colluded in a conspiracy of silence on this point, as
though there were something shameful about it –
except for a few maverick works like *Tristram Shandy*.
Proust, Eliot, Kafka and Beckett, though, affect us as
they do precisely because they break the silence on this
point. They assert that this inability to connect
anything with anything, this failure of the will to
organise language so that it can express what we feel
and want to say, is perfectly natural, is in fact *the*
natural condition of man. Here, they say, is where we
must start from, not the ideal of the finished, the well-
made work. And by so saying they release us from our
sense of personal failure and give us back hope. This, it
seems to me, is the true heart of Modernism.

(pp. 191-3)

Insofar as Josipovici understands these passages as
reflective upon the whole work itself, rather than simply as
a kind of shrugging attitude within it, he has in effect both
secularised Moody's metaphysical transcendentalism and
radically reinterpreted Leavis's emphasis upon the poem's
self-contradiction. Leavis's detailed pinpointing of the
disavowal of human creativity and the poem's
paradoxically compelling yet dismissive evocation of
natural beauty is nevertheless not necessarily dissolved.
His diagnosis of what is 'wrong' can remain largely
persuasive insofar as the reader finds unsuccessful the

allure of Eliot's 'music' or deliberately resists the seductions of Eliot's tactics of conversion. But whereas Leavis sees a self-cancelling counterposition between Eliot's actual creative practice and his repudiation of the power of human creativity, what Josipovici claims as the core impetus of the poem is precisely its negotiation of the dilemma which he more generally sees as shaping or even defining the modernist endeavour: the endemic problem for the writer, composer, or painter, of finding the very possibility of creative articulation while, and in the very act of, confronting the apparent impossibility of such creative effort, the danger that every beginning is immediately an end, that no word is right, that all attempts to write are inevitably wrong. In other words – my inadequate words rather than Josipovici's or Eliot's – what several passages in *Four Quartets* explicitly confront is precisely an intensification of the dilemma which *The Waste Land* had already presented.

Elsewhere, Josipovici has memorably explored this fundamental motif in the work of Becket and of Kafka, and even as informing the whole of Proust's work, and he convincingly argues that the artist's always provisional, fragile, and barely achievable temporary resolution, formally specific to each work – rather than any finally satisfactory and generally applicable solution – of this persistent and unavoidable impasse is repeatedly to take that very impasse or double-bind as indeed the subject, object, focus, both beginning and end, of the work itself. In that respect, he is close to both Adorno's insight that every effort is a formally different kind of failure, and Eliot's emphasis that for all of us now there is only the trying.

Let us try then. But what?

## viii : having to construct something
## upon which to rejoice

At this point, with considerable reservation, I want briefly to consider my own attempted reconciliation of both acquiescence in Leavis's overall critique of Eliot and my recognition of the force of Josipovici's critical position. I have already suggested that one appropriate response to Eliot was not only to write criticism but also to attempt a kind of counter-poem. The dilemma, for me, of how to negotiate the impossibility of writing was in part resolved by a re-writing of Eliot's own work, by in effect treating Eliot's *oeuvre* as providing the scaffolding which Eliot himself had found in part in Dante. By adopting and adapting Eliot's own words, lines, and voice, I was assuming an Eliotic *persona*, both deploying Eliot's work as the basis for a classical *imitatio* and setting myself a OULIPO-type formally restricted task, while also paying homage to the Situationist device of *détournement*. It was, at least for me, an enjoyable form of attempted exorcism.

My starting point for writing an Eliotic poem was hearing Eliot's voice as I read and wrote. As with my version, above, of the opening of Eliot's essay on *Hamlet* I found myself both matching and replacing or displacing Eliot's own characteristic way of writing. Let me quote some brief indicative instances:

The history that is past and the history that is present
Will together, we presume, determine the history to come
And those histories are always before us.
For to be fixed in a permanent present
Is only a dead repetition, a fatal denial.
What might be and what can be
Are not merely some slight thought in advance
But practical, difficult, delicate paces before us.

What might be and what could be
Stem from determined decisions, from more than decision.
The calls of the dying reach out at us
From brick walls trickling with blood,
Moments of misery, outrage and upsurge,
Courage defeated, efforts that failed. Such calls
Break on us still. ...

and:

A terrible coming we had of it,
just the worst time of the year
for a journey, and such a dangerous journey,
the border uncertain and the front-line constantly changing,
the dead all around us.
My sister and I, exhausted and crying,
lying down and refusing to budge.
There were times we remembered
the quiet village on the hill, the fields,
and the summers bringing the harvest.
Then the road-blocks and patrols, cursing and threatening,
beating and raping, looting what little we had.
And the water running out and the absence of sleep,
aircraft zooming low and tanks rumbling by,
minefields without warning and the sudden explosions.
A harsh time we had of it.

And so on.

I was trying to appropriate some of Eliot's stylistic
characteristics, but in spelling out, and making prosaically
clear, what the political intent of my own 'poem' was upon
my reader, I was seeking to undermine the way in which,
as I read them, Eliot's poems including *Four Quartets*,
though covertly, indirectly and seductively, enacted a
process of an ultimately political persuasion as well as a
more explicitly religious conversion upon its readers.

Clearly, I was also seeking to develop a variant upon the dual composition I had explored in relation to Pound and Eliot, a blending of my own voice and Eliot's. Not, however, as a way of relying upon or endorsing Eliot's authority. On the contrary, I was trying to appropriate Eliot's authoritative status in order to oppose it. I was thereby both acknowledging that Eliot could give me a starting-point out of the dilemma which Josipovici had emphasised while also putting into effect a variation on the self-cancelling construction which Leavis had identified. Effectively or not, I was using Eliot as both target and support for my own attempts, in a way related to how I saw Eliot as utilising Dante and the entire range of European literature 'from Homer onwards' as a substitute for a coherent philosophical system.

I am not, of course, claiming that I succeeded in my various aims, and – as this book testifies – I have certainly not succeeded in wholly exorcising Eliot, but the process of writing my *Eliotics* had at least provoked some further considerations with which I can bring these remarks to a *diminuendo* conclusion.

I'm not confident that my own response to *Four Quartets* wasn't merely an unsatisfactory compromise or oscillation between Leavis's and Josipovici's readings. However, I would now suggest that there is a certain parallel between my notion of 'literary conversion', as a temporal process undergone by the reader while actually reading, and the working experience of composition, if what one is seeking is a form specific to the work in progress – in that in both cases it is the process already undergone, the work already partly completed, which shapes and even enforces upon both reader and writer a decision whether to continue, to follow through the implications of the premises already implicitly or consciously accepted, and thereby complete the process which one finally endorses only in a retrospective affirmation. What began for me as an unbidden re-write of the opening of *Burnt Norton* led to an entire volume of *Eliotics.*

Arguably, this is most deeply the structure of any form of major decision-making: a retrospective endorsement of what one recognises that one has already become committed to, which may only then take definite and conscious form as a specific project, a sense of vocation or profession, or even a firm belief. At some level, this was indeed the structure of emotion which Eliot had confronted in looking back in 1921 upon the events of 1915: he was voluntarily committed to an ongoing hell. And my account of Eliot's decision to authorise the publication of *The Waste Land* in a form which he perhaps at that point did not himself wholly grasp would be a variation upon this structure of validation. I might also suggest that Eliot's later poem *Ash Wednesday* enacts this process in relation to religious conversion, both as formal structure and as a pattern of experience: the arrangement of the overall poem is such that in a kind of guided cyclical repetition the reader is brought increasingly into the process of acceptance of a belief in the elusive reality of the world which the poem presents.

One alternative option for a reader *in medias res* is to stop reading, to resist the text's conversion tactic, to suspend assent, in effect to go back and reject the premises which have so far been guiding the reading, though only, one might then recognise, as a provisional acceptance thus far. This is perhaps what Leavis ended up doing, not simply deciding that there was a discernible moment of failure but that the underpinning premises, which had previously evaded his critical dissent, were what was most basically at fault in the poem. The corresponding option for the writer is to abandon the work in progress, as not only unfinished but unfinishable.

Again, it may be worth recalling that Eliot, rather unusually, explicitly included 'unfinished poems' in his *Collected Poems.*

In the case of *Four Quartets*, Eliot had completed *Burnt Norton* as early as 1935 with no notion of any kind of sequel, but in later undertaking *East Coker* he allowed the shape of *Burnt Norton* to act retrospectively as a template or formal model for the new poem. Thereafter, there was a kind of emergent logic about writing a further poem consonant with the first two, and once the notion of 'quartet' had taken hold there had to be four quartets, though the difficulty of matching or aligning the fourth with the previous three proved more difficult than he had anticipated.

The more general problem of the 'genuinely new' today, which Josipovici's wider argument highlights, is the difficulty of getting sufficient of the first stage of this compositional process off the ground at all, to reach the substantial point at which one has adequately constructed a partially effective process, such that what gradually emerges before one is a sense of where the material itself is taking you. However, to begin repeatedly from the compositional premise that there is nothing to express – not of course primarily a logical premise but an experienced *impasse* – involves one in having to negotiate the further difficulty of avoiding a mere repetition of the solution or resolution which one had previously found in earlier attempts, while still resolutely beginning from that same recognition.

In writing *Eliotics*, my own partial solution to this familiar impasse, in a very minor key, was a variant on the OULIPO tactic of setting oneself a slightly absurd constraint – in this case, to match Eliot's poems line-by-line – combined with taking each one of Eliot's existing poems as a given template for a consonant composition, yet trying to avoid mere parody or pastiche. This recourse was in my case no adequate remedy or recompense for lacking individual talent, and to some extent, of course, was only a variation upon accepting one's location within a given or chosen tradition: to find a starting point for a poem in a received form, to write a sonnet or compose a villanelle. Ezra Pound's early poems wonderfully exemplified this relation to a variety of traditions, using Provençal or Chinese poems as the template or starting point for his own, an often consummate blending of voices. From a certain perspective, such forms of composition always involve an element of dual authorship, a conflating of different voices, which can also be found in the process of translation, or even a close reading form of criticism. Again, my tactic in *The Literary Labyrinth* of imagining unwritten works in order to review them had allowed me to play with a medley of interwoven voices, none of them necessarily my own, but the peculiar process of 'reviewing' my 'own' work, however imagined, raises the issue of self-judgement, which returns us to Adorno.

Insofar as criticism in a Leavisite mode involves a dialogue of at least two voices in interactive partial dissent – 'yes, but' – the compositional problem for any solo critical writing is intimately involved in the difficulty of confidently arriving at one's own critical judgement. Eliot once rightly claimed that very few people have a first-hand judgement of Shakespeare. When Eliot remarks of a draft of part IV of *Little Gidding* that he is too close to it to know whether it is fundamentally right or fundamentally wrong, he points to or even exemplifies one of the central problems involved in the widely current forms of literary blogging or of solo self-publishing (as in this book): without critical feedback during the compositional process one is reliant upon resolving the paradoxes of self-judgement – but perhaps one always is. Eliot's notion of achieving 'impersonality' is a further variation upon this core problematic, as indeed is Plato's definition of any form of thinking as the dialogical conversation of the soul with itself.

One might even approach the problem of critically assessing *Hollow Men* and *Ash Wednesday* somewhat along these lines: now that Eliot lacked a sympathetic interlocutor of Pound's calibre, his own self-judgement as to the success or otherwise of these faltering compositions was to some extent warped by the need to produce an adequate follow-up to the success of *The Waste Land*, perhaps further complicated by his uniquely awkward position as also the publisher of that previous success. It may even be that he could persuade himself in the case of *Ash Wednesday* that the very process of searching for the grounds of religious conversion (that peculiar combination of retrospective endorsement and future commitment) would bring into play the justifying grace of critical approval for a persistently inchoate composition from a rather more elevated source of feedback than any humanly available co-creator. It was perhaps this emergent religious belief itself which eventually allowed him to trust in the otherwise almost serendipitous conjunctures which had gradually emerged upon the page, the process which he recounts of writing disparate short poems and then seeking somehow to constellate them together. The crucial compositional decision, not unlike that of a painter before a constantly re-painted canvas on the easel, was again to know when and how to stop, as Adorno was to recognise.

Perhaps one of the tendencies which emerged for aspiring writers 'after modernism' was a reversion – not least under those twin pressures of celebrity and commerce which had so converged upon Eliot himself – to an apparently more self-confident and even arrogant self-judgement (though endemically vulnerable and fragile), operating to sustain the individual writing self, even when perhaps only a commercially-oriented literary agent or a commissioning editor was available as the primary or possibly sole critical interlocutor during the compositional process, a variant upon Eliot's own dual role at Faber. One thinks perhaps of Joyce's Stephen already anticipating the enthusiastic commercial reviews before the work is even begun.

If you inherit and emulate a compositional or formal model, you can in the writing process gradually adjust and consciously revise your working drafts to match the model, to fit the received form. The most obvious example would be the poetic *imitatio*, the traditional pedagogical exercise of classical humanism. But once you have – in a general sense – broken the pentameter, made the first heave, you confront the problems of 'free verse', in whatever actual medium you are working. What may then primarily emerge to take the place of any externally authorised formal cohesion is simply one's own characteristic voice, which in Eliot's case seems to have been an almost immediately recognisable (and invitingly imitable) audible combination of cadences and rhythms in the individual line-unit and the persistence of a preferred paragraph unit, sometimes half-cloaked, of roughly seven lines, a relatively long breath shaping his characteristic syntax. Noticeably, Pound's local and sometimes drastic interventions in Eliot's drafts too frequently overrode or disrupted precisely this Eliotic voice-print.

The early Eliot quite quickly established his distinctive voice in the flow and timbre of individual poems, but after the somewhat odd-man-out exemplar of *The Waste Land* Eliot neither constructed nor bequeathed any specific formal innovation at the level of the poem as itself a unit of composition, his contribution in that respect being rather to authorise and endorse a variety of unexpected formal organisations which, somewhat frustratingly for his critics and successors, have seemed to provide no transparent model for structural analysis or convincing emulation. The successive four quartets clearly did become formal models for each other, but even in them one can perhaps see a temptation for Eliot to trust that his characteristic voice was strong enough in and by itself to sustain the poem as a whole, while its overall formal patterning remained an elusive and unlikely model for successors.

How far these considerations might also apply to the practice of criticism, with its own received models of appropriate form yet also its distinctive individual voices, Leavis, Adorno, Williams, Eagleton, Josipovici, Eliot himself, I can leave for another occasion.

*

# Coda / Cadenza : thinking

*the work of T. S. Eliot in an age of...?*

To invent techniques that shall be adequate to the ways of feeling, or modes of experience, of adult, sensitive moderns is difficult in the extreme. Until it has been once done it is so difficult as to seem impossible. One success makes others more probable because less difficult. ... That is the peculiar importance of Mr. T. S. Eliot. ... he has solved his own problem as a poet, and so done more than solve the problem for himself.

F. R. Leavis

*Portfolio : La Figmenta*

Lay across the frame just off-diagonal
Wrap delirious limbs around the latest model
Flash, flash the sun-lamp of your smile
Clasp the current product with caressed delight
Partly open moistened mouth and pout
With softened passion in your lidded eyes
But flash, flash the sunshine of your smile.

So I would have you, dear,
So I would have you moan and pant
So they all would have you
As the mind mingles in the *mise-en-scene*
And imagination weaves an old *scenario*.
I should devise
Some novel pose incomparably pure-provocative
Some pro-position we all can knowingly endorse
Obscene and obvious as a fingered thigh
or lingering tongue.

She's discontinued now, but through the autumn season
Still compels consumption many times
Many ways and many places.
Hair over the eyes and lips lewd with promise.
I wonder how we ever got along without it.
We have shaped a pastime, art form, and a product.
Manifold manipulations still arouse
The satiated custom and the bored consumer.

Eliotics

I have found it convenient to put my remarks in the
form of disconnected paragraphs.

Eliot, 'Prose and Verse',<br>The Chapbook: nr.22, April 1921.

### *i : distracting from distraction by distraction*

This final segment of an already rather meandering book
may seem to stray very far indeed from Eliot's poetry. As
indeed it does. But it has developed from trying to think
through the implications of issues already broached,
particularly those concerned with copyright, and from
considering what might now constitute a diagnosis of our
current cultural landscape and, perhaps, point to some
emerging alternative formation. Let me begin with an
overstated suggestion.

The peculiar importance of Eliot for *The Dial* editors who
bought *The Waste Land* may well have been primarily
commercial: to boost the circulation of *The Dial*, which
would in turn boost its advertising revenue. Which may
help further to explain why, since they were spending the
considerable sum of $72,000 a year subsidising the re-
launched periodical, which they had taken control of only
a year before, they were willing to award $2,000 to secure

Eliot's new poem, almost sight un-seen: it was probably a canny investment. Rainey (*Revisiting*, p. 91) outlines a suggestive comparison between the proportion of revenue from subscribers and from advertising in the annual accounts of *The Dial* and of *Vanity Fair*, as part of a larger argument about the commercial aspects of literary modernism.

Interestingly, of course, the crucial cultural role of advertising had been anticipated by that other major modernist text of 1922, in which Leopold Bloom earns his insecure income by soliciting adverts for a newspaper.

A century or so later, the pervasiveness of advertisements, increasingly in the commercial colonisation of websites, as well as already entrenched in newspapers, television broadcasts, and public spaces, means that we are now unremittingly immersed in a variety of enticing virtual objects. It is not simply that we are continuously being subjected to persuasion to buy the actual objects depicted, and thereby indirectly to pay for the further penetration of our whole environment by this form of inescapable invasion, but also that even when we have no intention or desire to make an actual purchase, our mental, visual, and aural experience is continually filled with imagined objects, and even complete scenarios, which saturate our sense of what constitutes the world we live in. The overall effect is not unlike being involuntarily incarcerated or perhaps even permanently incarnated within the imagined world of a literary text, an almost nightmare variation on a once-familiar kind of profoundly involved and deeply absorbed reading experience, and at the same time an anticipation of some future all-encompassing virtual reality world already partly implemented. Perhaps we will eventually become the muzak we hear.

It is arguable that contemporary advertising has by now wholly appropriated, and even further developed, for its own purposes, many of the formal devices and literary and visual techniques first invented by successive twentieth-century avant-garde artistic movements, though some modernist techniques were themselves already indebted to advertising. These include attention-grabbing typographic versatility, as in the lay-out of Victorian theatre posters and in Wyndham Lewis's *Blast*. The insistent use in advertising of eye-catching images or enigmatic visual compositions can be partly derived from Cubism and Surrealism. An advert's unexpected ironic interplay between text and image, or image and image, attuning us to a momentary shock or a fleetingly sympathetic amusement, may often recall Magritte or the impossible visual configurations of Escher.

*ii : these fragments we have ...*

Above all, advertising deploys techniques of compositional collage and fragmentary narrative, whether in a television advert apparently offering 20-second glimpses of an ongoing domestic drama, or a speeded-up version of a whirlwind romance, or an exotic journey compacted into momentary jump cuts – with such disparate fleeting scenarios rapidly and inexplicably succeeding each other in an intensely compressed five-minute composition, the television advertising break. These miscellaneous yet constantly repeated, uncoordinated yet consistently cross-supporting, advertising episodes and tableaux constitute an insistent and almost inescapably pervasive articulation of a single compelling message, fragmentarily infiltrated into our memories: that the desirable world is fundamentally constituted by purchasable commodities, and that there is always an alluring alternative to our actual reality, one which is enticingly only a credit card away from realisation.

Each advert presents itself almost as an already half-familiar quotation from a permanently attractive other reality, another world not only (but not otherwise) accessible through a receptively responsive imagination which almost instantly constructs that alternate dimension, but one which is constantly yet elusively glimpsed and ever-present in our mundane perception of the actual world around us: billboards and advertising hoardings, printed posters and scrolling electronic displays, broadcasting interruptions and interleavings, website pop-ups and self-starting videos, strident sponsorship slogans or demurely located logos.

### iii : we do the police in our own voices

In another sense, too, adverts act as memorable quotations: they offer to insinuate themselves into our own voices, as we ask for a named brand in a shop, find ourselves involuntarily reciting a jingle, or repeating a catchphrase. Even with the sound turned defensively to mute, we can often supply, *sotto voce*, the dialogue to an endlessly repeated television advertisement repertoire. We can find ourselves becoming ventriloquised personae of those figures who fleetingly but permanently inhabit this strange territory of the endlessly projected ad-world, semi-voluntary avatars of an ongoing dual composition, a passively collaborative endorsement.

In some respects, this permeation of our conscious and unconscious by the lures of advertising seems no longer even directed towards any actual purchases, but pervasively enacts a collusive celebration of the commodity form itself, presented in a self-reflecting circularity as the image of itself. Since in any case we will not, and indeed cannot, purchase all the myriad objects, activities, and experiences which so enticingly invite us, we are nevertheless recruited into a vicarious enjoyment and routine acquiescence in this overwhelming provision of imagined satisfactions, despite knowing that in our actual experience such promises are permanently postponed or remain personally unreachable.


## *iv : a golden age of eliotics*

There is, I would now mischievously suggest, a definite continuity and underlying affinity between these various features of familiar advertising techniques and several aspects of Eliot's *oeuvre*. It is relatively easy to see in *The Waste Land,* with its abrupt transitions of texts, its juxtapositions of images and scenes, its brief dramas and interweaving echoes of many different voices, once so startling and almost incomprehensible, some definite formal precursors of the current tool-box of advertising tricks and techniques.

More elusively perhaps, *Four Quartets* itself can also occasionally feel like a subtly inventive commercial promotion, or perhaps an unusually intelligent political campaign pitch, an understated but sophisticated design upon us, persuasively deploying the magic of impossibly beautiful landscapes, a midwinter spring or a magical garden, with sounds of children laughing in the shrubbery, while the quietly authoritative and inwardly trustworthy voice tells us that there are three conditions which often look alike and that the way up is the way down.

Above all, the peculiarly indefinable reward which somehow prevents us everywhere in *Four Quartets* can be caught only in sidelong glimpses and half-guesses, yet would constitute for us both the desired still point of an ever-turning world and the lost home to which we want always to return, like a photogenic Cotswold cottage or a Texan farmstead. Those long lingeringly ruminative lines, subtly inviting acquiescence and even identification, are a considerable development from and an insinuating improvement upon the overly didactic and rather too crassly explicit evangelising assertions of *The Rock,* but the divinely commissioned brief remains the same: to convince us, reluctant and wavering as we are, that we are lacking an ineffable experience permanently on offer, a moment of the unimaginable, a future something always somehow beyond words, perhaps never to be achieved or attained – except at the price of everything else.

Any such mischievous account, of course, which it would nevertheless be possible to pursue much further, traduces and partly misrepresents the overall character of Eliot's poem and its consummate attractions, not least because the delights and allurements dangled before us by commodity advertising are basically rejected by the poem itself.

Yet insofar as the poem as a whole – and this, as we have seen, was the burden of Leavis's ultimately devastating critique – endorses the repudiation of embodied human living, and even of the natural world itself, in favour of a transcendent condition to be reached primarily by a way of negation and deprivation, there is in my response to the poem – as in my habitual response to all forms of advertising – an element of resistance to its seductive techniques. I react by wanting not merely to analyse or critically dissent from but actually to undermine and oppose the intended effect of Eliot's later poetry.

That is, I now recognise, why I had once found myself unexpectedly inclined to rewrite the whole poem, and then a number of Eliot's other poems, almost as a personal exorcism of their attraction. I may also have been partly motivated by the recognition that a training in literary critical analysis, or even more in the semiotics of popular culture, has regrettably become no barrier to but almost a sought-after qualification for writing advertising copy.

271

Of course, to blame Eliot's generation for the appropriation of their innovative literary techniques by the global advertising industry is no more just than to attribute to Bertholt Brecht the merely superficial adoption by the entertainment industry of his Berliner Ensemble's *verfremdungseffekts*. Nevertheless, the de-radicalising incorporation of avant-garde formal innovations challenges the optimism of Walter Benjamin's contention that the progressive writer is not the propagandist but the practitioner from whom other writers can learn to deploy improved tools of their trade.

I suggested earlier that, with the almost accidental exception of *The Waste Land* itself, Eliot's legacy as poet now seems to include little in the way of specific formal models which later poets have been able successfully to develop further, and much that once seemed startlingly new in local technique can in any case be derived not only from Pound or Corbière but traced back to Wordsworth and Browning, or even to the denigrated Tennyson. One might rather claim that what remains provocatively exemplary in Eliot's small poetic *oeuvre* as a whole is precisely its diversity of formal modes while maintaining a recognisably Eliotic voice-print.

In any case, the most insistent challenge left to us by Eliot's deep ambivalence about the very possibility of creativity in our contemporary cultural wasteland is not primarily whether anyone can write a *Waste Land* or *Four Quartets* for our own time, but whether the leverage for cultural change which Pound and Eliot located in literature and criticism has since been rendered wholly ineffective, or should be regarded as simply misconceived. Or perhaps now to be located elsewhere? In whatever has succeeded the age of modernism and of merely mechanical reproduction, what concluding reflections does looking back upon Eliot's work now provoke?

## v : MacObvious

Let me first take up the comment that Eliot constructed and retained an individual voice across a range of different modes and forms, a characterisation which might also be applied to, say, Duchamps and Picasso or, in a different range of media, Stravinsky or David Bowie. One could claim that almost the opposite situation prevailed in the early days of digital multimedia composition. The possible structure and organisation of, for example, any individual hypertext presentation was so constrained by the built-in features and programmed assumptions of each specific authoring software (most notoriously in the case of PowerPoint) that in design circles and art colleges the term 'MacObvious' was rapidly baptised as shorthand for indicating that a particular piece of work not only must have been put together on a Mac computer but also that it had made the most obvious and predictable use of standard Mac software such as Photoshop.

The tricky challenge for an artist or designer was to deploy the most advanced features of the widely available software in such a personally imaginative way that one could not easily identify the specific programs used in the production. Correspondingly, the most egregious mistake was enthusiastically to utilise as many as possible of the inbuilt features and options provided by the software, without knowing when to stop.

The difficulty in the digital domain of following the injunction implicit in Adorno's dictum, that any serious work of art must invent its own specific form, is that any such innovative digital composition must involve the dual contribution of programmer and artist, the one in constant co-creative dialogue with the other throughout the whole authoring process, even if both roles are incarnated in the same person. The most flexible examples of experimental film production have rarely involved redesigning the camera while shooting a scene, and even the highly collaborative teams involved in the complex evolution of cutting-edge interactive video games might shy away from adopting Adorno's *desideratum* as their company motto.

However, beyond the immediate demands of any specific product development, there is now a wider territory of feedback, exemplified in the Open Source movement, involving relatively *ad hoc* and often globally dispersed temporary communities of volunteer programmers implementing free versions of useful software and responding to suggested input from active end-users not themselves necessarily proficient in programming skills. From one perspective, in line with some of Benjamin's notions, this might be seen as a contemporary version of a reciprocal relationship between the editor of a traditional newspaper or periodical and its readers, with not only ongoing dialogical responses between contributors, but also regular readers' suggestions to the editor, whether published or otherwise, acting as stimulus and prompt, criticising or approving current articles and suggesting future contributors and topics. The online comments sections of some newspapers or in a different domain the development of Wikipedia and similar sites offer current examples of such dispersed and collaborative content input, but only within the given formal constraints of the host apparatus. Though the same might be said, after appropriate re-reformulations, of such anonymously collective achievements as mediaeval mystery play cycles or Gothic cathedrals.

One crucial difference from the patterns of cultural collaboration and the networks of contacts which Eliot assiduously nurtured in his roles at *The Criterion* and Faber is that of scale: the index of persons in Eliot's collected letters covers a considerable percentage of the national and even international circle of cultural practitioners he was aiming to influence and to draw upon, whereas a debate about the strategy and priorities of an organisation such as Avaaz or 38 Degrees may now involve the input of several hundred thousand individuals. In these circumstances any notion of a 'clerisy' has been fundamentally transformed

*vi : collectors items*

Another aspect of the after-life of Eliot's work can now be considered by returning to copyright-related issues. Among the very earliest adopters of Internet-based commerce were dealers in second-hand books, since a physical book, as an item or object, is precisely appropriate to the kind of search routines which enable a would-be purchaser to find a very specific book, identified and located through a variety of filters – date, place of publication, first edition, previous owner, etc. – across a truly global marketplace. And some of the earliest innovative uses of the World Wide Web were the online provision of digital text data-bases which allowed researchers, students, and general readers to access literary and other out-of-copyright texts, first through specialised websites and then more generally through consolidated search engines.

That the 1922 date of publication of *The Waste Land* fortuitously allowed it to remain in the American public domain, and therefore subject to free digital reproduction, brings into focus some of the intriguing issues concerning texts in the new digital landscape of cultural production. The 'same' text – *The Waste Land* – can now be downloaded and distributed for free, yet at the same time remains in other forms both a valuable collectors' item and a copyrighted commodity. The disparity between the almost cost-free copying and digital distribution of Eliot's pre-1923 texts and the fact that some of those same texts were once only available as luxury or limited editions, reinforces awareness of the intrinsically odd relationship between the physical commodity form and an intellectual articulation, the poem 'as poem', which can be realised in such different modes or formats, and raises issues about the very nature of intellectual 'property'.

If I search on the various internet second-hand book-dealer sites looking for a 'first edition' of Eliot's *The Waste Land*, most of the relatively few items I will find on offer are either the Boni & Liveright 1922 American edition, or less commonly the Hogarth Press edition of 1923. It is, however, rare to find the publication of the poem in *The Dial* for November 1922, and still rarer to find the actual first appearance in print of *The Waste Land*, in the launch issue of *The Criterion* for October 1922. Prices for these varous 'first editions' range between a few hundred dollars and several thousand pounds.

However, to avoid paying these high prices, I can now order instead a printed-on-demand facsimile copy of the 1922 Boni & Liveright edition, for about five dollars, or simply download a free digital copy of that same edition from the Internet Archive and similar sites – some copyright implications of which I have already considered.

That the writing and publishing of printed literature was almost always, directly and indirectly, a component of a profit-oriented commercial business was clear not least from the encounter with Mr Nixon in *Hugh Selwyn Mauberly*, and the often hard-up Modernists were no more reluctant than previous generations to encourage expensive limited editions, not only in the interests of enjoying printing and binding excellence but also in the hope of enhanced financial reward.

While one can admire the extraordinary quality of John Rodker's editions of the early *Cantos*, and register that they were in that case apparently published with no expectation of ever breaking-even, it is also the case that Joyce's *Ulysses* was from the first deliberately published with an eye on the collectors' market, which very rapidly developed around the first few hundred copies printed on special paper. When Watson arrived in Paris in 1922 it was partly to take delivery of several copies of a first edition *Ulysses* which he had cannily pre-ordered at an advance price, but which within a few months was reselling at considerably more.

Eliot at least demurred at some of these temptations: on one occasion he almost sarcastically reproved an enquiring clergyman who wished to add to his collection of Eliot signed copies, while on another, when shown a signed Pound volume by his dinner-party host, Eliot graciously took it, asked for a pen, added his own signature to the flyleaf, and returned it with the poker-faced remark that it was now worth *twice* as much.

Given the unlikelihood of any repetition of the extraordinary success of Eliot's career as the icon of 20th century English literature, at least in part as the unrepeatable result of his own successful strategies of self-publicity, and the fortunate fact that he was (however de-nationalised in 1926) an American poet, it is hardly surprising that, as financial and cultural hegemony has increasingly migrated across the Atlantic, the 1922 American book publication of *The Waste Land*, albeit in a rather drab and ordinary binding, has become as sought-after, particularly by moderately well-heeled American collectors, as even *Ulysses* itself. That the poem is so explicitly situated within the City streets which have spawned so many bankers' bonuses and speculative fortunes may also have contributed to its singular attractiveness as an investment item. But it may be doubted whether well-heeled bankers or penurious pupils would, or even could, now read *The Waste Land* as quite the transformative challenge and paradigmatic break-through it was once so persuasively adjudged to be.

The easily-ordered Print On Demand hard copy facsimiles of that once-scarce 1922 American first edition (though there are none – as yet – of the English Hogarth Press edition of 1923) are not, it seems, the product of some accredited corporate publishing house, but probably the work of an enterprising individual downloading a free online copy, and then utilising the kind of self-publishing software which has also produced this very book you are now reading. It may even be that such current legal 'pirate publishers' are motivated as much by a love of Eliot's poems as by the profitable recognition of a gap in the market to be easily filled with a few mouse-clicks. But the action of self-publishing a book, even if by someone else, is part of a much wider development.

### vii : to what purpose disturbing the dust?

Eliot once remarked (and here I quote *verbatim* – adding to my copyright count – though admittedly out of context) 'the poetry does not matter'. In a sense not intended by Eliot, this seems to me increasingly the case. I would suggest that, from one pessimistic perspective, the current writing and publishing – whether in a book, periodical, online blog, or any other forms – of an enormous range of critical and oppositional writing, both political and cultural, equally 'does not matter', much. And even if the mainstream media were also full of articulate, cogent, and intelligent economic counter-arguments and alternative political policies, opposing the present neo-liberal economic and financial orthodoxy and its vicious global application, it is doubtful whether any effective agency now exists for implementing any such counter-proposals. This argument also applies, of course, to the burgeoning of self-published books like this one.

However, this may be pertinent only if we assume the traditional model of leverage, whereby a written intervention into some residual public sphere was intended to have an influence or effect upon some central bastion of power. But it may instead be the case that it is now the very act of so writing and disseminating which constitutes part of the difference it is actually making. There is perhaps a certain parallel with the earliest days of the Gutenberg Galaxy, when writers seized upon the new technology of the printing press in order to argue some particular case aimed at a ruling Prince or at the People at large – but without fully registering for some time that it was the development of the printing press itself that was making a long-lasting and even epochal difference.

From one viewpoint it is, of course, increasingly the case that when any individual can publish a daily blog to be disseminated to a potentially global on-line readership, or send numerous tweets on an hourly basis, to record and publish not just family news, baby photos, or celebrity gossip, but instances of blatant corruption, or upload searing eyewitness accounts of an appalling atrocity to a video-streaming website, then one can be reasonably certain that none of this may 'make much difference' – in the old sense. Precisely because so many thousands, or indeed millions, can also do the same, in a myriad different voices, prompting a myriad of in-different responses.

Moreover, even if such instances of proliferating serious political communication and reporting are not simply swamped by the much greater floods of trivia and chit-chat that also spill over from the mainstream media, the sheer explosion of 'writing' means that the hope of any such intervention exercising a leverage upon the centres of power is not only largely unrealistic – but also perhaps curiously unnecessary. In a sense, Eliot's *The Sacred Wood*, with its titular gesture towards the replacement of one reigning monarch by a coming upstart, was consonant with its date of publication: *Prufrock* appeared in the year of the Leninist *coup d'état* in St. Petersburg and *The Waste Land* in the very same month as Mussolini's march on Rome. But such models of regime change may now have been partly superceded.

Already, Ezra Pound's strategic approach was somewhat different from Eliot's. Rather than attempting to capture the commanding heights of the cultural apparatus – to write leading reviews for the *TLS*, for example – Pound was prepared again and again to establish his own organs and outlets, to discover, encourage, and put into prompt circulation by whatever means available, the writers, artists, and musicians whom he selected for encouragement. In effect, Pound constituted himself as a peripatetic whirl-wind one-man publishing house, not so much launching an assault upon the priests of the sacred wood as inventively proliferating an impressive range of alternative plantations.

The very fact that everybody is now technically able to self-publish a book suggests a tiny glimmer of an alternative to be explored, even a potential shift in the dominant economic form of production itself. As we have seen, Eliot was himself a self-publisher in a somewhat different mode: to write a poem, all he needed was a pen and paper, or a typewriter, but to publish his poems he mainly deployed the resources of Faber and Faber, and it was more than a useful bonus that he was himself a director of what became a major publishing house. But though one now needs the global (and mainly capitalist) resources of the Internet, and perhaps those of Google and of Amazon, in order to disseminate digitally one's individual writings or other contributions, it is no longer necessary to own a publishing house or even to convince those whom Coleridge once called 'The Gatekeepers' to approve, accept, and propagate one's work.

We can here bring into play Terry Eagleton's contrast (in *Eliot in Perspective,* p.285) between Eliot's and Raymond Williams's different notions of a 'common culture':

> ... it is precisely because Eliot's idea of culture involves unconsciousness in the majority that he can consciously prescribe [traditonal] values: since the people are excluded from active remaking, the essentials of the culture can be said to exist already. Eliot does not need to wait and see what will emerge spontaneously from a common collaboration, since in his schemes there will be no such collaboration.

And (my emphasis):

> It is useful to compare Eliot's model of a common culture to one which, despite many points of contact, ultimately opposes it. In the conclusion to his *Culture and Society 1780-1950* (1958), Raymond Williams places a similar emphasis on the unconsciousness of a lived culture, but links it to a different structure of values:
>
> > A culture, while it is being lived, is always in part unknown, in part unrealized. The making of a community is always an exploration, for consciousness cannot precede creation, and there is no formula for unknown experience. A good community, a living culture, will, because of this, *not only make room for but actively encourage all and any who can contribute to the advance in consciousness which is the common need.* . . . We need to consider every attachment, every value, with our whole attention; for we do not know the future, we can never be certain of what may enrich it.

To extrapolate from Williams and Eagleton: what we are currently witnessing, or perhaps participating in, is a recognisable but also quite new development, a different model of a cultural avant-garde, one which is attempting not only to modify the inherited tradition but radically to imagine and to construct alternative forms of cultural production, now transformed by the sheer scale of involvement, variety, and accessibility of what might in the past have been micro-movements and dispersed groupuscules, with short-lived 'little magazines' struggling for miniscule circulation, and all vying for the unpredictable patronage and passing attention of the established cultural institutions and powers.

Rather than an assault upon the existing cultural citadels, what is increasingly possible through digital production and internet distribution is to by-pass traditional channels altogether and to stake out, occupy, and simply implement quite new domains. Rather than attempt to take over entrenched institutions or even exercise leverage upon them, it is possible to develop a replacement model, or at least to riddle the dominant cultural landscape with multiple emergent alternatives – even if, in practice, the capacity as yet for actually inventive and innovative alternative forms seems disappointingly under-utilised, as old cultural modes and formal models continue to maintain their sway.

However, the technologically-enabled proliferation of decentralised cultural production is significant not simply for the cultural sphere itself, however redefined. The model and practice of self-publishing, on the net and in digitally distributed texts and images, video and music, is one small indication of an emerging alternative to the entire existing forms of production, perhaps even to the dominance of capital itself and its mode of production for exchange and for the extraction of profit rather than directly for use.

The commercially-motivated copyright restrictions which I have already discussed in this book are instances of a more general component of capitalism: the control of products through patents, whether in traditional manufacturing sectors such as pharmaceuticals or new technologies like mobile phones. Indeed, one might see even the creation of capital itself, in the form of *fiat* currency, as essentially the application of a legal copyright over the financial medium itself: the right of a private bank (and the Bank of England remains a private bank) to issue credit is an exercise in restricted copyright, as evidenced most clearly in the prosecution of bank-note forgery. The only contrast between a forged and a legitimate banknote may not be any discernible physical difference but a different relationship to authorisation, in effect a false signature on a signed edition rather than the authentic limited edition.

One of the emergent problems for the current financial system is that, not unlike the digital downloading of identical copies of texts, most financial transactions now take a variety of fundamentally digital forms, including the instantaneous transformation, whether by simple addition and subtraction or through complex automatic algorithms, of digital numbers denoting financial assets. Eliot's daily task at Lloyds Bank, keeping track of the fluctuating financial viability and credibility of banking institutions and national economies throughout Europe, could now be accomplished by updating a spreadsheet on a laptop, while the transfer of Germany's reparation debts could be implemented by the click of a mouse.

The entire complex system of what we call Capitalism is, at the most basic level of both analysis and practice, structurally driven by the ongoing attempt to generate a return on investment, even when the investment is in a planet-destroying activity or is itself a dangerously derivative financial speculation. The present system of production is certainly not organised to distribute goods free at the point of consumption but to ensure if at all possible a surplus of return over investment, a marginal difference between cost of production and price of product, whatever the product. But in the domain of digitally identical copies, the unit cost of which is effectively nil at the point of reproduction (leaving aside the global overhead costs of the internet itself or the costs of one's own computer apparatus), not only is the model of copyright control which has previously obtained becoming rapidly obsolete and increasingly difficult to maintain, but the mode of patent-controlled production is also under threat as all forms of intellectual property, of authorised 'objects', become digitally reproducible and increasingly available, technically at least, for free and immediate dissemination.

More widely, it can be suggested that we are now at the very earliest stage of a development in which production may not be primarily for exchange at all. When I transfer a physical object to another person I no longer have that object in my possession. Insofar as capitalism is based upon an exchange of goods under conditions of exclusive but transferable ownership, one long-standing alternative has been to try to develop forms of possession which are communal, whether of a power station or a national health service. But now, in the expanding domain of digital reproduction, I can in effect both give someone else and at the same time retain for myself the very same identical item – a text, a song, an image, a program, a design – so the very notions of exclusive possession or even of shared ownership become inapplicable.

And what has all this to do with reading T. S. Eliot?

But – of course! – this core feature of 'gift exchange' was once predominantly the case with poetry itself. We are now habituated to the practice of reading poetry silently to ourselves from a printed text. Yet if I recite a poem aloud to someone else, particularly if he, she, or they, memorise that poem, I have in effect created multiple free copies of the poem – and my audience may range from a single person to a packed stadium at a poetry festival or several million radio listeners. The very nature of spoken language means that what is said is intrinsically shared, while any actual conversation – this is so, isn't it? – inevitably involves the reciprocal modification of what each contributes to an 'exchange' which is not at all an exchange in which the giver no longer has what is given and the recipient takes exclusive possession of the given, but rather each may retain what is mutually produced, each free to make their own 'use' of what is now a common possession, a dual composition.

If we have almost abandoned the once familiar practice of reciting poetry aloud to others, we can at least recognise that in telling a joke or singing a song I am indeed 'passing it on' while certainly not depriving myself or my listener of the pleasure of repeating the joke or again performing the song in any variety of personalised modifications.

It would take us too far afield even to sketch the complex interactions between oral, manuscript, and printed modes of literary production, reception, and criticism. Though it might be interesting to speculate, for example, how our current conception of 'impersonal' critical writing has been shaped by a pedagogical practice rarely characterised by any reciprocal recitation of poetry, even when the emphasis still falls upon 'the words on the page' instead of contextual scholarship. But the primary point I am making here is that the emergence of digital forms of production, re-production, and dissemination may prove as significant as the transitions from oral to manuscript to print, and not only for what we call literature.

Let me now elaborate the point in relation to Eliot himself. It might be instructive to explore Eliot's relation to that interesting moment of transition between writing poems by hand and making a typed fair copy, such as we see in the facsimile material for *The Waste Land*. The emergence of the typewriter (admittedly, first patented in the early 18th century!) as a working tool of the literary practitioner perhaps even had some subterranean influence upon Eliot's very notion of 'impersonality', insofar as the poet's own composition could now have the instant look of a quasi-printed page, a machine product stripped (almost) of identifying individual traits, though Ezra Pound rose valiantly to the challenge of idiosyncratically personalising his own typewritten output. But it is, instead, one of Eliot's Oxford tutorial essays that I want to bring into the argument.

In the Trinity term of 1915, that pivotal period for Eliot, he wrote a paper for Joachim on 'Matter and Form in Aristotle's *Metaphysics*', which explored, as I mentioned earlier, the problem of whether it is matter or form which effects the particularisation or individuation of an object, or indeed subject. Involved in this question is the apparent oscillation in Aristotle's own usage of ὕλη [Eliot had to insert the Greek characters into his typescript by hand and even now my version of Word cannot efficiently handle rough breathings or Greek accents], normally translated simply as 'matter', as indicating both 'substance' and 'being'. Since no matter can be found without form and it is the combination of form and matter, of matter specifically in-formed, which makes an object what it is, for any change to occur there must be a trans-formation of matter, from the general potentiality which for Aristotle seems to conceptually characterise 'matter' into the new formally actualised object. The 'matter' in question is not of course to be identified with what we normally think of as physical material, and Eliot offers an interpretation which comes close to identifying the distinction between ὕλη and μορφή (form) with the logical division between genus and species, while at the same time suggesting – somewhat oddly – that we should think the problem in terms of 'degrees of reality'. (When Eliot writes of an 'Unreal City' or presents unreal encounters in the poems he is partly influenced by Bradley and is partly, I suspect, responding to Pound's presentation of palpable encounters with the 'gods' of the Cantos, but that is yet another story.)

The details of Eliot's argument in this tutorial essay don't particularly matter, but it is worth singling out three remarks. The problem of change, of the transformation of potentiality into actuality, only occurs, says Eliot, 'when there is a genesis of time, because in imperishable substances it is meaningless to separate the form and matter'. We can here see an affinity with Eliot's insistence upon Dante's quasi-Thomist notion that the punishment of the imperishable damned is for them to be eternally fixed in a voluntarily unchangeable identity. This is consonant with his concern in the strange prose piece of 1917 *Eeldrop and Appleplex* 'to apprehend the human soul in its concrete individuality', to probe by different means what makes an individual this specific individual, neither a generic type nor a merely fleeting epiphenomenon – a problem he was to confront in the profoundly problematic individuality of Vivien, and of himself.

Second, in discussing Aristotle's example of a statue actualised in bronze which might have been actualised in some other material, just as the bronze might have been trans-formed into some other object, Eliot almost parenthetically notes that in the case of the artist since 'the conception varies with the medium in which it is worked out, the separation of form and matter becomes impossible.' Again, we can see the full realisation of this position in Eliot's repeated and almost Adorno-esque search for the specific, unique, and unprecedented form for the intractable matter of his poems.

But the most interesting element in Eliot's paper for my present concerns is Eliot's tussling with Aristotle's account of mathematical matter and form. Since Eliot's discussion is largely conducted in Greek quotations, let me paraphrase in English. Aristotle does speak of the 'matter' of mathematics but this, says Eliot, may be only an analogical usage, inasmuch as in mathematics there are properly no 'individuals' and therefore no 'accidents', in the sense of those features of an object which are not its 'substance' but in one sense only 'accidental' to this particular instance of the object – such a distinction cannot, it seems, obtain with a mathematical object. Moreover, since we conceptualise a mathematical object as a-temporal and un-changeable, we can ask both what is occurring in a mathematical transformation and what it might mean to refer to, for example, 'this' circle. Eliot resorts at this point to simply quoting Aristotle 1036a2, which I can translate as:

When it comes to a specific object, such as *this* circle, one of similar circles whether perceptible or intelligible (I call mathematical circles intelligible and those made of bronze or wood perceptible), we cannot offer a definition of it but only grasp it by intuitive intellect or immediate perception, so that when it no longer has this instantiation it is not clear whether it persists in existence or not, since we can only speak and understand it with reference to the universal term ['*a* circle'].

One can see why Eliot was drawn to the co-author of the *Principia Mathematica* and would proceed from Russell and Whitehead to Husserl and Meinong. One might also, incidentally, trace from this same passage of Aristotle the undeniably unique Jacques Derrida's trajectory from *The Origins of Geometry* to *La carte postale* and *Papier machine.* Another entwined tale of text and technology.

What is intriguing – but, of course, wholly fortuitous – is that this fragment of Eliot's thinking (some pages of an incomplete typed version supplemented by a handwritten draft) probes some of the issues central to the digital domain. In one sense, the 'ones' and 'zeros' which appear in conventional representations of 'the digital' are not numbers at all but simply serve to signify the distinction between 'on' and 'off' in electronic circuits, or more abstractly that between 'true' and 'false' in a logical argument. Yet the processes (programs) which govern these intermissions of electrical flow are indeed mathematical calculations ('computations', at utterly unimaginable speeds, several billion per second) by the repeated application of basic mathematical procedures. Through a complex layering and inter-action of many such processes, from 'machine language' instructions to 'graphical user interface' levels, a sequence of switchings takes almost instant visible, audible, even tactile, form as images, text, sounds, in 'the real world' of the computer user, specific instantiations of 'ones and zeros' taking now accessible shape as this text, this song, this tool, this spreadsheet, this segment of a map, this character, this pixel, this full stop. In what sense the forms we see and manipulate on our screen 'exist' when not so realised or instantiated would have exercised both Aristotle and Plato, in their different ways.

There is, of course, an intricate interdependence between our daily use of taken-for-granted and apparently almost a-material digital processing and such formidably material activities and industries as mining and transport, launching satellites and laying cables, manufacturing circuit boards and advanced research in electronic engineering. And correspondingly there is a distribution of expertise which has constructed a hierarchy of power and knowledge not wholly dissimilar to that of the mediaeval church. There may have been as much of a difference between Aquinas's understanding of theology and that of a peasant parishioner, as there is between, say, David Gelernter, designer of supercomputers and author of *Mirror Worlds,* and a teenager on a mobile phone, but the teenager no more needs to know how the system of global communications works in order to send a text than Samuel Beckett needed to know about radio technology in order to write his radio plays. And though indeed it may 'take an army to make a movie' this does not preclude the making of a film as stunningly personal as Andrei Tarkovsky's *Andrei Rublev.*

*The Waste Land* now exists as a hyper-text on numerous websites and as a downloadable 'App' for the iPhone. Much of the 'material' for this present book was accessed on-line from a laptop by merely clicking on a mouse and, arthritis having rendered me even more incapable of typing, most of it was 'written' by dictating to a voice recognition system. What we generically call 'information' may be the ὕλη (matter) of the digital world we have been rapidly creating and – leaving aside much further elaboration – the point to be stressed in relation to some of the themes of this book is that not only does 'information want to be free' but that the digital processes already available have indeed so reduced marginal costs that the production, reproduction, and dissemination of 'information' in its various forms is indeed already effectively free, apart perhaps from the price of printing material – and the deeply embedded 'copyright' charges which generate the super-profits.

In a purely oral system of communication (an imaginary construction, of course) the only physical equipment required would have been the human body itself and any notion of copyright would be somewhat problematic, but from 'Homer' onwards modes of memorability were developed through devices of rhythm and rhyme, mnemonic techniques combined with variably formulaic recitation, to create communal lore and cultural transmission. The slow impact of writing systems had widespread ramifications for storage and retrievability, recording and verification, long-term accumulation and more or less exact multiplication, but literacy was always a laborious skill, basic reading and writing still requiring tedious training, while more expert proficiency encouraged a possessive individualism, sometimes intertwined with income-generating accredited 'authorship', the foundation of copyright. Technologies of printing and mechanical reproduction, including the once-dominant forms of audio-visual communication in photography and film, radio and television, extended these possibilities while reinforcing several divisions of cultural labour.

While some critics, most notably Gabriel Josipovici, have illuminatingly argued for striking affinities between the late mediaeval moment and that of high Modernism, it may be that the digital era is now revitalising certain aspects of a predominantly oral mode, as a smart-phone becomes almost a prosthetic and the mere act of speaking can access an unprecedented memory-bank or initiate a global conversation – though one might well imagine Ezra Pound's reaction to the use of instant translation apps: it may be possible to order a meal in Albanian or a rail ticket in Serbo-Croat, but one would not like to see Google Translate's Persian rendition of *Finnegans Wake*.

And while a Ray Kurzweil may once have successfully set out to invent a whole series of user-friendly programs for the physically disadvantaged and mentally challenged, it is also terrifyingly possible for paedophiles to disseminate or fundamentalist fanatics to propagate their respective barbarities through global social media, not to mention the political trash purveyed by online Fox News.

A salutary anecdote from M. A. Screech is also worth recalling: after he had repeatedly failed to locate a particular remembered phrase in the collected works of Saint Augustine (the Montfaucon edition runs to seventeen elephant folios), a colleague's teenage son found the phrase in seconds by searching online; Screech responded gratefully but ruefully with the remark "Well, at least *I* knew what the Latin *meant*."

If, to further adapt Eliot's own derivative phrase, the process of writing was once, at its most ambitious, the hoped-for intersection of time with timelessness, of present composition with future quotability, the current ease of communication and cultural production perhaps favours the instantaneously thoughtless intervention and the instantly forgettable contribution, but it also no longer requires anyone who aspires to be a poet after the age of 25 to sign up for the privilege of a ticket to the British Museum Reading Room, which in any case no longer exists. It is now possible to have the whole of literature 'from Homer onwards', if not yet in one's bones, at least on one's flash drive. Needless to say, to adapt another dictum of Aristotle, while anyone can make a pair of shoes, a cobbler is one who makes good shoes.

So let us return to poetry. What most essentially gives a poem its continuity over time is not the particular material upon which it is transcribed, nor indeed the particular form of the inscription, though a variety of poems, from Islamic or Chinese calligraphic arts to Anglo-Saxon riddle verses have explored a multitude of possibilities. Nor is it the perhaps intractable matter of a person's own individual experience which necessarily constitutes the 'matter' of a poem as such, but, as Eliot's practice insists, the whole of previous literature can enter into the material of a poem. In Eliot's case I have tried to trace the complex interactions of both form and matter in the unique configurations of *The Waste Land* and, more briefly, *Four Quartets*. I am now suggesting that it is possible to hope that quite new kinds of 'poetry' may be created from the formal possibilities of digital composition combined with the almost overwhelming availability of so much existing cultural material.

It may still, I admit, be over-optimistic to discern in the shared enjoyment, common possession, and freely exchanged transmission of a poem, the implicit features of a whole future mode of production.

The current forms of digital production and reproduction can certainly be primarily implemented simply for personal use rather than for commercial exchange, for individual self-consumption by the immediate producer. I can now create and publish a book, even a book of my own 'poems', using the most recent technical developments, and my print-on-demand product may be simply a more convenient or attractive way of shelving my own writing in a pleasantly readable form, a harmless variation on a vanity press publication. Or I can have a few copies printed mainly to send to friends as gifts. And though the technical process would remain exactly the same in both cases, my print on demand self-published book could, but need not, be marketed for a mass consumption readership, which probably doesn't in any case exist.

But this range of possibilities is increasingly viable not only for physical books. I can envisage using emerging technologies such as 3-D printing to make for myself many of the everyday physical objects which I regard as useful, and even some that I might regard as beautiful, for my own use and enjoyment, and to be also given freely to friends – bearing in mind that those friends may be as global as the reach of the World Wide Web. Once the copyright-free design, the basic but flexible form, of an everyday household object, for example, is easily downloadable to a local micro-manufacturing machine, of which 3-D printers are only a primitive example, then the required basic physical material, the matter, may be largely provided by local recycling of waste material or at minimal actual cost. Even an entire 3-D printed car is now available, with, of course, the possibility of more personalisation and optional extras than the standard automobile production line.

What would be thankfully unnecessary in such newly possible domains of production and distribution is the role of conventional advertising. Arguably, the fundamental function of commercial advertising is to keep in constant process a cycle of production for exchange, of purchase for additional consumption, of endless replacement shaped by manipulated fashion rather than by actual obsolescence, and most crucially in order to maintain an increasingly unavoidable reliance upon temporary cycles of purchasing on credit which almost inexorably are transformed into accumulating indebtedness, which as a pervasive form of 'financial product' has become pivotal to the overall economic structure, displacing the manufacture of physical objects and even other material provisions as the most profitable sector of investment.

As is already clear from the global on-line trade in books, it is possible for the familiar modes of consumer advertising to be almost entirely made redundant, by sufficiently powerful forms of search engine coupled with adequately organised databases of globally available items. In the case of digital downloads the procedure for finding a desired item is almost identical with the action of transfer: a viewing of a website is actually the momentary realisation on one's own computer system of a myriad of almost instant digital copies of the components of that website.

How far the emerging models of production for use, through digital reproduction and free exchange, can be enabled by such capitalist organisations as Google and Amazon remains to be seen, but the Open Source software movement offers freely available alternatives to corporate-controlled and patented programs, while the new micro-manufacturing possibilities may easily allow us to make even extravagantly unnecessary objects, simply for the pleasure of what is possible: luxury books, or illuminated manuscripts, though quite how the notion of a 'limited edition' would be applicable is amusingly unclear.

To reiterate, the possibility increasingly exists of extending the application of digitally-based production methods to a wide range of what up till now have been commercially produced and distributed commodities. The consequences of such developments for a post-capitalist society may be as interesting as the application to many other products of the mass-manufacturing of identical objects which, we often forget, was first pioneered by the printing press at the close of what we now think of as the 'middle' ages.

So, finally to conclude these ruminations prompted by thinking about various facets of 'Eliot': whoever is currently responsible for those cheaply available print-on-demand facsimile 'first editions' of *The Waste Land* may even – not entirely unlike Eliot's own adventurous inclusion of his almost accidental, covertly co-produced, and self-published poem in the first issue of *The Criterion* – be also making a small contribution towards a transformative paradigm and perhaps even a potential cultural remedy or alternative, to be imitated and extended. Today's global financial capitalism did not emerge primarily from treatises trying to persuade the Vatican that Usury was now theologically legitimate, but from small and dispersed groups taking initially sporadic and local advantage, under the radar as it were, of being able to implement increasingly long-range transactions bearing officially illegitimate interest.There are more interesting avenues to explore with the currently new technologies than amassing a big data-base of how people read texts.

Of course, whether anybody does now produce freely disseminated digital versions of, say, a multimedia *Waste Land* or an interactive operatic *Four Quartets* and whether you or I would ever hear about them, or indeed want to, is a further question. But let us now go and find out. . .

*

14092519R10175

Printed in Poland
by Amazon Fulfillment
Poland Sp. z o.o., Wrocław